KYM MCCONNELL first set foot in Tibet more than ten years ago not long after finishing his final university exams. He has been travelling in the region on and off ever since, one visit including a six-month stint in northern India working for the Tibetan Government-in-Exile.

Kym grew up in Blenheim in New Zealand and currently lives in London. He believes travel to be the gift of our generation and any opportunity to explore another part of the world to be priceless. He does not claim to be a cycle guru: he bought his first mountain bike only three weeks before arriving in Lhasa to research this book.

He continues to take an active interest in Tibetan issues and to maximize every opportunity that presents itself for travel to remote regions of the world.

Tibet Overland
First edition 2002

Publisher
Trailblazer Publications
The Old Manse, Tower Rd, Hindhead, Surrey, GU26 6SU, UK
Fax (+44) 01428-607571
info@trailblazer-guides.com
www.trailblazer-guides.com

British Library Cataloguing in Publication Data
A catalogue record for this book is available from the British Library

ISBN 1-873756-41-0

Editor: Henry Stedman
Series Editor: Patricia Major
Typesetting and layout: Bryn Thomas and Anna Jacomb-Hood
Index: Jane Thomas

Important note: Travel by road in Tibet is unpredictable and can be dangerous.
Every effort has been made by the author, contributors and the publisher to ensure that the information contained herein is as accurate as possible. They are, however, unable to accept responsibility
for any inconvenience, loss or injury sustained by anyone as a result of the advice and information
given in this guide.

Printed by
Star Standard (☎ +65-861 3866), Singapore

Cover photo: The Potala Palace, Lhasa © Kym McConnell & Wendy Miles

TIBET
OVERLAND

**A ROUTE AND PLANNING GUIDE FOR
MOUNTAIN BIKERS AND OTHER OVERLANDERS**

KYM McCONNELL

TRAILBLAZER PUBLICATIONS

Dedication

For Wendy
who shared the dream and tolerated my trivia and scribblings along every kilometre
and
All Tibetans, may you one day be truly liberated

Acknowledgements

Two people provided the key inspiration for this book. The first is His Holiness the Dalai Lama, who embodies the global image of Tibet and continues to illustrate to us all the true meaning of the word 'compassion'. I first met His Holiness while working in Dharamsala and presented him with some personal accounts of the way many Tibetans inside Tibet, against extreme odds, are continuing to live as he would prescribe. I am grateful to His Holiness for writing the Foreword for this book and I hope he can soon return to his wonderful homeland.

Secondly, overland travel in Tibet is about adventure and I have been fortunate in the past to work with Graeme Dingle, one of the world's leading explorers and humanitarians (we once jumped out of a helicopter together on to the summit of Mt Nicholas in New Zealand). Graeme has achieved many alpine 'firsts' but I remember him more for his maxim 'it's not the summit that's important – it's the journey'. Graeme, along with his close friend Sir Edmund Hillary, has managed to explore remote parts of the world and, at the same time, give something back to the local communities he has visited. Graeme has kindly written the Preface for this book.

There is also a diverse cast of characters each of whom I would like to thank for her or his assistance and support along the unorthodox path that I took to complete this guidebook. First and foremost Wendy, who is the unsung hero of this book, she cycled every kilometre with me throughout Tibet and not only wrote the section for women travellers but helped with much of the text and kept me focused on finishing each chapter whenever I strayed.

I also particularly want to thank Claude André, from the Tibet Map Institute, who freely gave his time to create the detailed maps in this book. Claude lives in the lovely village of Eze on the Côte d'Azur and is one of the world's leading Tibetologists. Additionally, I wish to thank the following people for their support along the way: Peter Stewart, Kathmandu's mountain-bike guru who wrote the Nepal mountain-bike section; Jamie McGuinness, a kiwi also living in Kathmandu, who wrote the Kashgar–Lhasa route notes; Coen Koomen who provided valuable input for the Xining–Lhasa route guide collected during his cycle ride from Beijing to Kathmandu.

Dr Mick Goodwin, a fellow All Blacks supporter, who provided the medical advice and some free antibiotics; Bryn Thomas, my publisher, for belief in this project from the outset and his continuing patience at the multiple deadlines I missed en route; also at Trailblazer: Henry Stedman for editing the text, Jane Thomas for the index and Anna Jacomb-Hood for layout; Dr Prativa Pandey for writing the invaluable section on altitude sickness; Tenzin Chokey, Lobsang Nyandek and my other co-workers at the Tibet Centre for Human Rights and Democracy; Kate Saunders and Louise Fournier at the Tibet Information Network in London; Jamyang and Christophe from the Amnye Machen Institute who provided the general maps of Tibet; Mel, Nick, Karin, Fiona, Mike, Patricia, James and Gus for sharing plenty of banter in Dharamsala; All the regulars from Colonials' Café in London; James Scully and Andy Wood for building my website (🖳 www.tibetover land.com); Louise Thomas for introducing me to rooibos and assisting with the appendices; Ben Plant for providing floor space in London when it was most needed; Tracey Mifflin for safely carting a very heavy box of my research notes from Delhi to London; my family for never questioning and always encouraging my random travels.

Finally, I wish to say 'thank you' and *tashi deleg* to the many Tibetans and Chinese inside Tibet who provided us with butter tea, food, shelter or simply warmth from their campfire along the way. Travel is never remembered by the amazing sights and exploits 'ticked-off' along the way but rather through the hospitality and kind faces of those people you encounter.

A request

The author and publisher have tried to ensure that this guide is as accurate and up to date as possible. Nevertheless things change. If you notice any changes or omissions that should be included in the next edition of this book, please write to Kym McConnell at Trailblazer (address on p2) or email him at kym.mcconnell@trailblazer-guides.com or kym@tibetoverland.com. A free copy of the next edition will be sent to persons making a significant contribution.

Updated information will shortly be available on the Internet at 🖳 **www.trailblazer-guides.com**

FOREWORD

THE DALAI LAMA

Travel to and within Tibet has always been a challenge. The country is surrounded by the highest mountains in the world that are traversed by some of the most inhospitable passes. Once they are crossed, the high altitude is only one of the obstacles a traveller might face. Others might include, depending on the time of year, heavy snow, fierce sunshine, biting winds and gruelling sandstorms. None of them are insuperable. Tibetans, of course, are used to these moods of the landscape and climate and take appropriate precautions.

This book prepared particularly with mountain bikers in mind contains a wealth of advice for coping with the many difficulties an overlander in Tibet might face, as well as informed advice about places to visit, what to see and how to get there. It is ironic that, although the Chinese forces occupying Tibet proudly boast about the roads and other infrastructure they have built, the restrictive regime they preside over prevents both Tibetans and foreigners from using them as freely as they would like. Nevertheless, it is still possible for an observant and astute traveller to get out and about and develop a feel for the situation that currently prevails in Tibet, and I encourage anyone who wishes to go to do so. What's more I believe that, despite the destruction that has taken place everywhere over the last forty years, once you get out of the cities much of Tibet's landscape retains the clear wide-open quality that has filled Tibetans with a sense of freedom for centuries.

I congratulate Kym McConnell and Wendy Miles, dedicated friends of Tibet, for the work they have done compiling this book. I am also happy to know that it contains detailed colour relief maps that are the result of the efforts of the Tibet Map Institute. I am sure that the book will serve the worthy purpose of promoting greater awareness of Tibet and of providing valuable guidance to those who wish to travel there, both those who remain in the comfort of their armchairs and others who actually get on their bikes.

PREFACE

In 1985 I was a member of one of the first foreign mountaineering expeditions to be given permission by the Chinese to approach Everest through Tibet. What I saw made me weep. Tibetan faces everywhere that showed the pain of the Chinese occupation.

Once grand ancient structures reduced to piles of rubbish. Of the ruins of the previously incomparable walled mountain town of Shekar Dzong, I wrote, 'the remains poked skywards like a giant skeleton picked clean by vultures…as I watched a small group of Tibetans rebuilding their *gompa* from the rubble, I wept.'

Not much I thought, apart from the fabulous mountains or to help the people in some small way would attract me back to one of the most fascinating lands on earth. But Kym's book, *Tibet Overland*, has my Tibetan juices bubbling again.

Although *Tibet Overland* is designed for the mountain biker, it is so comprehensive that it will be of interest to the armchair traveller, useful to those planning an excursion to the Himalayan region and a must for those intending to bike on the Roof of the World.

Graeme Dingle
ONZM, MBE

Graeme Dingle has been one of New Zealand's leading mountaineers for many years and is one of the world's foremost adventurers and humanitarians. He has achieved over 200 mountaineering and adventuring firsts throughout the world including:

● *First ascent in one season of all six 'classic' European north faces including the Eiger and Matterhorn.*
● *First traverse of the Himalayas, 5000km in 265 days.*
● *A 400-day, 28,000km circumnavigation of the Arctic in two stages.*

Graeme has chronicled his many adventures in more than 10 books and has received numerous international awards, including the 'Antarctic Service Award'. Graeme was made Officer of the New Zealand Order of Merit in 2001 and is currently Executive Trustee of Project K – New Zealand's first national youth development programme.

CONTENTS

INTRODUCTION

'Tis the Dreamer whose dreams come true! **Rudyard Kipling**

Hundreds of books written in contemporary times wax lyrical about the lure of Tibet. Nonetheless, no matter how many people visit Tibet, it remains an extraordinary destination.

The purpose of this book is to help travellers to explore Tibet in a new way and, where possible, avoid the commercial trappings of 'bottled tourism' that have become commonplace in the region. With this guide, a bit of independence and a decent measure of determination and good humour, you can have a unique overland adventure on the Roof of the World.

TIBET – A DESTINATION AND A JOURNEY

The magic and mystery of Tibet have lured travellers for years. Until the turn of the 20th century, Tibet was one of the few destinations in the world that was so unattainable that it would tantalize adventure travellers from all corners of the globe. Its geographic isolation on the highest plateau in the world and unique culture and religious beliefs have for centuries moulded the lives of a very special people. For years, hearsay and Pundit rumour were all that the outside world could learn about this secret land and its inhabitants.

The Tibetan civilization is one of the oldest in the world, dating back 5000 years at least. It is almost certainly much older than this. The mythical history, according to Bon tradition, describes the Tibetan people as descendants of a Simian father and a mountain ogress. The offspring inherited their father's compassion and their mother's stubborn character. When travellers meet the Tibetan people living on the plateau today, they may wonder if there is some truth to their mythical ancestry.

Of equal importance is the environment that has shaped the Tibetan people. Tibet is bordered to the south by the Himalayas and to the west by the Ladakh mountains and the Karakoram ranges. To the north are the Kun-Lun and Tang-La ranges. The sole gap between the magnificent mountains that isolate the plateau is to the east where three mighty rivers flow. These are the three main rivers in Asia that find their source in Tibet: the Indus, the Brahmaputra and the Yangtse.

Tibetans call their home 'Land of the Snows'. It is often referred to as the 'Roof of the World'. Both names capture the extreme nature of the land. Covering an area of about 2.5 million sq km, the average altitude on the plateau is more than 4000m. The extreme climate renders 75% of the land uninhabitable, making Tibet one of the world's least populated regions.

Since 1951, just as the Western world was beginning to catch its first real glimpse of life in Tibet, the Chinese government closed its doors.

These remained closed until the early eighties. China's so-called 'peaceful liberation' of Tibet in 1959, promoted under the policy of 'Reunification of the Motherland', has impacted significantly on both the land and its inhabitants. The ancient civilization now coexists with Communist China.

Yet despite the difficulties created by the presence of the Chinese authorities, travel to Tibet is still completely worthwhile. China has recognized the economic value of tourism in Tibet and identified it as one of 'five pillars of industry' necessary for the economic development of the region. As a tourist you are able to take advantage of this approach and travel relatively freely in all open areas.

Although the policies introduced in the country since 1959 have transformed Tibet's cities, the land and the people outside the city centres continue to retain many aspects of traditional Tibet. The thin mountain air creates an almost surreal effect on the landscape. The mountains and lakes have an overwhelming presence and remain enduringly holy and sacred to the people. These things have not changed since 1959. In many ways, the Tibetan way of life, particularly outside the major cities, continues in the same manner as it has done for thousands of years. Unfortunately, Chinese policies are extending into remote rural areas, and it is possible that these ancient traditions may become a thing of the past – and that would be a tragedy.

If you have any doubt that your presence as a tourist in Tibet may contribute to the decline of the traditional Tibetan way of life and condone the Chinese presence and control over Tibet, consider the advice of His Holiness the 14th Dalai Lama, who is recognized by most Tibetans as the spiritual and temporal leader of Tibet. The Dalai Lama maintains that informed and aware tourists have an important role to play in the preservation of Tibetan culture and he has a clear message for travellers to his homeland, as stated in the Foreword to this guidebook:

> . . . I encourage anyone who wishes to go to do so.

OVERLAND TRAVEL IN TIBET

Tibet is the ultimate overlander's paradise in terms of the scope for excitement and adventure. Adventure travellers and visitors to Tibet are often of the same mindset. Any individual who seeks an exciting travel experience that permits a real insight into a culture should consider an overland journey to Tibet – the cream of 'off the beaten track' travel.

Mountain biking in Tibet is the ultimate off the beaten track adventure. There is nowhere else in the world where mountain bikers are able to cycle alongside 8000m-plus peaks and conquer 5000m-plus mountain passes – almost daily. It's even possible to bike to the foot of the highest mountain on earth. Tibet boasts the world's longest downhill run – from a high point of just under 5000m at Lalung la to below 800m in Nepal, in just over 160kms of incredibly exhilarating descent. To add to that, road quality and extreme weather conditions make mountain biking in Tibet technically challenging – particularly off the main routes.

Mountain biking on the highest roads in the world is a physically and mentally demanding challenge but the rewards are extraordinary. The personal satisfaction and thrill achieved from such a trip can be enormous. Difficult and often exhausting conditions combine to test your fortitude. But the view of the world from the dizzying heights of Tibet and the long, lonely expanse of solitude that envelops you is a humbling experience. Inevitably, your view of the world, and of yourself, will never be the same again.

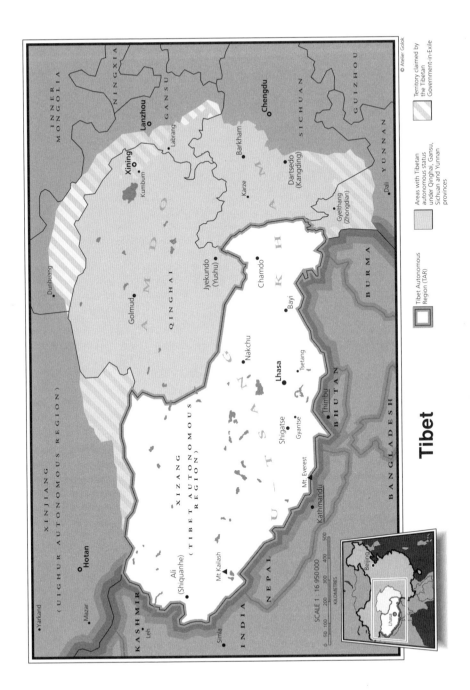

Tibet

SCALE 1 : 16 950 000

KILOMETRES
0   50 100   200   300   400   500

© Atelier Golok

Territory claimed by the Tibetan Government-in-Exile

Areas with Tibetan autonomous status under Qinghai, Gansu, Sichuan and Yunnan provinces

Tibet Autonomous Region (TAR)

Regardless of your chosen mode of transport, Tibet is a perfect setting for an adventure. The secret, jealously guarded by the few travellers who have already travelled overland in the region, is that this mode of travel makes it possible for travellers to live with the Tibetan people and discover the traditional Tibetan way of life outside the big modernized cities. For example, on most overland routes recorded in this book it is not possible to reach the next major township within one day of cycling. Accordingly, mountain bikers will be required to camp with nomads or negotiate accommodation at local villages or monasteries. In doing so you will catch an insight into nomadic, village and monastic life that is very difficult to achieve unless you have completely independent transport.

In an overland travellers' (particularly cyclists') daily search for food outside the main towns, the renowned hospitality of the Tibetan people is inescapable. Bikers are frequently invited off the road to share a cup of butter tea and a bowl of tsampa. It would be misleading to suggest that all of these aspects of overland travel in Tibet are entirely pleasant. In particular, some of the most magical, and at times most frustrating, characters encountered by mountain bikers are the local children. Tibetan and Chinese children literally mob cyclists passing schools and villages. The playfulness of the children on the plateau will drive you to distraction. But look at it from their point of view: mountain bikers are an exciting and refreshing sight in their isolated environment and a welcome distraction from schoolwork and the never-ending task of collecting yak dung for the fire. If you spend the time winning the favour of the village children, you will inevitably find that their parents are much more willing to accommodate your needs!

HOW TO USE THIS GUIDEBOOK

The aim of this book is to provide overland travellers in Tibet with the most accurate maps and route descriptions. The overland routes on pp63-146 were researched by me and are accompanied by maps, elevation profiles and km-by-km route descriptions. The routes on pp147-71 were compiled from a mixture of my own research and other friends' and travellers' notes.

Maps

The maps included in this book have been painstakingly created by Claude André from a voluntary group in France called the **Tibet Map Institute**. M. André has been involved with cartography on the Tibetan plateau since 1967; the Royal Geographical Society published some of his early research. The impetus for his recent work is the lack of credible maps produced since the 1950s identifying and locating the Tibetan villages and monasteries destroyed by the Red Guards during the Cultural Revolution.

The Tibet Map Institute (🖳 www.tibetmap.com) has now produced over 80 maps (scale 1:310,000) together with a database of over 7000 toponyms. The maps are based on NASA Landsat photographs superimposed onto international aeronautical maps and they incorporate the most accurate altitudes/features available from various sources (including everything from the earliest explorers' and Pundits' notes to the most recent traveller data).

At my request for assistance, M. André kindly adapted some of his maps to illustrate the key overland routes detailed in this book including distance and altitude readings. Scales for the maps are as follows: Maps 1 and 3 (1:450,000), Maps 2, 4-8 and 10 (1:500,000), Map 9 (1:300,000). During my research I found various road maps (see p32) but none had the accurate distance readings or elevation profiles required by cyclists. Whilst a 20km error is generally irrelevant for motorists it can mean two or three hours of extra cycling at the end of an already hard day for mountain bikers!

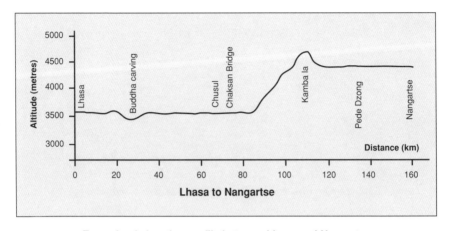

Example of elevation profile between Lhasa and Nangartse

Elevation profiles
The elevation profiles in this book are generated from the altitudes recorded religiously along the way and should assist you in anticipating the severity of your daily route.

Relative or absolute It is the relative, not absolute, heights that are important when travelling in Tibet. The accuracy of any map series is only relative to the 'base' or reference coordinates upon which it is created. Because the Chinese have not allowed anyone to officially 'map' Tibet for 50 years, the altitude readings provided by the different recognized topographical map series vary (see 'Maps – topographical' pp31-2). For example, the height of Mt Nyenchen Thangla (north of Lhasa) is recorded at the varying heights of: 7090m (Russian World Series); 6986m (US Tactical Pilot Chart Series); 7111m (US Joint Operations Graphic Series); and 7117m (Chinese Series).

Also, the recorded altitudes for Lhasa city vary between 3600m and 3680m. **For the sake of simplicity all altitudes in my route descriptions are based on an altitude for Lhasa (Barkhor Square) of 3600m**.

Another example of inconsistencies is the stone marker readings on top of most passes in Tibet, which never seem to agree with (or differ by the same amount from) any traveller's altimeter.

Route guides (🚲)
The route guides in this book provide a km-by-km breakdown of popular overland routes including points of interest, villages, mountain passes, possible campsites, and the main places to buy food (🍽), water (ⵟ) or seek accommodation (🛏). They are not exhaustive as there are many additional compounds or groups of houses where you could also barter for sustenance or shelter. Firstly, tours are described that travellers will be able to complete in less than one week (to Ganden, Nam Tso or the Yarlung Valley) using Lhasa as a base. Secondly, there is a detailed description of the 'classic' overland route in Tibet from Lhasa to Kathmandu including the side trip to Mt Everest North Base Camp.

The final route guides in Part 3 cover the long overland journeys into Lhasa from Xining, Kunming and Kashgar and provide an overview and indication of the distances and main passes between key villages along the way. Note that these routes do not always contain information such as road markers, and some altitudes may not be exact where they have been collated from secondary sources.

NANGARTSE to GYANTSE

CYCLOMETER READING (KM)	ROAD MARKER (KM)	ALTIMETER READING (M)	NOTES AND KEY POINTS OF INTEREST
1	153	4410	First 'road marker' out of Nangartse
7.9	160		Road fork – go right to Karo la *(left road goes to Taklung monastery 17km)*
13.5	165/166	4550	Possible campsite – next to river *(past Langla village and around spur into narrow valley)*
59	211	4240	Lungma village ⬤, ⍩, ↝ *(valley leads north to Rong Valley and Rinpung Dzong)*

Extract taken from route guide between Nangartse and Gyantse

Distances All the distance 'cyclometer' readings originating out of Lhasa commence from Barkhor Square. It is anticipated the daily distance measurements could vary up to 1km per day between different individual cyclists, depending upon how straight cyclists ride, especially on uphill sections of the passes.

Road markers In Tibet there are very few road signs but most of the main overland routes have stone markers on the shoulders of the road, supposedly at 1km intervals. The distance readings on various markers can be a little confusing as they can commence from different origins (some start from Beijing!). Also, as the roads are redeveloped the stone markers get updated or replaced and a new system may be totally unrelated to the old one. At least four different marker systems (in black or red) are in use just between Lhasa and Kathmandu.

The kilometre marker readings are recorded in the route guides throughout this book. Sometimes an approximate reading is given where the marker is missing. Where a particular 'point of interest' lies between two markers, both markers are recorded (eg 165/166 as seen in the above extract). Remember that the cyclometer on your bike or the odometer reading in your vehicle may not always equate with these markers.

Cycling times

Approximate cycling times (excluding rest breaks) are also given to allow you to plan the maximum or minimum time it will take you to get between points (weather dependent, of course!). I had full rear panniers throughout Tibet but cyclists on organized tours (where all gear is usually carried by a supporting vehicle) can expect shorter times.

🚲 CYCLING TIMES 🚲

ROUTE TAKEN	JOURNEY TIME*
Nangartse to Samding monastery (side route)	1hr
Nangartse to Karo la	2.5-3.5hr
Karo la to Lungma	2-3hr

*ESTIMATE WITH FULL PANNIERS; NOT INCLUDING REST STOPS

SPECIAL ISSUES FOR TRAVELLERS IN TIBET

It is important for travellers to the region to understand something about the political situation in Tibet. The political climate is turbulent and rules and regulations governing individual travellers are liable to change with little or no notice. If you understand something about the historical facts that led to the current situation, you will better appreciate the reason why certain things are as they are. Whether you intend to or not, your very presence there will have an impact both on the lives of the Tibetan people and of the Chinese living in Tibet.

Most people contemplating travel into the region will have heard of the Dalai Lama, the Tibetan religious leader who fled from his homeland in 1959 when the Chinese army took control of the capital city of Lhasa. See p181-91 for an introduction to Tibetan history (which I have tried to relate in an objective manner). The unfortunate reality is that the events since the Dalai Lama fled to neighbouring India cannot be dismissed purely as a matter of historic interest only. Those events, and the continued presence of the Chinese people in Tibet today, have an immediate effect on the lives of both the people living on the plateau and the tens of thousands of Tibetan refugees currently living in exile. Each year thousands of new Tibetan refugees arrive in Dharamsala, Northern India, the home of the Dalai Lama and his Government-in-Exile. Many more enter other Tibetan refugee camps in India, Nepal and Bhutan.

Chinese policies continue to undermine Tibetan culture. Things that are fundamentally Tibetan, such as Tibetan Buddhism, the nomadic way of life, monastic living, the Tibetan language and food, all comprise a living and breathing culture that is quite different from the culture and traditions of the Chinese. This poses a threat to China as it strives to redefine Tibetans as a 'minority ethnic group within China' to be preserved by a 'Cultural Ministry' for display on appropriate state occasions and to tour parties. Whilst some of the major monasteries are undergoing reconstruction, largely funded by the Chinese administration, ancient scriptures also are being redrafted so as to exclude the doctrines that the Chinese find offensive or 'separatist'. The new open religious practice is in fact very severely constrained.

For example, in 1996 a campaign of 'patriotic re-education' commenced in all major monasteries in Tibet. Monks were forced to denounce the Dalai Lama and destroy all photographs of His Holiness. Since 1996 more than 12,000 monks and nuns have left or been forced out of monasteries and nunneries because they were unwilling to comply with China's demands. Religion is only one aspect of repression in the 'new open Tibet'. There were reported shootings by the Chinese authorities in Lhasa in April 1998, leading to the deaths of seven monks. In 2001 there were at least six reported executions in Tibet as a result of a renewed wave of the so-called 'Strike Hard' campaign which aims to crack down on crime.

Travellers to the region need to be aware of the political issues – it is possible that you could become involved (directly or indirectly) with such issues. Travellers on

---

TIBET ONLINE

The best organizations providing up-to-date information on recent events and the political situation in Tibet are:

Tibet Information Network (💻 www.tibetinfo.net)
World Tibet Network News (💻 www.tibet.ca)
Tibetan Centre for Human Rights & Democracy (💻 www.tchrd.org)

For other information, including how you might assist the Tibetan struggle, check out:
Free Tibet Campaign (💻 www.freetibet.org)
Office of Tibet (London) (💻 www.tibet.com)
Tibetan Government-in-Exile (💻 www.tibet.net)
International Campaign for Tibet (💻 www.savetibet.org)
International Support Group (💻 www.tibet.org)
Milarepa Fund (💻 www.milarepa.org)

bicycles must be particularly cautious as they will often avoid the controls that have been established by the authorities to shield the Tibetan people from foreign visitors (and vice versa).

Awareness of the issues and a sensitive and sensible approach to your environment and the people in it will enhance your Tibetan experience. It will help you to understand why people behave in a certain way and how they react to you – a foreign visitor. Try to be aware that conversations in major centres, such as Lhasa, may be monitored. The Potala Palace in particular is equipped with an extensive video and infra-red sound surveillance system. In addition, there is a far-reaching network of 'informers' operating in major tourist spots and monasteries. Conversations of a 'political' nature will be most likely to draw the attention of the authorities. There are accounts of nuns and monks reporting travellers to the authorities on the grounds that they illegally engaged in political conversations or distributed banned material (such as photographs of the Dalai Lama or Tibetan flags). In 1995 a guest at the largest tourist hotel in Lhasa was detained for 48hr by police for speculating about a bomb explosion in a facsimile that he had sent home. In October 2001, three foreign tourists were detained in Lhasa after displaying a Tibetan flag and shouting pro-independence slogans in front of the Potala.

In reality, the worst thing that is likely to happen to a tourist who is suspected of 'unlawful' activity is that he or she will be interrogated and deported. Any Tibetan who is caught receiving or distributing incriminating material is liable to a lengthy term of imprisonment and, possibly, torture at the hands of the Chinese authorities.

Admittedly, the growing number of tourists in Lhasa makes it increasingly difficult for the Chinese authorities to monitor everybody. The key is to keep a low profile in the major city centres. If you do not draw attention to yourself then you and your mountain bike will be permitted to move about virtually unhindered by the authorities (also see the visas and permits section, pp20-2).

TIBET – A MULTI-SPORT DESTINATION!

Tibet is becoming a haven for individuals seeking extreme multi-sport challenges in addition to mountain biking.

Raid Gauloises

The tenth Raid Gauloises international multi-sport event, including 69 teams from 18 countries, was held in Tibet for the first time commencing in May 2000 from Shekar Dzong. The 827km course initially followed a route similar to the Lhasa–Kathmandu road, reaching a high point of 5150m, before entering Nepal via Kodari. Inside Nepal contestants headed on to Dolalghat and then through Manthali and Harkapur along the Sunkosi River, then descended south into Rajbiraj before reaching the finish line at Janakpur (near the India-Nepal border).

Kayaking the Brahmaputra

A team of intrepid explorers attempted to kayak the entire length of the Brahmaputra (from Kailash to the Bay of Bengal) but were stopped in their path by canyons.

Everest Marathon

The Chinese Tourism Board has hosted a 'world's highest marathon' event near Mt Everest North Base Camp to compete with a rival event held in Nepal from Mt Everest South Base Camp. The event was run twice but has not been held since 1995.

Qinghai-Tibet Bicycle Stage Race

The Chinese Cycling Association hosts an annual Qinghai-Tibet Bicycle Stage Race each September. International competitors participate in the ten day, 1000km race from Xining to Lhasa.

Windsurfing at Nam Tso

The Chinese Tourism Board recently sponsored a Chinese windsurfer to windsurf on the great Lake Nam Tso – anything is possible!

PLANNING

1

Overland travel options

Just leaving one's homeland is to accomplish half the Dharma **Tibetan adage**

There are several options for overland travel in Tibet. Flights are available into Lhasa (except during the winter months) and many independent travellers opt to fly one way then travel overland once in Lhasa. However, given that there are no internal flights in Tibet, in order to visit any main sights travellers will need to arrange some form of overland transportation (public bus, hired 4WD vehicle or bicycle).

JEEP TOURS

The most common trip is to fly one way and join a group with a jeep-hire to travel the Friendship Highway in the other direction. These trips can be organized through package-tour companies in Kathmandu or Lhasa. Alternatively, independent travellers can make their own way to Lhasa by bus, hitching or cycling (and do the same by way of return). (See pp58-9 for information on renting a four-wheel drive vehicle and public buses).

MOUNTAIN-BIKE TOURS

First, there are tour companies in Kathmandu that run organized and authorized mountain-bike tours from Lhasa to Kathmandu. The operators will arrange all permits and visas and transport you to Lhasa. You then cycle back to Kathmandu, followed by a support vehicle, which will carry your gear – and you if required.

The benefits of organized cycle tours are three-fold. First, you will not have to deal with any permit issues and will not be confronted with the risk of finding yourself permit-less in a region. Second, the support vehicle makes life altogether easier because carrying panniers full of food and gear is hard work at 5000m-plus. The support vehicle and guides are available to deal with any emergency posed by traffic accidents or altitude problems. Third, it is almost invariably quicker to undertake, for example, the Friendship Highway, in an organized tour group.

The downside is expense and lack of freedom to alter your course or spend an extra few days at particular places. A reliable operator in Nepal is Himalayan Mountain Bikes (www.bikeasia.info) – see p173 for details.

INDEPENDENT CYCLISTS

Alternatively, you can 'go it alone'. Independent cyclists in Tibet are still rare enough for the Chinese authorities not to pay them too much concern. Therefore, unless you do something particularly stupid to draw attention to yourself, the likelihood is that you will be left alone to quietly meander through the countryside. The downside is that if you run into any trouble with the locals, or become involved in an accident or medical emergency, you may find that the authorities are not particularly sympathetic. The risk is relatively small and if you are properly prepared in terms of equipment, safety and local political issues, it should not be too difficult to minimize it even more.

If you do decide to go it alone, you need to think carefully about the best way to get to your starting point. See pp43-46 for the main options, and the pros and cons of each. Your decision will depend a lot on where you are arriving from and the amount of time available to you. You will also need to consider what type of bike and gear to take. All of these issues are covered below.

When to go

Tibet has an extreme climate and harsh conditions. It was created from the Indian continent colliding with the Eurasian land mass around three million years ago. The collision thrust up from the bottom of the sea what is now the Tibetan plateau and moulded the landscape to produce the Himalayan mountain range.

The altitude in Tibet ranges from 2000m to over 8000m. In central Tibet, the average altitude is almost 4000m. The height brings with it extreme temperatures and the land is often covered in snow. The lowest temperatures in winter will reach around -40°C. Midday in summer can be as hot as 38°C. The rainfall is limited to 25-50cm per year, most of it falling within a three-month period (from June to August).

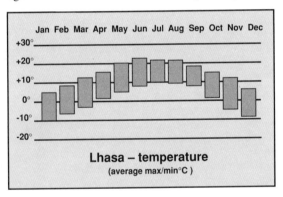

Lhasa – temperature
(average max/min°C)

Essentially, travellers may visit Tibet at any time of the year and cyclists have made the journey from Golmud to Lhasa in the middle of winter. However, the climatic conditions in Tibet are harsh at best and, accordingly, weather-related obstacles may be minimized by travelling at certain times of the year. The spring and autumn months are the best time for overland travel in Tibet. The ideal window for mountain biking is from September to November.

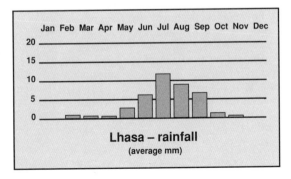

Lhasa – rainfall
(average mm)

SEASONS

Spring (March-May) – Cold, dry and windy

Spring is exceedingly windy and sandstorms make travel, particularly by cycle, extremely unpleasant. Cyclists have been known to make the trip at this time of the year but usually the only way to tolerate the shocking sandstorms is to cycle by night when the winds have dropped. This is not a good way to take in the scenery and visibility problems at night make cycling dangerous.

Summer (June-August) – Cool and wet but hot at noon

Summer is very wet. The rainy season is from June to August and many of the rivers flood during this period, making them impossible to ford by bicycle (and often even by four-wheel drive vehicle).

Autumn (September-November) – Cold and dry

Autumn is the ideal season for overland travel in Tibet. The rains are usually over by the end of September and the rivers subside by October. By arriving in Tibet during September you will benefit from the long hot sunny days of summer's end and miss the rain. In early September it is better to make shorter trips to the north and east, saving the Friendship Highway and other routes heading south until the end of September or beginning of October. The Friendship Highway journey can be made comfortably until the end of November – after that time it becomes too cold and heavy snow on the passes makes crossing impossible.

Winter (December-February) – Cold and extremely dry

Winter is just plain cold. There are no problems with rain or sandstorms during the winter and the visibility on clear days can be spectacular but it is simply too cold to be out in the open – particularly over exposed mountain passes – without serious equipment for those conditions. Another problem in winter time (from November to February) is that Lhasa airport is closed. At the same time, the high mountain passes on the roads often become impossible to cross.

FURTHER INFORMATION

The current weather in Lhasa (plus forecast) can be checked online via:
- www.weather.com/weather/local/CHXX0080
- www.wunderground.com/global/stations/55591.html

Visas and permits

How much a dunce that has been sent to roam
Excels a dunce that has been kept at home!
From *The Progress of Error*, William Cooper

Getting in and out of Tibet without incident requires planning and preparation. The two key considerations are where and how to obtain a **visa and permit**, and which **entry point** to use.

For political and security reasons, China has actively discouraged independent travel into Tibet. Group travel is often the only 'official' way to enter the country. Besides a Chinese visa, a travel permit is required just to enter Tibet. Once inside Tibet, many places are closed to individual travellers and an Aliens' Travel Permit (see p21) is required to get around.

Travel to Tibet is subject to an important caveat. **Things change and the official position in relation to foreign visitors is extremely fluid**. Certain key anniversary dates, such as the Lhasa Uprising (14 March), lead to increased security controls over tourists in Lhasa. Events such as the escape of the 10th Karmapa Lama in December 1999 caused an immediate crackdown on border security. There are no guarantees with China and a policy on visas and entry points that applies one week may change completely the next (check out 🖥 www.tibetinfo.net or any of the other websites listed on p15 for the latest travel regulations in Tibet).

The main overland routes into Tibet are from Kathmandu in the south, Kashgar in the west, Golmud in the north and Chengdu (Sichuan) or Kunming (Yunnan) in the east. The only overland border that is officially open to individuals is the border on the route from Golmud. However, intrepid individuals, including cyclists, have successfully made it across each of these overland routes (albeit sometimes under cover of night).

Where and how to sort out your visa may depend on whether you intend to travel overland or fly into Lhasa. Many travellers decide to visit Tibet after they arrive in Kathmandu, Nepal. If your intention is to join a tour or organized group cycle tour, Kathmandu is an excellent place to book such a trip. However, until recently the Chinese embassy in Nepal would not issue visas for tourists wishing to travel independently in Tibet but currently independent travellers are reporting that they are being given visas here. Note that this could change at any time.

To enter Tibet you must have a **Chinese visa** and a **travel permit**.

VISAS

You may apply for a Chinese visa in your country of origin or somewhere else en route such as Hong Kong, Delhi, Islamabad or Bangkok. Most Chinese embassies will grant independent travellers a 30-day Chinese visa without too much difficulty.

Where to get your visa
Local Chinese embassy To apply for a visa your passport must be valid for at least three months after the period of the intended visit. When applying, it is advisable not to mention that you intend to travel to Tibet (state anything else such as Beijing, Xian, or Shanghai). If you require a visa for more than 30 days, and this may be necessary if you intend to embark on overland routes other than the Friendship Highway, you will need to shop around a little. For example, the Chinese embassies in Amsterdam, Paris, Birmingham and Hong Kong issue three-month visas to independent travellers. Most other Chinese embassies, including London, Wellington and Sydney, will offer only one-month visas.

While applying for your Chinese visa, you may also wish to obtain a visa for the country that you are likely to enter upon your departure from Tibet (although short-term transit visas can be obtained for Nepal and India at the border crossings).

Chinese embassy in Nepal It is probably best to avoid trying to obtain a visa in Kathmandu unless your intention is to join a tour group. The on again, off again policy relating to issuing individuals with a visa is frustrating and although it's currently possible the situation may change at any time, in particular during politically sensitive periods. If the embassy is not issuing visas to individuals when you arrive you will be forced to travel with an organized tour group and you will only be able to obtain a 5-14 day visa through a travel agency. Note that the embassy will usually cancel any other valid Chinese visa in your passport.

Chinese embassy in Hong Kong Hong Kong is the most reliable place to obtain a three or even six-month Chinese visa. Bear in mind that, post-1994, Hong Kong is once more a part of China so you will first need to check that you can enter Hong Kong on your passport without a visa. Chinese visas are obtainable from the Ministry of Foreign Affairs visa office, 5th floor, Low Block, China Resources Building, 26 Harbour Rd, Wanchai. The 30-day visa costs HK$100 for next-day service or HK$250 same day.

A reliable and more convenient place to get a visa in Hong Kong is Shoestring Travel (Flat A, 4/F, Alpha House, 27-33 Nathan Road, Kowloon; 🖳 shoetvl @hkstar.com). A three-month visa costs HK$180 (single entry) and can be processed over two working days, while HK$380 ensures same day delivery. A six-month visa can also be arranged within a few days for HK$700 without the usual requirements for business invitations and references.

Visa extensions

It is possible to extend a tourist visa at the 'Foreign Affairs Section' of the Public Security Bureau (PSB) in most main cities inside China including Chengdu, Xining, and Kunming. Usually you will get a one-month extension the first time and two to four weeks the second time. A third extension is difficult to obtain.

However, once inside Tibet it is difficult to get any extension, especially in Lhasa. If you can get an extension in Lhasa it may only be for a week and you'll almost certainly have to provide evidence that you will be leaving Tibet (eg a flight ticket to Kathmandu). Some travellers have had more success going through travel agents or trying in Shigatse. It is best to assume that you won't get an extension in Tibet and you should therefore try to obtain the longest possible visa you can before arriving.

TRAVEL PERMITS

Group Travel Permit

Foreigners are told they officially require a travel permit in addition to their visa to enter Tibet (this is not the case for other provinces in China), but most travellers have never seen one of these permits.

When you purchase an airfare (eg Chengdu/Lhasa or Kathmandu/Lhasa) or bus fare (eg Golmud/Lhasa) along the main overland routes the travel agent acquires both the ticket and permit on your behalf (as part of a 'five-person group'). There is no indication of the permit in your passport and inspections are rarely carried out to check for it. Basically the travel permit is a piece of paper outlining the 'group itinerary' and sometimes (but not always) listing the names of the group participants. It is advisable to ask for a photocopy of your group permit in case you do get separated from your group.

Aliens' Travel Permit (ATP)

In the Tibet Autonomous Region (TAR) many places are officially closed to foreigners. Before you visit key sights outside Lhasa (such as Samye or Chongye) you need an Aliens' Travel Permit (ATP) indicating your destinations. This is obtained from the local Public Security Bureau (PSB) in each region.

An ATP is not required for some main open towns, including Lhasa, Shigatse, Tsetang, Nyalam, Zhangmu (in Tibetan Dram), Purang, Nakchu and for other sites such as Ganden and Lake Nam Tso. If you go to the PSB and ask, they will either tell you that you need one and take your money accordingly or say

中华人民共和国

外国人旅行证

The People's Republic of China

Aliens' Travel Permit

No.

Aliens' Travel Permit

you need one but won't issue them to individuals. In the latter scenario you may be able to obtain the relevant ATP by chartering a vehicle (via a travel agent). The situation gets even more confusing when the PSB abruptly changes the open status of key destinations (usually following some anti-Chinese activity).

In reality, ATPs are not checked at many places and most people simply do not obtain one. However, if you are planning to travel along the Lhasa-Kathmandu road (known as the Friendship Highway) and, in particular, make the side trips to Everest North Base Camp and Sakya, you may be checked for a permit. Other areas where the PSB have become more thorough in their inspection for ATPs are at Samye (ferry depot), Mt Kailash and bigger towns along the main overland roads. If you do not have an ATP you will be fined and possibly not permitted to enter those places (the amount of fine depends on the place and the official). Those foreigners who rent 4WD vehicles for specific tours (eg a visit to Mt Kailash) will obtain the required permits automatically via their travel agent.

If you do arrive in a closed area it will pay to be inconspicuous and leave swiftly. If you require accommodation many towns allow foreigners to stay at designated hotels only, which generally charge foreigners outrageous prices. Also the PSB may visit and enquire why you are there before fining you and making sure you depart as soon as possible. Because of the difficulties in arranging ATPs for individuals in Lhasa many overlanders wait until they reach Shigatse to apply for a permit from the local PSB. At the time of research the Shigatse PSB were more favourable to issuing ATPs (for a fee) and would even include specific reference to the fact that you are permitted to travel by bicycle (if you ask nicely and pay even more). Make sure the PSB officer writes down every town you intend to pass through or visit on your intended trip.

Cyclists and ATPs It is legal to travel independently from Lhasa to Shigatse without a permit (because they are both open areas). This is normally a 5hr bus ride. However, for cyclists who travel the Southern Friendship Highway (and nearly all do), it can take up to six days to reach Shigatse. Clearly the current policy does not take into account the time-scale for cycling, and as a result cyclists seem to be able to take advantage and make the trip from Lhasa to Shigatse without a permit. However, to be on the safe side, some cyclists still have gone to the effort of visiting Shigatse for a day from Lhasa (by bus) to obtain a permit prior to commencing their cycle tour from Lhasa.

It is possible to book an organized cycle tour in Tibet. The tour operators will arrange the necessary visas and permits for you. Generally, such tours take 5-10 people and are for the duration of approximately 15 days – which will take you from Lhasa to Kathmandu. A guide and support vehicle will be included. The support vehicle will carry your panniers and equipment and also assist slower riders.

Independent cyclists travelling overland into Tibet will not have the correct permits and could be turned back, fined and/or have cycles confiscated by vigilant PSB officers at any point during their trip. Most cyclists try to overcome this problem by passing through particular 'checkpoints and hot spots' under the cover of night. (See the Route Guide in this book for more information on these longer overland routes including the location of main checkpoints).

OTHER PERMITS

For certain areas an ATP is not sufficient and other permits may be required as well, particularly in border areas or military zones (eg 'military permits' are required for Aba prefecture or the Kyirong region). Other special permits include cultural permits to visit sites of cultural importance. All military and other special permits can only be obtained through a travel agent.

Costs and money

COSTS

The cost of your visit will, of course, depend upon the type of trip you choose. Tibet (and China) is generally more expensive for the visitor than neighbouring India or Nepal. At the lower end of the market, most foreigners can get by on £7-10/US$10-15 per day (food and accommodation only). If you're not cycling or hitching rides on trucks, transport costs can be high: since there are not many buses you'll have to rent a car and driver. See p59 for some sample prices and itineraries.

MONEY

Tibetan money was replaced in the 1950s by the Chinese *renminbi* system (RMB) which has the unit of currency called *yuan*. One yuan (Y), also called *kwai* in Tibet, is divided into 10 *jiao* (or *mao*). The FEC (Foreign Exchange Certificate) was finally abolished in January 1994, causing the black market for hard currency to virtually disappear.

❏ Rates of exchange	
	Chinese Yuan
Aus$1	Y4.72
Can$1	Y5.44
Euro€1	Y8.04
NZ$1	Y4.08
UK£1	Y12.46
US$1	Y8.28
For up-to-the-minute rates of exchange check: ❏ **www.oanda.com/convert/classic**	

Officially, all foreigners (since mid-1997) pay the same price as Chinese residents for trains, flights and tourist attractions. Having said that, most travel costs and entry fees for monasteries or sights of interest in Tibet are three-tiered (with vastly different fares for Tibetans, Chinese and foreigners).

Main foreign currencies (but preferably US dollars) and travellers' cheques (especially Thomas Cook or American Express) can be exchanged in Tibet at the Bank of China. However, outside of the main cities you will rarely find a Bank of China branch. Cash advances are possible on credit cards in Lhasa.

One US dollar is approximately 8.28 yuan (July 2002) and this rate has been very stable since 1996 (when it was also 8.28).

Mountain-biking in Tibet

WHAT BIKE?

In Tibet, I have met cyclists riding everything from single-speed Chinese-made bikes (brand name 'Flying Pigeon') to full suspension carbon bikes and aluminium tandems – all successfully completing the trip from Lhasa to Kathmandu.

There is no such thing as the ideal overland bike. Some bikes, however, are more appropriate than others. As around 90% of the roads are just dirt and the passes are steep and drawn out on switchback roads, some form of mountain bike with a strong frame, knobbly tyres, and an extra low 'granny gear' is best.

Flying with your bike

If you are flying your bike to Tibet, bear in mind that the transportation of that bike, not to mention the trip itself, is going to be extremely hard on the frame and equipment. Most international airlines require cycles to be boxed before check-in but the policy constantly varies on China Southwest Airlines, which is the only airline that flies into Lhasa.

Buying a bike in Lhasa or Kathmandu

You can buy a multi-gear mountain bike in Lhasa for about US$100-150 and also basic spares like wheels, tyres and tubes. However they are all low quality and tend to cause problems such as pedals breaking off. Nevertheless some people have made reinforcements and successfully made it over the Friendship Highway (and even go on to sell their bike for a small profit in Kathmandu).

If you choose this option, consider taking with you a lightweight pump (old 'big' valve) and some panniers (both of which are virtually impossible to buy in Lhasa). Also check out the notice boards around the hotels for other bike items for sale.

BICYCLE EQUIPMENT

I recommend **front shocks** for cycling in Tibet to lessen the body/hand stress.

You will need to take the standard cycle touring **tools** that fit every nut and bolt including a **multi-tool set** (with chain breaker, relevant Allen keys, spoke wrench), a few spare chain links and a 15mm adjustable crescent. Make sure you can turn every nut (including the 10mm hex bolt that may be holding the crank arms onto the bottom bracket spindle). Consider taking one spare **rear derailleur** per group.

You will also need extra **spokes** (in two lengths – back and front wheels are generally different), spare gear and brake **cables** and numerous **puncture patches** with **adhesive**. Take one spare **tyre** between two people and two spare **tubes** each (make sure you test all spare tubes before leaving home!).

Take a decent lightweight **lock**. Having a **cyclometer/altimeter** adds to the fun. With Tibet's dry and dusty terrain you will need to **lubricate** your chain and front shocks regularly.

Helmets are optional but do make riding downhill with the weight of full panniers behind you a lot safer. Whether or not you take a helmet will really depend on how much you value your head and what is in it. They add no extra weight and, if it's on your head where it should be, it will not take up any room.

Know all the sounds your bike makes and when a new sound appears figure out the source and eliminate it as soon as possible. If you don't already know how to repair your bike, contact your local bicycle shop and ask them to run through a one-day maintenance workshop with you. You must know at least how to repair a puncture, and change spokes, cables and chain links.

For the ride from Lhasa to Kathmandu, you should only need **rear panniers** with a **front handle bag**.

For a **full equipment list** see pp30-1.

PREPARATION AND RISK LIMITATION

There are stories about cyclists who made a decision in Lhasa to buy a Chinese bike to ride to Kathmandu – and succeeded in doing so. There are also stories about deaths of ill-equipped and unprepared cyclists on mountain passes. Happily, the latter stories are rarer than the former.

KEYS TO MOUNTAIN-BIKING SUCCESS IN TIBET

Get fit

Get fit before you go. Success will be partly the result of your fitness but, perhaps more important, how you manage your health and the altitude.

Stay healthy

Stay healthy (ie well nourished) by eating as much as you can as often as you can and boiling everything. Food can be scarce so grab it when you see it.

Cycle high, sleep low

The way to manage the altitude (apart from adequate acclimatization in Lhasa) is to remember the adage 'cycle high – camp low'.

As with any sort of travel or sport in extreme climates, some risks can be minimized by careful planning and preparation and by proper training. Others, such as drunken Chinese truck drivers, landslides, snow storms or a bad reaction to altitude, cannot be prepared for and are just part of the adventure.

The fitter and stronger you are, the easier you will find travelling overland and mountain biking in Tibet. However, fitness does not lessen the risk of altitude sickness (indeed some 'fit' people will try to do too much too quickly, instead of waiting for their bodies to acclimatize and therefore will be more prone to altitude sickness). Furthermore, a lean and muscular body shape might be ideal for cycling in, say, France, but a little extra body fat is better for your Tour de Tibet, simply because extreme exercise in these conditions will inevitably eat away at your body's stores.

The best way to train for a long and difficult cycling trip is to cycle. Start cycling as a regular form of exercise as early as possible prior to your departure.

ROUTES – LEVELS OF DIFFICULTY

There are varying levels of difficulty on the various routes covered in this guide. The **Southern Friendship Highway** (see pp96-127) is the most popular route and the easier **central route** (see p128) can be undertaken by any reasonably fit and healthy person with the will to do it. The **southern route** adds two more passes – the first being the longest (and possibly hardest) of the entire trip. Having said that, it is almost always possible to push or hitch a ride up this (or any) pass if you feel so inclined.

Some of the routes involve a degree of technical mountain-bike skills. The **Everest Base Camp** side route(see pp131-7), for example, has some difficult downhill patches where the gravel is very deep and slippery, the gradient is extremely steep and the road zigzags sharply over a deep ravine in parts. Again, it is possible to push your bike over these parts but that really does take the fun out of it. There'll be enough pushing up hills en route to Everest without getting off to push downhill as well!

ROAD CONDITIONS

There's a full range of road conditions in Tibet. From Lhasa to Tsetang there's a pristine tarmac road; and the road from Golmud to Lhasa is basically all sealed. Then there are the dirt/loose stone roads everywhere else and they can be dry and packed one day and muddy and unrideable the next. There are also roads that are really trekking routes not much wider than your tyres.

Generally if you avoid the rainy season most of the main roads in Tibet are rideable, even with full panniers. The road from Lhasa to Kathmandu is 90% dirt (built for

STRATEGY FOR CYCLING OVER PASSES

For the main passes on the Friendship Highway (and there are at least six close to or above 5000 metres) a recommended strategy is as follows:

● The day before you intend to cycle over a pass, make sure you find accommodation or make camp as near as possible to the foot of the pass. (If you can, camp at about 4300m – but no higher).

● The next day, start your ascent at sunrise and cycle to the summit (which could take up to five hours). Descend as quickly as possible back down to below 4500m.

This becomes more important (and more apparent) when you are faced with heavy snow on the pass because you are simply not going to want to be caught up there for the night.

That is the strategy in theory. In reality, there are some routes where the road simply does not come back down below 4500m (eg around Lake Nam Tso). In other places, the road will not descend as quickly. Both of these factors will lead to some unavoidably chilly (and sometimes sleepless) high-altitude nights.

Chinese cadre trucks) and you shouldn't have any trouble, although you may need to hug the edge of the road to get the best traction (and avoid the odd vehicle at the same time). The side road into Everest Base Camp can be difficult with full panniers but is worth the extra effort.

HAZARDS ON THE ROAD

Dogs
Tibetan dogs can be ferocious, particularly to cyclists, and they can run faster than you can cycle with full panniers! Many people throw stones at the dogs or wave their pump in the air, which does deter them. Always try to put your bike between you and any dogs (sometimes pushing your bike appears less threatening to the dogs). You need to be particularly careful approaching villages/nomad camps at night as this is when the dogs are most lively.

Rabies is known to be present in neighbouring India and Nepal, but there is inconclusive evidence as to its presence in Tibet. However, given the proximity of India and Nepal, and the steady flow of refugee traffic to and fro, you should consider taking rabies immunization shots (see p40). Immunization does not prevent you catching rabies but it does give you more time before you need to report to the hospital for the second series of shots. The best plan is to avoid being bitten.

Children
The other gauntlet cyclists must run in Tibet is children. Unfortunately, a favourite game (which seems to be condoned by parents) is to try to push cyclists off their bikes or steal something off the rear rack as cyclists pass by. If they are not successful at either of these pursuits, the children then start hurling rocks at you as you race away! This is all genuine fun for the children but very annoying for tired cyclists.

FOOD AND DRINK FOR CYCLISTS

It's often difficult to get enough food to eat in Tibet; this makes you more susceptible to illness and will hinder your progress on the bike. On the road, food options are limited. Restaurants may be closed by the time you reach them at the end of a long day. Alternatively, you may be travelling in regions where restaurants simply do not exist.

There are stretches along the Friendship Highway where you will pass a shop or small restaurant each day. On other sections you will have to carry your own supplies

---

CULINARY TIPS FOR CYCLISTS IN TIBET

Thermos flask for a quick start

One way to get a quick start each morning (when it is generally cold) is to buy a thermos flask in Lhasa and fill it with boiling water each evening; you can then use it in the comfort of your tent to make up a quick brew the next morning (make sure you check the thermos is reliable before leaving Lhasa).

Buy two, eat one later

Another tip is to buy two plates of egg-rice, or whatever lunch you choose, eat the first plate and ask for a 'carry bag' for the second plate. This way when you arrive at your campsite each night you can just quickly heat up the second serving for dinner – saving time, fuel and weight (since you need to carry less rice).

---

to last a couple of days. The route guides in this book are designed to ensure that you know where food is available and where it is not. However, always have something by way of back-up in your panniers. It is safest to always carry at least two days' food.

You will generally be able to buy **biscuits**, **rice** and some Tibetan dishes, such as **toasted barley flour** (*tsampa*), **noodles** (*thukpa*) and meat/vegetable **dumplings** (*momos*). You should stock up on **soup powder**, **biscuits**, **muesli**, **powdered milk**, **tinned tuna**, **chocolate**, and **dried fruit** and **nuts** in Lhasa and Shigatse. You will need to bring your own **tea/coffee** and **vitamin supplements**.

Hot milk (made up from milk powder) and muesli is a great way to start in the mornings. At the end of the day, a mug of hot soup is warming and easy for campers.

You can find cans of **Coke** and **Sprite** seemingly all over Tibet even in small villages where nothing else is available. You can purchase bottled **water** in many places but help the environment (and save money) by adding iodine drops to tap or river water instead. Giardia is prevalent in Tibet so do not drink untreated water – even if it looks to be from a pristine mountain stream. See p39 for more information on water purification.

Be wary of the local *chang* (traditional fermented barley beer) – it packs a powerful punch and is made from untreated water.

What to take

The following information is primarily targeted at cyclists. If you intend to travel overland by vehicle only or if you are trekking you will need to vary your luggage accordingly. If you are on a tight budget you might consider buying some clothing and equipment along the way in mainland China or Kathmandu but the quality will generally not be as good. Tibet is not a place you want to be caught out with low-performance gear.

CLOTHING

The range of possible temperature changes during any month (or day) in Tibet means you must be prepared for both below freezing and burning sun conditions. You will also need to have an excellent set of 'full body' wet-weather gear.

What to wear is very much a personal choice so stick with what works for you. However, many overland cyclists do carry too much equipment, particularly clothing. I took only two long sleeve tops for all my time in Tibet. You can easily wash your clothes daily and dry them in a few hours hanging on the back of your bike.

Apart from the obvious all-weather clothing and equipment, be sure to take some warm waterproof gloves with mitten inners, and a balaclava. Also take one lightweight long sleeve top to walk/cycle in under the burning midday sun. Avoid very bright colours – day-glo lycra gear is not really appropriate in Tibet. You may wish to consider throwing in a scarf or bandana for the really dusty and windy afternoons. Be sure to take strong sunscreen and a good pair of sunglasses.

- **Footwear** – one pair of lightweight mountain bike shoes that you can also walk in (sandals/thongs are optional – but it's normally too cold to use them at night)
- **Socks** – two pairs of warm woollen socks (one pair of light-weight cotton socks optional)
- **Long trousers/pants** – one pair medium-weight thermals, one pair of lightweight cotton pants
- **Long sleeve shirt** – two (eg Icebreaker superfine range: 100% New Zealand merino)
- **Shorts** – one pair cycling shorts and, for modesty, one pair of cotton shorts to wear over your cycling shorts
- **Underwear** – three pairs of whatever you usually wear
- **Gloves** – one pair warm/waterproof ski-type, one pair thermal mittens
- **Waterproof jacket** – one parka with hood, waterproof is the key word!
- **Over-trousers** – one; must be waterproof
- **Balaclava** – lightweight
- **Hat/cap** – should also shade your neck
- **Bandanna/scarf** – one; to avoid road dust on windy days
- **Towel** – one small hand-towel size
- **Pile jacket** – one 300 weight fleece
- **Sunglasses** – essential for Tibet

EQUIPMENT

For camping, you need to have a multi-fuel stove suitable for kerosene, the most readily available liquid fuel in Tibet. Consider taking a spare one-litre fuel bottle to use for stocking up on fuel in Lhasa (as it can be difficult to get any outside the capital). Obviously, you will need a reliable tent that can endure alpine-like conditions. You will need a compact and light sleeping bag (or a heavier-duty bag if you are primarily just trekking) and a sleeping mat. A silk sleeping bag liner adds very little weight but can add a season to your sleeping bag (plus it can be easily washed and dried). Remember to take a good head torch (plus spare batteries) which can be worn for walking/cycling at night if need be. It is important to have at least one durable water bottle for your travels. Also, a larger than normal first-aid kit is essential for overland travel throughout Tibet (see the 'Travellers' health' section pp35-41).

Sleeping equipment
- **Tent** – alpine quality (eg Macpac Microlight – one person; Macpac Expedition – two people)
- **Sleeping bag** – compact and light (eg Fairydown Superlite S with 450mg down)
- **Sleeping mat** – optional but adds warmth/comfort (eg three-quarter length Thermarest)
- **Silk liner** – adds warmth and up to one season to your sleeping bag

Cooking equipment
- **Cooker** – must run efficiently on kerosene (eg MSR-XKG II stove with cleaning kit/nylon bag)

- **Fuel bottle** – one-litre size
- **Pot** – compact lightweight 'canteen' style – with handle and lid (one between two people), steel wool for cleaning
- **Knife** – 'Swiss army' pocket knife type (get one that includes scissors/tweezers)
- **Metal spoon**
- **Water bottle** – one-litre size (must be durable and fit into bike holder)
- **Mug** – optional but great for a late cuppa

Miscellaneous equipment

- **Backpack** – optional, superlight/small (maximum 25litre) for trekking/around Lhasa etc
- **Flashlight** – head torch with spare batteries (eg Mini Petzl)
- **Lighter** – small (eg mini Bic)
- **Candles** – two for starting fires or if your flashlight fails
- **Camera** – personal choice (with extra battery)
- **Film** – print and slide film available in Lhasa/Shigatse (eg 10-15 rolls per month)
- **Maps** – see pp31-33
- **Compass** – to use with maps
- **Mirror** – small hand mirror 5cm across
- **Toilet paper** – keep restocking in the main towns
- **Soap** – can also purchase along the way
- **Toothbrush/toothpaste**
- **Tampons/sanitary pads** – some sanitary pads are available in Lhasa
- **Sewing kit** – two needles plus selection of thread (for fixing clothes/tent/panniers etc)
- **Tape –** two rolls of duct tape (for multiple uses/repairs)
- **Nylon cord** – optional but always useful
- **Stuff sacks** – two for clothes, two for food
- **Notebook/pens/pencils** – some pens may not work in Tibet
- **Plastic bags** – five heavy-duty freezer bags
- **Comb** – optional
- **Tibetan phrasebook** – optional but useful
- **Reading book** – optional
- **Pictures/postcards from home** – always a handy icebreaker

Important documents

- **Passport** – with Chinese visa, plus four spare passport photos
- **Credit card** – can use in Lhasa for cash withdrawals if required
- **US dollars** – budget around $10-15 per day for food and accommodation (extras include travel, vehicle rental, permits, souvenirs etc)
- **Travellers' cheques** – optional (eg American Express or Thomas Cook)
- **Airline tickets**
- **Photocopies** – passport details, airline ticket, travellers' cheque numbers etc (give to travelling companion)
- **Money belt** – to carry your important documents, essential for any traveller

PHOTOGRAPHY EQUIPMENT

You do not need to be an expert or have a long-range zoom to get a great picture in Tibet and it would be a crying shame to return home without any. It is useful, even on instant cameras, to have a zoom (around 35-110mm). Most importantly, bring a camera that's portable (with a spare battery) and plenty of film. Print and some slide film are available in Lhasa and, to a lesser degree, Shigatse but make sure you take plenty with you once you leave Lhasa (10-15 rolls should last a month). Remember to always ask permission before taking photographs of people or inside monasteries.

BICYCLE EQUIPMENT

The following lists include my suggestions for mountain biking in Tibet – but every cyclist will have their own preferences.

● **Frame** – steel (maybe cro-moly), easier to fix/weld on the spot and strong enough to cope being carted on top of a bus or truck (I used my 12-year-old Gary Fisher Montare!)
● **Components** – love them or hate them, I use Shimano components for gear shifts, front/back derailleurs
● **Rims** – double walled
● **Brakes** – start with new or nearly new ones, they could save your life!
● **Tyres** – thick knobblies (eg Kujo DH from IRC, 26x2.25)
● **Tubes** – there are two types of cyclists in Tibet – those with numerous punctures and those with very few. The difference is in the quality of their tubes and tyres. I used medium-weight Kenda tubes with wide, and heavy, Kujo DH tyres and had only one puncture the whole time! The problems really mount up when cyclists run out of tubes bought from home and start using the Chinese-made tubes: they are just not good enough for touring.
● **Pedals** – strong pedals with toe clips (to help on all the climbs)
● **Shocks** – front shocks only is sufficient
● **Gear cogs** – aim for one low 'granny gear' (ie small chain ring at pedal to have fewer teeth than the largest rear gear, on say, a 11-30 rear cluster)
● **Seat** – personal choice (I have Giro fi'zi:k, which is very narrow)
● **Spokes** – thick stainless steel (eg Swiss DT)
● **Handlebar grips** – comfy, well-padded grips to protect hands against stress
● **Rack** – preferably steel with three supports (eg Blackburn Expedition or Bruce Gordon)
● **Panniers** – two rear and one front handle bag – 100% waterproof, dustproof, easy to remove (eg Ortlieb), you shouldn't need front panniers for the Friendship Highway
● **Speedometer/altimeter** – you'll regret not taking one (eg Avocet/Sonata)
● **Bottle cage** – one should be enough (to fit a one-litre bottle)

Spare parts
● **Brakes** – one set
● **Cables** – one brake and one gear cable
● **Tubes** – two per person (test them all before leaving home!)
● **Tyre** – one between two people
● **Spokes** – five front and five back (both different lengths)
● **Ball bearings** – for hubs/headset/pedals
● **Rear derailleur** – optional
● **Bolts** – for rack

Accessories
● **Lock** – decent length for use everywhere (plus spare key!)
● **Helmet –** optional, but necessary for steep/windy downhills on a heavy bike
● **Elastic straps** – bungy type for tying down anything on the back
● **Zap straps** – many uses (eg for repairing broken struts on pannier: tent peg with zap strap)
● **Water bottle** – one-litre PET bottle

Tools
- **Pump** – multi-valve (eg Blackburn Mammouth MTN)
- **Glue** – for nuts/bolts (eg Loctite/Seamgrip)
- **Puncture repair kit** – multiple patches plus adhesive
- **Multi-tool** – including Allen keys, chain breaker, tyre levers, spoke wrench (eg Top Peak)
- **Lubricant** – will need to lube regularly in Tibet (eg Finish synthetic)
- **Grease** – small tub (eg Judy snot)
- **Crescent/screwdriver** – optional, but useful when you least expect it
- **Metal wire** – for DIY fixes (eg 10-20ft)
- **Tape** – duct tape
- **Freewheel removable tool**
- **Chain links** – six
- **Hacksaw blade** – small three inch, for cutting nuts off other metal bits
- **Metal 'U' clamps** – in case frame mounts break
- **Kevlar emergency spoke** – interim repair to break on cog side of rear hub – will get you through the day (and then repair)

MAPS – TOPOGRAPHICAL

Russian World Series
(Scales 1:1 million, 1:500,000 and 1:200,000) Produced by the former Soviet Union military in the early 70s to mid-80s these are the best topographical maps available for Tibet. Although they are only available in Cyrillic script, and names and locations of some towns and roads have changed slightly since production, they have excellent relief markings and contours (up to 100m).

This series is available from specialist map dealers including Därr Expedition Service, Librairie Ulysse, and Stanfords (see 'specialist map dealers' listed on p32). They usually have the 1:1 million and 1:500,000 series in stock but the 1:200,000 range may take a few months to order (Därr have a free catalogue that makes identifying the maps you need for your overland route easy).

For example, the NH-45 and NH-46 maps (1:1 million scale) provide an overview of south/central Tibet but the 1:500,000 scale maps required to cover the overland route from Chengdu to Kathmandu (via Lhasa) would include: NH-48-A, NH-47-r, NH-47-B, NH-46-r, NH-46-B, NH-45-r, NH-44-A.

TIBETAN PLACE NAMES

The naming of Tibetan places is sometimes complex and confusing. The difficulties of establishing any consistency are threefold:

Firstly, Tibetan is written in a script derived from Indian Sanskrit of the seventh century. Since then the spoken language has changed with respect to the written language (eg one name in Tibetan can be spelt 'RwaSgreng' but pronounced 'Reting').

Secondly, there has never been an attempt by Tibetans to establish a register of official places names in the Latin script corresponding to their spoken form.

Finally, with the arrival of the Chinese in 1951 there was a revision of all place names into Chinese script – characters were used to represent a collection of sounds without any reference to the meaning of the word. The translations of Chinese script into Latin (using the most common Pinyin system, which is like 'Romanized Mandarin') can considerably alter the pronunciation of each name (eg. 'Shigatse' is transliterally written from Tibetan script as 'gZis-ka-rtse' then transcribed from Chinese ideograms using Pinyin into 'Xigaze').

Some of the useful 1:200,000 maps covering popular trekking routes are:
● *Ganden/Samye & Yarlung Valley:* (08-46-20 Lhasa, 08-46-26 Nedong)
● *Tsurphu/Yangbachen & Nam Tso:* (08-46-07 Dongkar, 08-46-08 Nam Tso, 08-46-13 Yangbachen, 08-46-14 Damxhung, 08-46-19 Tolung)
● *Mt Everest region:* (08-45-33 Tingri, 08-45-34 Shegar, 07-45-03 Chomolungma – Nepal side only)
● *Mt Kailash:* (08-44-9 Kailash, 08-44-15 Manasarovar)
● *Yamdrok Tso:* (08-46-25 Nagartse)

US Defence Mapping Agency

The second-best maps for Tibet are the Joint Operations Graphic (JOG) Series 1501 produced by the US Dept of Defence with a scale of 1:250,000. Unfortunately, this series is semi-classified and difficult to obtain. To locate some try the map sections of large university libraries (particularly those with large Asian Studies departments). A number of these maps are partly reprinted in Victor Chan's *Tibet Handbook – A Pilgrimage Guide*. Some of the more common JOG maps are:
● NH46-9 Lhasa, NH46-10 Tsetang, NH45-11 Lhatse
● NH45-12 Shigatse, NH46-13 Yamdrok Tso, NH45-14 Tingri (Dingri)

Two other aerial maps produced by the US Defence Mapping Agency are the Operational Navigation Charts (Series ONC) and the Tactical Pilot Charts (Series TPC). Both of these series are pilot maps and are useful sources for obtaining an overview of a route but have limited use when you are actually on the ground. Both series were updated in the 1980s and are widely available from specialist map stores. The most commonly purchased maps are:
● ONC H-9, H-10 – South Tibet (scale 1:1,000,000)
● ONC G-8 – North/East Tibet (scale 1:1,000,000)
● TPC H-9A, G-7D – West Tibet, (including Kailash, Xinjiang) (scale 1:500,000)
● TPC H-9B, H-10A – South/Central Tibet (scale 1:500,000)
● TPC H-10B, H-10C – Kham (including Sichuan, Yunnan) (scale 1:500,000)
● TPC G-8D, G-8C – Amdo (including Qinghai) (scale 1:500,000)

Lanzhou Institute of Glaciology & Geocryology, Chinese Academy of Sciences

Another two series of maps becoming more widely available are those produced by the Chinese Institute of Glaciology and published by the Xian Cartographic Publishing House in the early 90s. With a scale of 1:100,000 these are suitable for trekking and the maps in the series more readily obtainable include the following: Kangrinboqe (Mt Kailash); Mount Qomolangma (Sagarmatha) (Mt Everest); Noijinkangsang (south of Lhasa); and Xixabangma (Mt Shishapangma).

MAPS – ROAD

The Chinese have produced a detailed 170-page road atlas for the TAR called *Atlas of the Tibet Autonomous Region* (Xizang Zizhiqu Dituceng) including one map per county (scale up to 1:250,000). Unfortunately the atlas is written only in Mandarin. A useful touring map, written in English but with some inaccuracies, is the *China Tibet Tour Map* (Mapping Bureau of the TAR, 1993 – scale 1:3,000,000). This fold-out map is available in Kathmandu or from tourist hotels in Lhasa. More detailed maps include:
● *Tibet Autonomous Region* (Tibet Information Network – scale 1:1,700,000)
● *Tibet and Adjacent Areas* (Atelier Golok, Amnye Machen Institute, 1998 – scale 1:3,200,000)
● *Road Map of Tibet* (Dept of Information & Planning Dharamsala, 1994 – now out of print)

SPECIALIST MAP DEALERS

United Kingdom
Stanfords, London (🖳 www.stanfords.co.uk)
Cordee Books and Maps, Leicester
(🖳 www.cordee.co.uk)
The Map Shop, Worcestershire
(🖳 www.themapshop.co.uk)
Cambridge University Library, Cambridge
(🖳 www.lib.cam.ac.uk)

France
Tibet Map Institute, Eze (🖳 www.tibetmap.com)
Librairie Ulysse, Paris (🖳 www.ulysse.fr)
L'Astrolabe, Paris (🖳 www.lastrolabe.fr)
IGN, Paris (🖳 www.ign.fr)

Switzerland
Atlas Travel Shop, Bern (🖳 www.atw.ch)

Germany
GeoCenter ILH Internationale Landkarten-haus, Stuttgart (🖳 www.geocenter.de)
Därr Expedition Service, Munich (🖳 www.daerr.de)

Nepal
Pilgrims Book House, Kathmandu (🖳 www.pilgrimsbooks.com)

USA
Maplink, Santa Barbara (🖳 www.maplink.com)

● *Map of the Mountain Peaks on the Qinghai-Xizang Plateau* (China Cartographic Publishing House, 1989)
● *Map of the People's Republic of China* (Cartographic Publishing House of China/Liber Kartor Sweden 1995)

Other more easily available (but less accurate) road maps include:
● *Himalaya* (Nelles Verlag – scale 1:1,500,000)
● *Tibet, Nepal, Bhutan* (GeoCenter – scale 1:2,000,000)
● *Tibet & Mongolia* (Bartholomew – scale 1:6,000,000)
● *Tibet Road Map* (Berndtson & Berndtson – scale 1:1,500,000)

Cycling maps
The two maps most commonly used by cyclists along the Friendship Highway are the *Biking Map: Lhasa to Kathmandu* (Himalayan MapHouse, 2000 – scale 1:400,000) and the 'original' *Map of South-Central Tibet* (Stanfords Map, 1992 – scale 1:1,000,000). Both maps can be purchased from specialist bookstores in the West.

GUIDEBOOKS

There has been a recent increase in the number of guidebooks providing information for travellers to Tibet. See also the Bibliography on pp194-7.

Trekking and pilgrimages
Easily the best resource for trekkers in Tibet is *Trekking in Tibet – A Traveler's Guide* by Gary McCue (The Mountaineers, 1999, second edition). The book covers numerous treks with accurate trail descriptions including those in the Mt Everest & Mt Kailash regions.

An encyclopaedic pilgrimage guide, taking ten years to research, is *Tibet Handbook – A Pilgrimage Guide* by Victor Chan (Moon Publications, 1994), which includes 60 pilgrimages and 200 maps over a whopping 1104 pages.

The Power-Places of Central Tibet – The Pilgrim's Guide by Keith Dowman (RKP, 1988) was one of the first Tibet overland guides, based on a traditional Tibetan pilgrimage guidebook, covering over 170 'power places'.

General Tibet (TAR only)

A worthwhile addition to the growing list of guidebooks is *Tibet – Travel Adventure Guide* by Michael Buckley (ITMB Publishing, 1999) written in an entertaining style. The book contains interesting bites on the ongoing political spin and a section on the Tibetan exile community from a well-seasoned Tibetan traveller. *Tibet* (Lonely Planet, 2002, fifth edition) is a significant improvement over the previous editions and now includes extended sections on trekking and travelling to Western Tibet. *The Tibet Guide – Central and Western Tibet* by Stephen Batchelor (Wisdom Publications, 1998, second edition) contains excellent descriptions of monasteries and Tibetan iconography from a Buddhist/cultural expert. The *Odyssey Illustrated Guide to Tibet* by Elizabeth Booz (Odyssey, 1997, second edition) is a nicely illustrated book in a flowing narrative style. *Tibet* (Insight Pocket Guides, 1995) contains a very limited description of the route between Lhasa and Kathmandu but it does contain a handy pullout map of Central Tibet and Lhasa.

TAR plus Kham/Amdo regions

The first Tibet guidebook to cover sections on the Kham and Amdo regions was *Tibet Handbook – with Bhutan* by Gyurme Dorje (Footprint Handbooks, 1999, second edition) and it includes a large number of maps useful for overland travel. *Mapping the Tibetan World* (Kotan Publishing, 2000) contains more recent practical information and also covers the wider 'Tibetan Cultural Region' with over 280 detailed maps.

Central Asia

Trailblazer has several other books on Asian destinations. If you're travelling in China there's *China by Rail*; there's also *The Silk Roads*, a guide to this web of ancient trade routes. For Nepal there are guides to all the main trekking regions. See pp202-4 for more information or 🖳 www.trailblazer-guides.com.

Language

The main languages of Tibet are Tibetan and Mandarin Chinese. Mandarin is now prevalent throughout urban Tibet and all Tibetans taking higher studies do so in Mandarin. English is spoken and understood in the big cities by both the Chinese and Tibetans. However, there are still many places in Tibet outside the main towns where it is difficult to get by on just English. Any effort to learn some basic Tibetan will be much appreciated by the local Tibetans and will make your visit more pleasant. A selection of useful Tibetan words is listed on pp198-200.

Tibetan is part of the Tibeto-Burmese language group. There are many dialects of Tibetan from the various regions but the one prevalent in Lhasa seems to be the one most widely understood. Tibetan is primarily monosyllabic and not tonal like Mandarin. The written form of Tibetan was derived from Sanskrit in the seventh century and includes 30 consonants and five vowels.

Some useful phrasebooks to get you started are:
● *Tibetan Phrasebook* (Lonely Planet)
● *Learning Practical Tibetan* (Snow Lion Publications); includes two audio cassettes
● *Say it in Tibetan* (Paljor Publications); also includes an audio cassette.

To practise your pronunciation you might also want to listen to the online Tibetan audio language guide at 🖳 www.wordbridge.com or buy the *Learn Tibetan* CD (Eurotalk Interactive).

Travellers' health

Many of the health and medical issues discussed below are relevant to travellers in any developing country. In Tibet there are further issues relating to the high altitude conditions and the isolation of the region. See p41-3 for health information relating specifically to women travellers.

BEFORE YOU GO

Pre-departure immunizations

No immunizations are officially required for entry into China (and therefore Tibet). However, as for any overland travel in developing countries you should update your **polio, diphtheria, rubella** and **tetanus** vaccinations. It is also recommended that you receive immunizations for **typhoid** and **hepatitis A**. Additionally, vaccination shots for rabies should also be considered (see the section on dog bites, p40). **Malaria** is not present on the high Tibetan plateau but you need to give some thought to it if you are entering or leaving Tibet via malarial areas such as south-east China or southern Nepal.

Give yourself plenty of time before departure to sort out all your jabs; the rabies vaccination, for example, involves three injections over a month.

For general travel health and vaccination information check out these websites:
- Centre for Disease Control & Prevention (🖥 www.cdc.gov/travel)
- Travel Health Online (🖥 www.tripprep.com)
- Travellers Medical and Vaccination Centre (🖥 www.tmvc.com.au)

First-aid kit

Overland travel in Tibet places all tourists, not just climbers, in a unique environment. The altitude of the Tibetan plateau coupled with the isolation (from assistance) dictates that you should be better prepared for self-treatment and carry a larger then normal first-aid kit. See p36 for what to take and when to use it.

TIBET-SPECIFIC HEALTH ISSUES

Key health issues, not unique, but particular to travelling in Tibet are: altitude-related illnesses; access to purified water, travellers' diarrhoea, possibility of dog bites and the lack of decent hospital facilities.

Altitude or attitude

A great deal of research has been undertaken into the problems associated with acute mountain sickness but it is extremely difficult to forecast who is likely to be struck down by it. It [Acute Mountain Sickness] can happen equally to the young or the elderly; to the fit of not so fit; to the experienced or the completely inexperienced. **Sir Edmund Hillary** (from his foreword in *The High Altitude Medicine Handbook* by AJ Pollard & DR Murdoch, Radcliffe Medical Press 1997)

Altitude starts to affect most of us above 3000m. Every year many thousands of tourists fly into Lhasa (3600m) from Kathmandu (1350m) or Chengdu (500m) and suffer mild to severe forms of altitude sickness, also known as Acute Mountain Sickness (AMS).

For example, a recent study on a group of people in a Lhasa hotel showed 93% had flown in from Kathmandu or Chengdu and 76% had symptoms of altitude sick-

FIRST-AID KIT AND TREATMENT

Prepared with assistance from **Dr Mick Goodwin**, experienced Himalayan trekker and guide, the following list will assist you in putting together a medical kit. Keep the antibiotics simple. There are often two or three different, but equally effective, antibiotics that are recommended for various treatments. Travellers need to be pragmatic about how many of these to carry. Remember the adage 'above the belly button use Augmentin, below the belly button use Norfloxacin' (and if your diarrhoea does not settle with Norfloxacin, try Tinidazole). Some of the pharmaceutical brand names that are used below may differ, depending on the country of purchase.

Altitude
'Too high too fast' (eg flying or driving into Lhasa). **Treatment**: Acetazolamide (eg Diamox – half 250mg tablet twice daily, starting one day before ascent, or even on the day of departure, and continuing for two days once in Lhasa).

Diarrhoea
Treatment: Bacterial diarrhoea (eg Norfloxacin: one 400mg tablet twice daily for three days). **Treatment: Giardia** (eg Tinidizole: four 500mg tablets as a single dose each day with food for two consecutive days, can make you nauseated). **Treatment: Amoebic dysentery** (eg Tinidazole: four 500mg tablets as a single dose each day with food for 5-10 days; can make you nauseated).

Constipation
No bowel movements, stomach cramps. **Treatment**: Laxative (eg Coloxyl – two tablets after evening meal for five days).

Nausea
Persistent vomiting (but not diarrhoea). **Treatment**: Anti-nausea tablet – Metoclopramide (eg Maxalon – one 10mg tablet orally every six to eight hours) **or** if you cannot stomach anything try Proclorperazine (comes in a tiny tablet that you can pop under your gum).

Chest/Sinus/Middle Ear
Runny nose or chest/sinus/middle ear infection. **Treatment**: Decongestant (eg Sudafed – one tablet three times a day). **Treatment**: Antibiotic (eg Augmentin – one 500mg tablet three times a day for seven days, do not take if allergic to penicillin).

Throat
'Khumbu cough' on dry/high Tibetan plateau **Treatment**: Plenty of throat lozenges

Allergies or itches
Treatment: Antihistamine/Promethazine (eg Phenergan – 10-20mg three times per day, makes you sleepy).

Pain or fever
Pain or inflammation. **Treatment**: **Mild** (with fever) – Paracetamol (two 500mg tablets every four hours, maximum eight per day). **Treatment**: **Hardcore** – Codeine Phosphate (30-60mg up to four times per day). **Treatment**: **Anti-inflammatory** (eg Diclofenac – take 50mg three times a day, must be taken with food).

Vaginal thrush
Intense vaginal itch plus white discharge. **Treatment**: Clotrimazole pessary (eg Canestan – insert one tablet intra-vaginally).

Skin
Skin or wound infection. **Treatment**: **Antiseptic** (eg Betadine). **Treatment**: **Antibiotic** (eg Augmentin – one 500mg tablet three times a day for seven days, do not take if allergic to penicillin).

Dental infection
Treatment: Antibiotic (eg Augmentin – one 500mg tablet three times a day for seven days, do not take if allergic to penicillin).

Other medical equipment
● Syringes/needles/scalpel (one or two of each)
● Digital thermometer (normal body temperature is 37°C)
● Bandages (triangular and wide crepe types)
● Gauze squares/swabs
● Tape (thin for dressings and wide for blisters)
● Knife/scissors/tweezers (all contained in many Swiss army knives)
● Safety pins
● Butterfly wound closures (sticky tape type)
● Band-aids
● Sun block/lip salve
● Cold sore cream (optional)
● Tiger balm (to soothe those tired muscles)
● Multivitamins (optional – useful for prolonged travel in Tibet)

ness (50% of those not suffering altitude sickness had used Diamox). The fact that most people arrive in Lhasa after such a rapid ascent means altitude sickness, which is primarily related to the rate of ascent, is likely to affect most travellers visiting the Tibetan plateau (not just climbers attempting the Himalayan peaks).

Anybody can get AMS, there is no predisposition according to age, gender, physical fitness, or previous altitude experience. Altitude sickness represents the body's intolerance of the hypoxic (low oxygen) environment at a particular elevation. If you know what to do if you get it you should be able to sensibly minimize the risks associated with AMS. **It is OK to get altitude sickness but it is not OK to die from it!**

It is likely that you will have invested a large amount of time (and money) just to reach Lhasa and it would be a shame if your itinerary did not allow some time (at least three days) to acclimatize before embarking on any overland routes. Many groups of travellers, with a team member experiencing health problems, leave after only one or two nights in Lhasa. Unfortunately, there are no known methods to forecast who will be most affected by altitude. Therefore, for some people 24 to 48 hours in Lhasa will not be enough to acclimatize and an additional day or two may be required. In any event, there are at least two to three days' worth of excellent sights to explore in Lhasa. Many tourists visiting Lhasa are hospitalized every year so do not underestimate the height and remember, from Lhasa just about anywhere in Tibet that you travel to will be higher – so go easy and take your time.

Altitude sickness
(This section was written by Dr Prativa Pandey – Medical Director CIWEC Clinic, Kathmandu, Nepal; Volunteer doctor, Himalayan Rescue Association, Nepal). Symptoms of altitude sickness can begin to occur at 2400m or lower, but serious altitude sickness is rare below 3000m. These symptoms occur due to our body not adapting to the lower atmospheric oxygen at high altitudes. At 5490m there is half the oxygen available as at sea level and it is about one-third on top of Mount Everest. The body tries to adapt to lower amounts of oxygen in the air mainly by increasing the rate and depth of breathing so you breathe deeper and faster. There is also an increase in heart rate. Both of these mechanisms try to bring more oxygen to the body. There is wide individual susceptibility to altitude, which seems to be genetically determined – how well someone does at altitude seems related to how well that person's breathing adapts to altitude.

What happens to the body in Altitude Sickness? Fluid accumulates in between cells in the two most important organs of the body – the brain and/or the lungs. Symptoms can be mild or severe.

Mild symptoms of Acute Mountain Sickness (AMS) are headache, loss of appetite, nausea, lethargy, lack of sleep and dizziness. Anyone with these symptoms should not climb higher. Often, spending another night at the same altitude is all that is needed to resolve symptoms of mild AMS.

As AMS progresses, the more general symptoms of AMS are replaced by **severe symptoms** that manifest due to fluid accumulation in the brain and/or lungs. These conditions are known **as High Altitude Cerebral Edema** (HACE) and **High Altitude Pulmonary Edema** (HAPE).

In **HAPE**, breathlessness comes first with exertion but later on with rest, also a cough that is dry in the beginning but then becomes wet with frothy blood-tinged sputum, chest tightness and extreme fatigue. There may be a low grade fever as well.

In **HACE**, there are symptoms of mental confusion, bizarre behaviour, and difficulty with balance and co-ordination with inability to walk in a straight line. Headache may or may not be present in HACE. As the symptoms worsen, unconsciousness or

---

RULES FOR AVOIDING DEATH FROM AMS

1. Know the symptoms of AMS
Learn the symptoms of altitude sickness and recognize when you or your travelling partner have any of them. Remember, you may be the only person in your group with symptoms.

2. Don't ascend to sleep higher with AMS
Never ascend to sleep at a new altitude with any symptoms of AMS.

3. Descend if symptoms get worse at rest
Descend if your symptoms are getting worse while resting at the same altitude.

---

coma and death can occur. HAPE and HACE are severe and descent must begin immediately. Physical exertion, even when it is for descent, seems detrimental to HAPE patients. Severe HAPE patients should be evacuated by helicopter and if this is not possible they should either ride a yak or be carried down.

Prevention
Having a **sensible itinerary** is the most useful and valuable way to avoid altitude sickness. It is recommended not to climb more than 300m a day above an altitude of 3000m and taking a rest day every 1000m. If the terrain is such that this is not possible (like flying into Lhasa, or driving into Tibet from Nepal), one needs to have a few rest days (eg two to three rest days are recommended if you have flown into Lhasa). Having **flexibility** with one or two extra days built into your schedule will allow you to rest when you are not feeling well and help avoid altitude sickness. It also helps to 'climb high' and 'sleep low'. A **good fluid intake** is very important.

Use of **acetazolamide (Diamox)** – Diamox blocks an enzyme in the kidney and makes the blood acidic, which is interpreted by the brain as a signal to breathe more. Diamox, therefore, enhances the physiological response to altitude by increasing the rate and depth of breathing. Side effects of the drug are tingling of fingers, toes and around the mouth and increased urination. People allergic to sulpha drugs ie Bactrim or Septra should not use Diamox. The dose of Diamox to prevent AMS is half a 250mg tablet twice daily. Contrary to popular perception the use of Diamox will not mask the symptoms of altitude sickness if it is to occur.

For the prevention of AMS in trekkers, gradual ascent without using Diamox is recommended. However, for travelling to Lhasa (3650m) by road or air from Kathmandu (1350m) or Chengdu (500m), where gradual ascent is impractical, using Diamox on a prophylactic basis (half 250mg tablet twice daily) starting one day before (or even on the day of departure) and continuing for two days once in Lhasa will help in preventing altitude illness.

Treatment
For **mild symptoms** stay at the same altitude to see if the symptoms will resolve and ascend when symptoms have resolved completely. Diamox can also be used to treat mild to moderate symptoms. If symptoms persist or are getting worse at this altitude, descent is required. For **HACE** or **HAPE** descent must begin immediately.

Other treatment modalities to help during descent:

● *Diamox* – Dosage of one 250mg tablet twice a day for moderate AMS.

● *Dexamethasone* – Dosage of 8mg initially followed by 4mg every six hours, a very potent steroid used in HACE temporarily to facilitate descent. This drug improves the symptoms without improving acclimatization. It is not recommended that you ascend while still taking this drug.

● *Nifedipine* – Dosage 10mg three to four times daily, useful in HAPE for lowering pressure in the pulmonary blood vessels and thereby decreasing fluid in the lungs. This is a very potent drug used in treating high blood pressure.

● *Gamow bag* – This is a portable bag which, when inflated, converts into a high pressure bag in which an individual with severe HACE or HAPE is put and air is pumped in with a foot pump. Pressure created inside the bag increases the oxygen tension and a person can improve rapidly. This is used to hold people during an acute crisis before descent is possible or pending helicopter evacuation.

Water purification

When travelling throughout Tibet it is best to assume all water is contaminated and to never drink untreated water (don't even brush your teeth with untreated water).

There are three ways to decontaminate water – by boiling, chemical disinfection (using iodine or chlorine) or filtration. Disinfecting water will kill bacteria, Giardia, amoebic cysts and viruses. Boiling and chemical disinfection are equally effective.

Just bringing water to a boil, at any altitude, renders it safe to drink. However, when you don't want to get your cooker out, I recommend using iodine to disinfect your water using Betadine (10% povidone-iodine) in a small dropper bottle. Fill up your water bottle from a stream, add four drops of Betadine per litre, and half an hour later it is ready to drink (an hour if the water is cloudy). You will rarely need water faster than this in Tibet and 30ml of Betadine is enough to disinfect 150 litres of water, ample for around one month of cycling/trekking (assuming this is supplemented with other fluids from shops/restaurants along the way).

Note that iodine should not be used by anyone with an allergy to iodine, persons with active thyroid disease, or during pregnancy.

Portable filters are quicker, although no filters remove virus particles (inc Hepatitis A) and many are inadequate even to reliably remove *E. coli*, the most common contaminant. Try to minimize your use of bottled water and aluminium cans in Tibet – both are creating a significant waste problem.

Travellers' diarrhoea

The mantra '**boil it, peel it, or forget it**' is basically sound advice when travelling in developing countries, including Tibet. Boiling water disinfects it and fruit and/or vegetables generally may be safely eaten once peeled. Also, any food item that is thoroughly cooked and is served hot should be safe to eat. However, whether you call it 'Delhi belly', 'Kathmandu quickstep' or the 'Tibetan trot', you are likely to contract some form of diarrhoea if you remain in Tibet long enough.

Diarrhoea has three primary causes: bacteria, giardia and amoeba (*Entamoeba histolytica*). The sudden onset of relatively uncomfortable diarrhoea is likely to be bacterial. A more gradual onset of prolonged, low-grade diarrhoea is likely to be protozoal (either giardia or *Entamoeba histolytica*).

Dehydration is the primary concern with diarrhoea. Fluid replacement is crucial and a rehydration solution is advisable such as oral rehydration salts (take one dose after each loose bowel motion). You can create your own rehydration solution by combining half a teaspoon of salt with six or seven teaspoons of sugar per litre of purified water. Try to drink at least as much fluid as you lose.

Bacterial diarrhoea Most forms of travellers' diarrhoea are due to bacterial infection and are usually self-limiting (meaning they go away by themselves). General symptoms include the rapid onset of uncomfortable cramping and uncontrollable urges to defecate. Fever, nausea, and vomiting can also accompany bacterial diarrhoea and mucus and blood may be present in your stools. Bacterial diarrhoea will normally clear itself in two to seven days. The problem is that there is no way to tell whether it will be two or seven and in the meantime you will be unable to contemplate getting on a bus, truck or bicycle. Bacterial diarrhoea can be relieved temporarily using bowel 'stoppers' (eg Loperamide or Immodium) or safely cured with an antibiotic (eg Norfloxacin – take one 400mg tablet twice a day for three days).

Giardia Giardia is relatively common in Tibet. However, unlike bacterial diarrhoea, giardia is generally milder with a more gradual onset. Giardia can commence up to a week after contracting it with one or two loose khaki-coloured stools but without fever or vomiting. Other symptoms include a rumbly stomach, sulphurous 'rotten egg gas' or burps, and upper abdominal discomfort. In contrast to bacterial diarrhoea, giardia can last for weeks or come and go over a few months if left untreated. The treatment for giardia is an antibiotic such as Tinidazole (four 500mg tablets all at once each day with food for two consecutive days).

Amoebic dysentery Caused by the water-born protozoa *Entamoeba histolytica*, Amoebic dysentery is not so common in Tibet. Serious amoebic dysentery causes severe, bloody diarrhoea and medical assistance should be sought. In its milder form, it can cause alternate 'on-off again' diarrhoea every day or two with days of normal motions or constipation in between. Other symptoms include losing weight and gradually feeling more tired. The treatment for amoebic dysentery is Tinidazole (four 500mg tablets as a single dose each day with food for five to ten days). Even if you recover fully it is advisable to see your doctor upon returning home.

Dog bites
Tibet is littered with mastiff guard dogs and bites are not uncommon. There are two things to consider after a dog bite – infection and rabies.

Infection You should thoroughly wash and dress the wound with soapy water (try to get out all the saliva as this is what transmits rabies). Be careful not to scrub the wound and push the infection deeper. Apply iodine and change the dressing as appropriate.

Rabies As there are conflicting reports about the presence of rabies in Tibet, it is best to assume that rabies does exist! So if you receive any animal bite that breaks the skin, commence a series of rabies vaccine as soon as possible (do not delay vaccination while waiting for the animal to show signs of rabies). The rabies vaccine is reportedly available from the TAR People's Hospital (Xizang Zizhiqu Renmin Yiyuan) in Lhasa and also many of the Kathmandu clinics.

If you have been previously vaccinated, the treatment is two doses of the rabies vaccine (preferably human diploid cell vaccine) in the upper arm (one dose on days zero and three).

If you have not been vaccinated you will require five doses of the vaccine in the upper arm (one dose on days zero, three, seven, fourteen and twenty-eight). You will also require rabies immunoglobulin (RI) to provide temporary protective antibodies while the vaccine takes effect (RI must be injected partly into the wound and the rest into the arm).

Hospitals
There are a number of hospitals scattered throughout Tibet of varying standard. The quality of service is generally poor and you are wise to avoid all of them if possible and ensure you have an adequate first-aid kit.

For emergency treatment, including altitude sickness, the best place for foreigners is the Emergency Treatment Centre (Jijiu Zhongxin) in the building next door to the TAR People's Hospital (Xizang Zizhiqu Renmin Yiyuan) in Lhasa where some of the doctors speak English. In Lhasa you can buy aerosol cans of oxygen to treat altitude symptoms upon arrival (ask at your hotel where to purchase some). There is no medical helicopter service within Tibet but an emergency ambulance service does operate from Lhasa.

Other smaller hospitals are located in Shigatse, Gyantse, Purang (near Mt Kailash), Tsetang and Shekar (closest to Mt Everest region).

Women travellers in Tibet

Wendy Miles

*I believe there are few greater popular errors than the idea we have
mainly derived from chivalrous times, that woman is a weakly creature.*
From *The Art or Travel* (1872), Francis Galton

Tibet is a relatively safe and easy country for women travellers. Generally speaking, Tibetan men will be more frightened of you than you need be of them. The religious issues are reasonably unobtrusive and often quaint – but not seriously threatening. For example, there is a particular room in Ganden monastery that women are not permitted to enter. The reason is that the demons and spirits painted on the walls are too terrifying for women to view. Nonetheless, there are health and physical issues that women travellers do need to take into account when travelling into the region. Many of the issues relate to either isolation or high altitude travelling.

PREPARATION
It is axiomatic that you should make sure you are fit before you endeavour to travel into the extreme high-altitude conditions of Tibet – particularly if you plan to travel by bicycle.

Training
Whilst there are some particular health and nutrition factors that women need to be aware of before travelling at high altitude, when it comes to training it is really the same for women as men.

Try to be in reasonably good shape when you leave home. Do not be too concerned if you are carrying a little extra weight. In fact, if you have been eating a high carbohydrate diet as part of your preparation, you will probably be a little heavier in any event. Your stores will be eaten into soon enough in the high altitude.

Try to build up strength in your arms as well as your legs. On the long mountain passes, you will need to use your arms to help pull yourself up. Try also to exercise for long periods at a time – endurance rather than speed is the key.

At the end of the day, the best preparation for cycling in difficult terrain is cycling. In the day-to-day bustle of life it is difficult to take time to cycle at all. Try to cycle to work or hop on a bike in the gym at lunchtime. Anything you do will help.

Equipment
There is a lengthy section earlier in this guidebook about choosing your bike (see pp23-4). All that needs to be added to that, for women, is that you must make sure your bike both fits and *suits* you. Your partner or a man in the cycle shop may tell you that one thing is better than another but it is you that will be sitting on it for days on end so make sure you are comfortable with it. One suggestion is that you take an expert women cyclist with you to buy your bike or ask a woman in the shop to advise. There are two particular items that do require serious consideration, and they are not unrelated: your seat and your cycle pants.

Seats Whilst men confidently claim that the pencil-thin rock-hard seat is more comfortable for them, such seats are not built for women. Try different women's seats to see what suits you. There are very broad seats with silicon gel pads in them that some women find extremely comfortable (as far as bicycle seats go). Others may not find them comfortable. You will need to sit on different seats and ride on them to get a feel for them. Once you select your seat, try some longer rides on it. If it is no good, change it before you leave for Tibet. One point about the gel seats is that the gel does become packed and hard after a while so they do not last forever.

Cycle pants Do not let a man tell you that women's cycle pants and men's cycle pants are the same. They are not. The padding in women's pants is cut differently and does not have the seam in the middle that men's pants have. You will be well aware of it if you ride for a day in men's pants. Find a cycle shop staffed by people who know what they are talking about.

Other things to take

For a general clothes list and other cycling gear, see pp27-31.

Underclothes Crop top bras (such as the Nike Dri-Fit) are very good. Support is not the big issue – it is comfort. Wear something that fits well and does not have any sharp straps or bits that could chafe when they get wet.

Sanitary napkins and tampons In most large cities in Nepal and China, you will be able to purchase sanitary napkins and tampons. It is slightly more difficult, although not impossible, to find tampons in large cities in Tibet. Outside the large cities in all three places it is virtually impossible.

Therefore, you will need to carry a large supply of your chosen product. This creates a significant issue. When travelling, particularly by bicycle, space is at a premium and weight really must be kept as low as possible. Tampons do not weigh a lot but three or four months' supply is significant. There is a risk that once your body hits the high altitude that your periods will become very heavy (although they may also stop altogether as altitude affects different people in different ways).

The other pressing issue is the disposal of used products. There is no Rentokil on the Friendship Highway (nor flushing toilets) and neither the locals nor fellow travellers wish to stumble upon your used products. Apart from the hygiene issues, there are environmental concerns attached to the disposal of sanitary products and their wrappings. One suggestion that can overcome all of these concerns is a single Canadian product that has won accolades from a multitude of women travellers. It is a product called the **Keeper Menstrual Cap**, produced by Health Keeper Inc. The manufacturers offer a number of health reasons, in addition to the sheer convenience and cost effectiveness of the product, to encourage women to use it instead of tampons (see 🖳 www.keeper.com for further information).

SPECIFIC HEALTH ISSUES

Symptoms associated with altitude sickness include headaches, nausea, dizziness, fatigue, shortness of breath, loss of appetite and extremely low energy levels are discussed in detail earlier (see pp37-8). Women are probably not significantly different to men with respect to their risk of altitude sickness, although there are some additional issues to take into account.

Nutrition and menstruation

Make sure that you eat well before heading up to high altitude. Try to maintain a healthy diet with plenty of fresh fruit and vegetables, cereals and meat for vitamins and minerals – especially iron. Start taking vitamin supplements before you leave and take them during the entire trip. Be aware that you are likely to feel the effects of altitude much more if you are underweight and malnourished and, unfortunately, during your period. Many women report extremely heavy periods at high altitude, whilst others report having had none at all. If you do have heavy periods up there, don't panic. Just take it easy and try not do exert yourself too much on those days. Most importantly, carry enough sanitary products for such contingencies.

Contraception

Some medical practitioners will recommend that, if you intend to spend prolonged periods of time at high altitude, you should not continue to take the contraceptive pill. The main concern is that high altitude increases the risk of a potential side effect of thrombosis (blood clotting), which can be extremely dangerous.

The suggestion is not absolute and will depend on your own personal medical record and history, including previous symptoms associated with clotting. You should speak to your medical practitioner about this. At the end of the day, with professional advice, you will need to weigh the risk of a blood clot against the possible risk of pregnancy, as sex does occur at high altitudes!

If you do decide to go off the contraceptive pill prior to travelling to high altitude, try to give your body a little time to adjust. The altitude, change in diet and change in climate may have an effect on your menstrual cycle anyway and, if possible, this should not be added to by the effect of coming off the pill immediately prior to travel.

SAFETY AND OTHER ISSUES

Obviously you should not walk around dark streets alone at night, but the biggest threat is of robbery rather than sexual assaults. Be sensible: keep yourself covered in temples (shoulders and legs) and have fun. Tibet really is a delightful place for women travellers. Unfortunately, life is not as pleasant for Tibetan women and there have been reports of brutal enforcement of China's one-child policy in rural and urban areas of Tibet. More information on this may be found on the Tibet Information Network's website (🖳 www.tibetinfo.net).

Getting to Tibet

Two roads diverged in a wood, and I -
I took the one less travelled by,
And that has made all the difference
From *The Road Not Taken*, Robert Frost

Once you hold a valid visa, you will want to enter Tibet via the most reliable and direct route, which will of course depend on your starting point – usually Hong Kong, mainland China or Nepal.

MAINLAND CHINA FROM HONG KONG

It is considerably more expensive to fly from Hong Kong direct to a city in mainland China, than to fly within the mainland. Fortunately, it is a brief and pleasant ferry, bus or train ride from Hong Kong to Shenzhen or Guangzhou, in the far south of mainland China. From Shenzhen or Guangzhou it is about half the price to fly to other cities in China (eg Chengdu or Lanzhou) than from Hong Kong. Also, travel agents in Hong

GETTING TO TIBET

Tibet Autonomous Region (TAR)

© Atelier Golok

SCALE 1 : 16 950 000

KILOMETRES

0 50 100   200   300   400   500

Kong can book you onward flights departing from Shenzhen or Guangzhou. If you are flying from Shenzhen try to time connections for flights departing on the same day as you leave Hong Kong as accommodation near the airport is relatively expensive.

Accommodation in Hong Kong

Many travellers stay in the numerous hotels and guest houses in the infamous Chungking Mansions or nearby Mirador Arcade on Nathan Road. They're in the heart of Tsim Sha Tsui where accommodation is cheap but the rooms can be pretty grim.

An alternative for those who are simply in Hong Kong to get a visa is the clean *YMCA Salisbury* (🖳 www.ymcahk.org.hk), 41 Salisbury Rd, Tsim Sha Tsui. It offers dormitory rooms on the fifth floor and a safe luggage room for bicycles. The airport shuttle will take you there from the Kowloon train terminal.

TIBET FROM MAINLAND CHINA

Once you are in mainland China, you can make your way by land or air to Lhasa. Most overlanders will try to reach Lhasa commencing from Chengdu, Kunming, Xining or Kashgar.

Xining to Lhasa

Overland The only overland route officially open for independent travellers is the 1969km **Qinghai-Tibet Highway** (see pp138-46) from Xining to Lhasa via Golmud (in Tibetan, Kermo). The road from Golmud is therefore the only 'guaranteed' overland route into Tibet, albeit from the most isolated starting point.

Very few cyclists or hitchhikers attempt the journey between Xining and Lhasa as water and food is scare and there are very few towns scattered along the main route. Most overlanders will take the train from Xining to Golmud then catch an overnight bus onto Lhasa as quickly as possible. The bus journey takes at least 36hr and is a long and uncomfortable trip.

By air A direct flight operates four times weekly between Xining and Lhasa; it costs approximately the same amount as the bus fare from Golmud to Lhasa. Individuals still have to purchase tickets from a travel agent and form a five-person 'tour group'.

Chengdu to Lhasa

Overland The **Sichuan-Tibet Highway** (see pp147-57) links Chengdu to Lhasa. The most direct 2166km southern route goes through Litang and Markham and the 2427km northern branch goes via Derge and Chamdo. Both branches merge again near Pomda and then continue west to Lhasa. From Chamdo there is also a rarely-travelled 1028km overland route to Lhasa heading due west via Nakchu.

The Sichuan-Tibet Highway is officially open as far west as Batang or Derge and can be reached by public bus from Chengdu. Thereafter, very little public transport exists and truck drivers face heavy fines for carrying foreigners. Keen cyclists and hitchhikers can usually reach Lhasa successfully by bypassing the main checkpoints during the night but they face the possibility of fines and being turned back at any village or hotel they stay in if caught. Food and accommodation is more widely available along the Sichuan-Tibet Highway than in most other parts of Tibet.

By air Flights from Chengdu to Lhasa depart twice daily in season. You must book your flight from a travel agent. The China Southwest Airlines office will not sell air tickets for Lhasa to individuals; the agent will arrange your ticket and permit by including you in a temporary five-person 'tour party'.

Chengdu is accessible by air and train from other main Chinese cities including Beijing, Xian, Shenzhen, Guangzhou and Hong Kong. International flights exist into

Chengdu from Bangkok and Singapore. There are also flights into Lhasa twice weekly from Beijing (via Xian or Chengdu), Guangzhou and Chongqing.

Kunming to Lhasa

Kunming is accessible by air or train from other main Chinese cities including Beijing, Xian, Shenzhen, Guangzhou and Hong Kong. International flights exist into Kunming from Bangkok, Yangon, Vientiane, Singapore, Osaka and Kuala Lumpur.

Overland The spectacular 2400km **Yunnan-Tibet Highway** (see pp156-7) connects Kunming with Lhasa via Dali. The last open town along the Yunnan-Tibet Highway is Zhongdian (or occasionally Dechen). Both towns can be reached by public transport from Dali. The route from Dechen to Lhasa joins the main Sichuan-Tibet Highway near Markham. From that point, the same issues of permit and travel restrictions will apply to overland travellers (as outlined above).

By air There's now a weekly Kunming–Lhasa flight (via Zhongdian) which independent travellers can book onto (as part of a group tour) with a travel agent.

Kashgar to Lhasa

Overland The journey along the **Xinjiang-Tibet Highway** (see p158-71) from Kashgar to Lhasa via Mt Kailash is a long and arduous 2884km. Only a handful of foreigners (cyclists or hitchhikers) have ever completed this truly wild overland route, which should only be undertaken by those with plenty of time and suitable equipment.

TIBET FROM NEPAL

Kathmandu to Lhasa

Overland – Friendship Highway (see pp96-137) It may be possible to cross the Zhangmu border, with a valid Chinese visa already in your passport, and rent a four-wheel drive vehicle from the CITS officials next to the Chinese immigration post, to take you plus any bikes directly to Lhasa. You can easily take a bus or hire a taxi to get you from Kathmandu to Kodari. Three British cycling friends of mine successfully entered Tibet this way recently. They were charged US$150 each to hire the four-wheel drive vehicle, arriving in Lhasa four days after leaving London.

Alternatively, you could book onto an organized overland tour with a travel agent in Kathmandu. Tours range from a basic three-day trip (US$200) direct to Lhasa, up to a week-long trip (US$450) with side trips including Everest Base Camp.

But beware: this 'door' into Tibet opens and closes regularly and relying on it can therefore be risky.

Overland – via Purang Since the mid-90s it has been possible to join a tour package entering Tibet at Sher (in Nepalese, Kojinath), near Purang, approximately 120km south of Mt Kailash. Sher is accessible via a five-day trek from Simikot, in western Nepal.

By air There are flights from Kathmandu to Lhasa three times per week. The flight, costing US$275 one way, lasts just over one hour and includes spectacular views of the Himalayas including Everest. Only China Southwest Airlines is permitted to fly the route and Gongkar Airport, which lies 95km south of Lhasa, is generally closed during winter (November-May).

Individuals cannot purchase tickets, so you must be part of a five-person 'tour group' and book through a travel operator. The catch with flying from Kathmandu is that because you are outside Tibet the agent takes your passport to the Chinese embassy, which issues you with a new visa (and usually cancels any existing valid visa issued elsewhere) but only for the duration of your tour (usually around 7-10 days). If you are lucky some of the travel agents manage to avoid this (see p20).

LHASA

2

City guide

One who does not get to Lhasa
Has only half a human life.
Tibetan adage

INTRODUCTION

Even travellers with a very limited knowledge of Tibetan history and culture will know that Lhasa ('Holy City') is the traditional seat of the Tibetan religious leader, the Dalai Lama, and the place from which he fled the Chinese to his current refugee base in India. With its people, the Potala Palace, temples and monasteries, Lhasa is synonymous with the Dalai Lama and, in a sense, with Tibetan Buddhism itself.

Since the Cultural Revolution in China there have been enormous population transfers of Han Chinese into territories such as Tibet. The presence of hundreds of thousands of Chinese immigrants is a ubiquitous reminder that Lhasa is no longer the seat of the Dalai Lama – it is now the westernmost regional capital of the People's Republic of China. Yet it is the infrastructure created by the Chinese, including the airport, transportation systems, communications networks and hotels, that make it possible for an ordinary traveller to visit Lhasa, historically an inaccessible part of the world.

The main construction of Lhasa's buildings occurred during the Yarlung Dynasty (7th-9th centuries) and the Gelug era (15th-20th centuries) but the whole landscape has undergone a vast expansion since Chinese occupation. Lhasa has become Sinicized, with ten-storey buildings and satellite communication towers. Numerous restorations have taken place in an effort to rectify some of the most tragic damage that occurred during the Cultural Revolution, and even the famous West Gate (once the primary entrance into Lhasa) was completely rebuilt in 1995 to commemorate the 30th anniversary of the founding of the Tibetan Autonomous Region (TAR).

Contemporary Lhasa has very heavy Chinese influences. The straight boulevards, utilitarian high-rise blue glass buildings and Chinese-style department stores dominate the city outside the Tibetan quarter. Travellers new to the area are often shocked at the numbers of Chinese migrants. But if you take the time to look carefully you will still see numerous relics of Lhasa's fascinating past, quite apart from the obvious and immensely impressive attractions of the Potala, the deserted residence of the Dalai Lama, and the atmospheric Jokhang, the most sacred temple in Tibet, and the Barkhor area.

HISTORY

Archaeologists uncovered relics near Sera in 1984 suggesting that Lhasa was inhabited thousands of years ago. Lhasa's dominance in Tibetan history, however, was primarily during two significant periods: the Yarlung Dynasty (7th-9th centuries) and the Gelug era (15th-20th centuries).

Songtsen Gampo and the conversion to Buddhism

King Songtsen Gampo (AD608-650) proclaimed Lhasa the Tibetan capital in the seventh century AD and built the first Potala Palace on Marpori. In doing so, he unified 12 small kingdoms. His father had earlier ruled the entire Lhasa region from his base in Chongye but before he was able to consolidate the country any further his ministers poisoned him.

Under the rule of King Songtsen Gampo, Lhasa prospered. The king made alliances with China and Nepal in exchange for wives. His Chinese wife, Wen Cheng, adopted daughter of Emperor Tai Zong (first of the Tang Dynasty), brought to Lhasa her dowry in the form of a gold Buddha statue. Songtsen Gampo's Nepali wife, Princess Tritsum (Bhrikuti Devi), was of equal status to his Chinese wife. Songtsen Gampo also took three Tibetan wives. The offspring of those marriages went on to found Tibet's Tubo Dynasty.

It was the combination of influences from the two foreign princesses that led Songstan Gampo to convert from the traditional Tibetan religion, Bon, to Buddhism. In honour of Buddhism, Songtsen Gampo built the Jokhang and the Ramoche, which were to house the sacred Buddha statues brought to Tibet by his wives.

Recognizing the importance of learning and recorded history, Songtsen Gampo sent a young scholar, Tonmi Sambhota, to India to learn a system of writing. Sambhota invented a script based on Kashmiri Gupta script, which was adapted to the Tibetan language. Within 20 years, the script was in general use for Tibetan religious translations. Many years after his death, for his role in the cultural and religious renaissance in Tibet, Songtsen Gampo was recognized as Tibet's first 'religious king', and declared an incarnation of Chenrezi (the Bodhisattva of Compassion), the patron saint of Tibet.

Rise and fall of Lhasa and of Buddhism

After early years of fighting as far away as Samarkand and Xian, **Trisong Detsen** (755-97) firmly established Buddhism in his country and eventually became known as the second 'religious king' of Tibet. He invited Padmasambhava (Guru Rinpoche), the great Indian tantric mystic, to visit Tibet and lead teachings. He also founded the first Tibetan monastery, Samye monastery, which was built in 779.

During the reign of Lang Darma (836-42), the monasteries were disbanded and the king sought to expel Buddhism from Tibet. A rebellious monk assassinated the king in 842 and the Yarlung Dynasty ended. For more than 100 years Tibet was in a period of civil war. Lhasa's importance diminished from that time and it remained only a nominal capital until the 15th century.

The Gelug Era and the revival of Lhasa

In 1409, when Tsongkhapa founded Ganden monastery and instituted the Great Prayer Festival (Monlam) at the Jokhang in Lhasa, he revived Lhasa as the religious centre of Tibet. Two other principal Gelug monasteries were then built nearby by disciples of Tsongkhapa. These were Drepung monastery (1416) and Sera monastery (1419).

Lhasa was fully restored as the capital of Tibet in 1642, when the Gelug sect asked Gushri Khan, leader of the Qosot Monguls, to defeat the King of Tsang and his Karmapa allies. The Great 5th Dalai Lama (1617-82) was installed as head of Lhasa and he reunited Tibet, establishing a theocratic form of government under the Gelug order that survived until the Communist forces arrived in 1950.

Before the 1940s Lhasa consisted of two separate quarters with trees and marshes in between. These were Shol (a village nestling below the Potala Palace) and the cluster of houses and alleyways around the Jokhang. A bridge known as Yuthok Sampa connected the two towns.

For an excellent account of the quest to be the first Westerner in Lhasa, read the thriller *Trespassers on the Roof of the World* by Peter Hopkirk (1982). In fact, the first Westerner to enter the country was probably Thomas Manning, in 1812. Tibet was not re-entered by a Westerner until the British army officer, Francis Younghusband, forced his entry through Gyantse in 1904 (see p107).

Lhasa today

Lhasa is now the capital of the Tibetan Autonomous Region (in Chinese: Xizang Zizhiqu), with six districts – Lhasa, Nyangtri, Shigatse, Ngari, Nakchu and Chamdo – which contain 77 counties. The area of Lhasa city is now over 20 times larger than it was when the Chinese took control in 1950 (now 53 square kilometres) with the Tibetan quarter making up less than one square kilometre.

Lhasa's population is around 230,000 with Tibetans a minority of only 25-30%.

ORIENTATION

Lhasa lies on the north side of the Kyi chu (Lhasa river) valley at an altitude of 3600 metres surrounded by mountains which average over 4800 metres.

The city is dominated by two craggy hills: **Marpori** (Red Hill) crowned by the Potala and **Chakpori** (Iron Hill) topped by a large antennae. Chakpori is one of the four sacred mountains of central Tibet and used to be the site of a 17th-century Tibetan medical college that was ruined by the Chinese in 1959.

INFORMATION

The travellers' network

Independent travellers in Tibet are fortunate to have a comfortable and secure base from which to organize trips. Although there are enough English-speaking Chinese and Tibetans in Lhasa to be able to help you make your arrangements, they will probably attempt to deter you from any 'off the beaten track' travel propositions. As a result, the unofficial travellers' network will be far more useful. That network can be tapped in all the usual ways.

Certain hotel courtyards, such as at the Yak Hotel, act as unofficial meeting places for travellers and drop-in advice centres for anyone seeking the latest intelligence. Notice boards around the Yak, Banak Shol, Snowlands and Pentoc hotels are also all useful. Often, individual travellers will post notices when looking for a travelling companion or seeking some equipment. Finally, certain restaurants (see p53-4) are good places for picking up tips on which trips are permitted and which are banned. Be aware that Chinese authorities sometimes plant spies in the more popular Tibetan restaurants. If you intend to discuss a trip or venture that you know is not officially permitted, it would pay to be discreet.

Maps

The most extensive map of Lhasa available in the West is the *Map and Index of Lhasa City* (Atelier Golok, Amnye Machen Institute, 1995). This excellent map, printed in English and Tibetan at a scale of 1:12,500, includes a gazetteer of about 600 locations

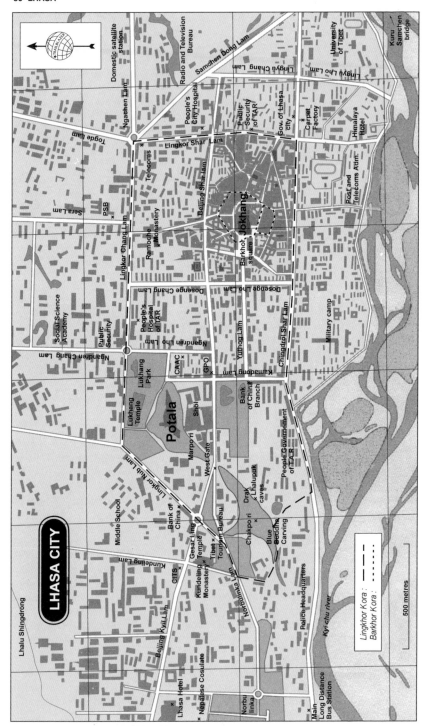

LHASA CITY

Lhalu Shingdrong

Domestic satellite station
Radio and Television Bureau
Samchen Dong Lam
Lingyu Chang Lam
Lingyu Lho Lam
University of Tibet
Kuru Samchen bridge

Ngachen Lam
Togde Lam
People's City Hospital
Public Security of TAR
Gov. of Lhasa city
Carpet Factory
Himalaya Hotel

Sera Lam
Lingkor Shar Lam
Lingkor Chang Lam
PSB
Telecoms
Beijing Shar Lam
Lokhang
Barkhot square
Post and Telecoms Atm.

Ramoche Monastery
Dosenge Chang Lam
Dosenge Lho Lam
Chingdrol Shar Lam
Military camp

Social Science Academy
Public Security
People's Hospital of TAR
Ngandren Lho Lam
Yuthog Lam
Kamdong Lam

Ngandren Chang Lam
CAAC
GPO
Lukhang Park
Lukhang Temple
Shol
Bank of China Branch
People's Government of TAR

Lingkor Nub Lam
Potala
Marpo ri
West Gate

Middle School
Bank of China
Drak LhalupK caves

Kundeling Lam
Gesar Ling
Kundeling Monastery
Tibet Tourism Bureau
Chakpo ri
Blue Buddha Carving

CITS
Norbulinka Lam
Police Headquarters

Beijing Kyil Lam
Kyi chu river

Lhasa Hotel
Nepalese Coslulate
Norbu linka
Main Long Distance Bus Station

Lingkhor Kora : ▬ ▬ ▬
Barkhor Kora : ·······

500 metres

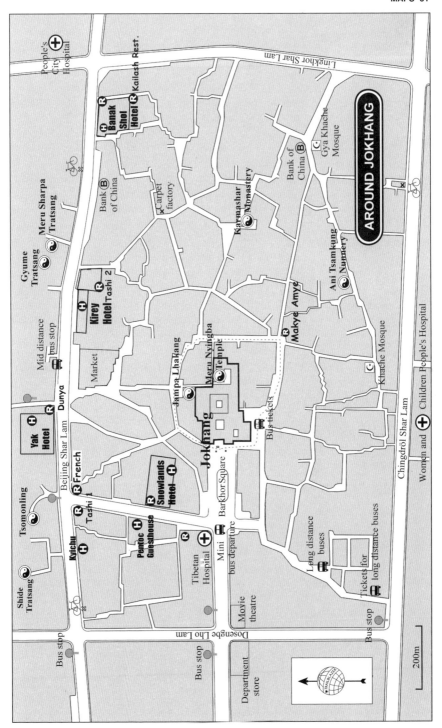

AROUND JOKHANG

in the city even including prisons and PLA bases. To purchase the map on the Internet visit 🖳 www.amnyemachen.org.

In Lhasa the most readily-available city map is the *Lhasa Tour Map* (Lhasa External Propaganda Dept, 1995). The map is in English and can be purchased from most of the foreign Lhasa hotels.

A more quirky but interesting map is *On the Spot* (International Campaign for Tibet, 1994), which has some interesting information on the history and tragedy that has gone into the creation of modern Lhasa.

SERVICES

Telecommunications
You can make **international phone calls** and send **faxes** from the main post office. Over the past few years a number of **internet cafés** have opened in Lhasa, such as the ones located near the Snowlands Hotel. You can also now check your email once you get to Shigatse.

Nepalese consulate
The Nepalese consulate is near Lhasa Hotel (see map on p50). You can get a Nepalese visa here in 24 hours and it's open Monday to Friday from 10am to noon.

Money
The main branch of the Bank of China, on Lingkor Nub Lam, gives credit card advances and is open daily. It closes at 3pm at the weekend. For travellers' cheques, the branch near Banak Shol Hotel is more convenient but it's only open on weekdays.

Hospitals
• **TAR People's Hospital (Xizang Zizhiqu Renmin Yiyuan)** This is the best place in Lhasa for foreigners. It is in a large building on the Lingkor North Road (in Chinese: Linguo Beilu). For emergency treatment, including altitude sickness, go to the Emergency Treatment Centre (in Chinese, Jijiu Zhongxin) in the building next door where there are doctors who speak English.
• **Lhasa City People's Hospital (Lhasa Renmin Yiyuan)** This smaller hospital is on the eastern side of Lhasa on Dekyi Shar Lam (in Chinese, Beijing Donglu) not far from Banak Shol Hotel.

OVERLAND SUPPLIES

Food
Basic food supplies can be found in the **bulk goods stores** behind Kirey Hotel or from the various supermarkets scattered across Lhasa. At **Pentoc Hotel** and at **Snowlands Restaurant** you can buy all sorts of treats, including American chocolate and imported sweets.

High priced but good quality trekking supplies can be purchased in the **Outlook Equipment Store** close to Kirey Hotel.

Bicycles and cycle parts
Multi-gear bikes are available in Lhasa for about US$70-100. The quality varies and is nowhere near as good as in the West. I know keen overlanders who have bought a bike in Lhasa and made it all the way to Kathmandu, but then I also know folk who have had to abandon their bikes a few hundred kilometres along the route so it's a bit of a lottery. The problems are usually with the pedals, saddles or other components.

The good news is that there are several small **bike repair shops** in Lhasa. There is always a chance you might find that missing part if you dig around long enough! Unfortunately, the quality of bicycle parts also varies significantly and Chinese tubes are awful.

● **Chuanwang Zhensuo** This clinic is about five minutes' walk west of Yak Hotel on Dekyi Shar Lam (in Chinese, Beijing Donglu). It may be possible to arrange for one of their doctors to visit your hotel.

● **Tibetan Medical Hospital (Mentsikhang)** The Mentsikhang is a Tibetan medicine hospital just west of Barkhor Square, but originally located at the summit of Chakpori (opposite Potala Palace). Traditional Tibetan diagnosis and medicines are used and some of the doctors speak English. The hospital is open 10:00-13:00 and 15:30-18:00, Monday to Saturday. It is well worth a visit just to see the wonderful display of traditional medical *thangkas* (paintings).

WHERE TO STAY

Budget hotels and guesthouses

Lhasa is probably the easiest Tibetan location for finding adequate accommodation at the lower end of the budget. There are several popular budget hotels, all of which are in the Tibetan quarter.

For the places listed below **costs** are similar: around Y20-30 for a bed in a dorm, double rooms from around Y50 with shared bathroom or Y100-200 with bathroom attached. Ask about discounts in the off season.

Yak Hotel (100 Beijing Shar Lam) is the traditional favourite and provides a range of options including some upmarket rooms with en suite bathrooms. The courtyard is a good place to meet other travellers and just sit around and let your body catch up with the altitude. The beds are comfortable and the communal bathrooms offer hot showers all day.

Pentoc Guesthouse (5 Mentsikhang Lam) is newer and has clean showers and toilets (Western ones) and a laundry service, but rooms near the road are noisy and the place is a little more expensive than the others in this area. The Pentoc does offer video nights and news updates. Even if you're not staying here you can attend these.

Snowlands Hotel (4 Mentsikhang Lam), *Banak Shol Hotel* (143 Beijing Shar Lam), and *Kirey Hotel* (105 Shar Lam) are all similar in price and facilities. They all have a choice of accommodation (dormitories or rooms). None seems to have the same ambience as the Yak but they are similar in style.

Tourist hotels

There is a multitude of alternative tourist-class hotels in Lhasa (including Lhasa Hotel which was operated by the Holiday Inn group until lobbying pressure forced the group to withdraw in the early 1990s). None of the tourist-class hotels is based in the Tibetan quarter and, to be perfectly honest, unless cheap, garish and inadequately cleaned Chinese-style hotels are your thing, none of them offers much more (room-wise at least) than the places down in the Tibetan quarter which are a whole lot cheaper. The only real advantage of the Chinese-run tourist hotels is that they may have reasonably good information and restaurant facilities – Lhasa Hotel, in particular. However, these facilities are also open to the public (including the Western toilets in the hall opposite the main restaurant inside Lhasa Hotel) so you don't need to stay in the hotel to use them.

WHERE TO EAT

The original *Tashi Restaurant (Tashi 1)*, on Mentsikhang Lam near Yak Hotel, is a great favourite with Western travellers. The highlight of dining in Tashi 1 is the *bobi* (pita bread rolled around fried vegetables with a cream-cheese sauce). The *momos* are not bad either and there are often delicious desserts such as apple pie or cheesecake.

The other restaurant in the Tashi chain is known as *Tashi II* and is located at Kirey Hotel. It has the same food but not the same atmosphere.

French Café, opposite Tashi I on Mentsikhang Lam, is an excellent place, particularly for breakfast. They serve superb coffee and home-made bread.

Kailash is the rooftop restaurant at Banak Shol Hotel. It offers some good meals and the cakes and coffee are delicious. It has great breakfasts of muesli, yoghurt and fruit and they will do their best to make you a pasta meal or pizza.

Snowlands Restaurant, at Snowlands Hotel, is one of the more upmarket restaurants in the Tibetan quarter. It offers everything from roast chicken to yak-meat hamburgers. It is also a great spot to stock up on dried soup mixes, muesli and sweets, all trucked over from Nepal.

Tibet Lhasa Kitchen (Mentsikhang Lam) is also popular. The food is good (particularly the apples pancakes).

Dunya Bar is next to Yak Hotel. The Dunya has a vibrant atmosphere and a large satellite TV that broadcasts all the big sports events.

A little further around Barkhor Square, at the south-east corner of the Jokhang, is *Makye Amye,* another rooftop restaurant and bar. This is an excellent place to sit and watch the world go by during the day, or for a drink or a meal in the evening.

JOKHANG TEMPLE, BARKHOR SQUARE & THE BARKHOR KORA

Jokhang temple is at the very centre of the Tibetan part of the city, an area known as Barkhor. This is also the name of the square in front of the Jokhang but 'the Barkhor' refers to the pilgrimage circuit around Jokhang temple. The whole area is fascinating and certainly not to be missed. It costs nothing to come here and it is a delightful pocket of Tibetan-ness in a city that looks alarmingly like any other Chinese town.

Barkhor Square

In this large square outside Jokhang temple there are neat rows of blue metal stalls selling everything from fruit and vegetables to prayer flags. The stallkeepers are used to tourists and will lay on some hard bargaining – but all with a smile. Enjoy the atmosphere but don't be fooled by claims made about the antiquity of some of the items.

After the 1989 Lhasa Uprising, and then again in 2000, the Chinese government completely redesigned the square and created uniformed, consigned stalls. The system permits the Chinese government to keep tight control over the area and the positioning of the PRC building, across from the front left corner of the Jokhang, with its security cameras and armed police surveillance, says it all. Be aware of the amount of surveillance that these people are under, particularly given their level of contact with Westerners. Respect their safety and do not engage them in political discussions.

The Barkhor *kora* (pilgrimage circuit)

The Barkhor, a neatly-paved road lined with little stalls selling 'Tibetan' artefacts, is one of three pilgrimage circuits in Lhasa. Remember the golden rule – always walk clockwise. Follow the flow of Tibetan pilgrims.

ENTRY FEES

In Tibet, the Chinese two-tier form of entry fee is prevalent. You may initially feel that it is not fair that the Tibetan pilgrims can enter the monasteries for free while you're hit with a Y20-40 entry charge. Instead, be grateful for the fact that, unlike the situation less than ten years ago, Tibetans are permitted the freedom to worship at all. They have paid more than enough for their faith over the years.

The Jokhang

Built in the seventh century by King Songtsen Gampo, the Jokhang predates even Samye monastery, making it possibly Tibet's first significant religious institution. It's an incredible place – Lhasa's (and Tibet's) spiritual centre – which you should not miss. The Jokhang is open until 18:00 and the rooftop is a beautiful spot to sit and watch the sun set over the Barkhor. If you are inside at 18:00, you will often be permitted to stay a little later.

The **side entrance** of the Jokhang, to the left of the main forecourt, will take you to the ticket office. Look around the courtyard. There is a magnificent display of burning butter lamps around the outside. At dusk, the lamps cast a beautiful and eerie glow across the faces of the Tibetan pilgrims as they add to the burning offerings. At the end of the day, a number of old women will conscientiously clean each butter lamp and stack them into neat little piles. The rhythm and calm of the task is in keeping with the atmosphere of the Jokhang.

If you tell the monks at the ticket office that you are only visiting the **first floor**, you will be directed to a particular entranceway and will be able to view the main courtyard and *kora* (circumambulation) with its prayer wheels around the outside perimeter of the inner sanctum.

On the **ground floor**, the corridor of prayer wheels provides welcome relief from Lhasa's unforgiving summer sun. As you follow the prayer wheels, the kora route, you'll see a door at the back. If it is open, ask someone if you can go in and see the kitchen area where a team of hardy nuns prepare the monks' meals.

The central **chokang** (offering hall) is the main building facing the courtyard, which the prayer wheels surround. It is dark inside and the smell of burning juniper and yak butter is pungent. You will soon associate this mixture of smells with Tibet. It is a smell that permeates every grain in the ancient timber of the temple, and the glistening butter coats the floors and beams throughout the temples. This is a smell that is missing from the temples of communities of exiled Tibetans in India, where highly-processed Indian ghee replaces the traditional yak butter as lamp fuel.

The sides of the hall are filled with separate chapels (*lhakang*). The four primary images inside the hall are the **Jowo Chempo** (Sakyamuni), the Buddha of our age; **Tujechempo** (Mahakarunika), the Bodhisattva of Great Compassion; **Jampa** (Maitreya), the Future Buddha of Loving Kindness; and **Drolma** (Tara), the Goddess of Devotion. These are known as the Four Deities Emanating Light. Of these four, the Jowo Chempo is the most sacred image in the Jokhang and represents the Sakyamuni Buddha not in his usual monkish garb but as a crowned Bodhisattva.

Outside and in front of the hall, the three-storey buildings to the right and left of the main entranceway and down the sides were originally buildings for the Dalai Lama's government, the *kashag*.

On the **upper storeys** of the Jokhang there are a number of additional chapels. If you keep following the stairs upwards, on some days you will be able to visit the two small temples on the very top of the Jokhang where the monks often have their *puja* (prayer) away from the bulk of the tourists.

Potala Palace

Potala Palace remains an enduring symbol of Tibet's past glory and is the building that symbolizes Lhasa. Surprisingly, it was spared by the Red Guards during the attack on historic, cultural and religious treasures throughout Tibet (and China) in the mid-20th century. The Chinese Foreign Minister, Chou Enlai, reportedly ordered the preservation of the Potala. Every visitor to the city will want to visit this vast building although without the Dalai Lama and his retinue in residence it is but a hollow shell, albeit an impressive one.

History The Potala is thought to have been named after Mt Potala, the sacred mountain in south India that is said to be the abode of the Bodhisattva of Compassion, Avalokiteshvara (in Tibetan Chenrisi). King Songtsen Gampo was considered to have been a reincarnation of Chenrisi. The choice of site for the Potala was subject to an historic town-planning exercise. The second option for its location was at Gongkar Dzong (near Gongkar Airport), which also has strategic fortifications fitting for a king's residence.

The 'Great Fifth' Dalai Lama commissioned the construction of the palace as it exists today, in all its glory. The White Palace was constructed first, between 1645 and 1653. The central Red Palace followed from 1690 to 1697. Unfortunately, the Great Fifth died in 1682 before building on the second stage of construction was commenced. Consequently, his regents concealed his death for 12 years while the work was completed.

The 13-storey structure is 118m high, occupies 130,000 square metres and contains over 1000 rooms. There were no steel frames or nails used in the original construction of the woodwork and the roofs were made of gilded copper. This magnificent building qualifies as an 'ancient wonder' of the world and was, accordingly, added to the UNESCO World Heritage List in 1995.

Visiting the Potala Unlike at the Jokhang there's an entrance charge (half price for students with a student card).

You reach the Potala from the south, through Shol village. Climb the long flights of steps to eventually reach the **White Palace** which contains the rooms once used by the Tibetan government and also the private quarters of the Dalai Lama.

The **Red Palace** was the religious centre of the Potala and contains numerous chapels and several reliquary chortens (tombs) of former Dalai Lamas. Highlights include the Potala's most sacred treasure, the **statue of Arya Lokeshvara** (the favourite deity of King Songtsen Gampo), located in the Phakpa Lhaghang (northwest corner of the top floor); the **rooftop views** over Lhasa and Kyi chu valley; the reliquary **chorten of the 13th Dalai Lama**; the large **assembly hall** on the ground floor and the ornate golden **reliquary chorten of the 5th Dalai Lama**.

Norbulingka

The Norbulingka ('Jewel Park') was built as a summer palace for the Dalai Lamas. About 3km west of the Tibetan quarter and 700m south of the Lhasa Hotel, it is well worth the visit – despite what some guidebooks might say. To get to the Norbulingka, make for the Dongkar intersection (near the confluence of the Tolung and Kyi chu rivers).

The 7th Dalai Lama founded the Norbulingka in 1755. The most modern building, the 14th Dalai Lama's **New Palace**, is the main attraction in the park. It stands inside a spacious walled garden and is built in a mixture of religious and contemporary styles. The rooms on view upstairs in the palace include a main **throne hall** above the entrance as well as the **Dalai Lama's private apartment**, an **audience hall** and his **mother's apartment**.

In the **reception hall** an elaborate mural details the history of Tibet, from its mythical beginnings through the early kings up to the discovery of the current Dalai Lama. It depicts the 14th Dalai Lama with his mother and ministers and relatives. Hugh Richardson, the British representative in Lhasa in the 1950s, can be identified by his

THE GREAT ESCAPE

'A soldier's clothes and a fur cap had been left for me, and about half past nine I took off my monk's habit and put them on. And then, in that unfamiliar dress, I went to my prayer room for the last time. I sat down on my usual throne and opened the Lord Buddha's teachings which lay before it, and I read to myself until I came to a passage in which Lord Buddha told a disciple to be of good courage. Then I closed the book blessed the room, and turned down the lights. As I went out, my mind was drained of all emotion. I was aware of my own sharp footfalls on the floor of beaten earth, and the ticking of the clock in the silence.'

Following the Monlam Prayer Festival in March 1959, the Dalai Lama, then 24 years old, had been requested to attend a theatrical show at the Chinese military camp near Lhasa. He was instructed to arrive with no armed bodyguard and the whole affair was to be kept secret. This summons was most unusual and a rumour spread throughout Lhasa that the Chinese were planning to capture the Dalai Lama. The Tibetans revolted and tens of thousands surrounded the Norbulingka Palace preventing the Dalai Lama from leaving. After a few days stand-off the Dalai Lama received a letter informing of the Chinese intention to shell the Palace and asking the Dalai Lama to indicate on a map where he would be 'so that the artillery could refrain from hitting whichever building within the Palace was marked'. That evening, on 17 March, the decision was made by the Dalai Lama and his Cabinet that he must escape at once.

'At the inner door of my house there was a single soldier waiting for me, and another at
the outer door. I took a rifle from one of them and slung it over my shoulder to complete my disguise. The soldiers followed me, and I walked down through the dark garden which contained so many of the happiest memories of my life.*

Leaving the Norbulingka, the Dalai Lama crossed the Kyi chu river then approached the Tsangpo via Che la. Crossing by coracle to Dungpu Chökar monastery in Chitishö village his followers continued south-east on horseback to the Khampa region via Chongye Riwo Dechen and Yarto Tag la and on to Lhuntse Dzong. It was in Lhuntse Dzong that the Dalai Lama received word of the extensive bombing of Lhasa and made a formal proclamation of a new temporary government before heading south to Jora.

'My followers helped me onto the broad back of a dzo, the cross between a yak and a cow, which is an equable animal with an easy gait; and on that primeval Tibetan transport, I left my country.

Finally, after three bitter weeks crossing numerous snow-capped passes the exhausted entourage reached Mangmang the last village in Tibet before entering Assam, India.

In India the Dalai Lama was warmly welcomed by the Nehru government which allowed him to establish his exile government firstly in Mussoorie and then finally in Dharamsala.

(All extracts above from *My Land and My People – The Original Autobiography of His Holiness the Dalai Lama of Tibet*, McGraw-Hill Book Company, 1962)

hat and tie. Other foreign dignitaries are also represented in the mural, including Russian, Indian and Mongolian officials.

In the Dalai Lama's bedroom stand his 1956 Phillips radio, an art deco bed and, off through a side door, a bathroom with state-of-the-art plumbing. In the reception hall is the carved golden throne that was used to carry the Dalai Lama during processions.

The other sites in the Norbulingka are also interesting. There are the extensive grounds, now overgrown and sad-looking, where Tibetans would come for picnics. There are several old stables and the 13th Dalai Lama's garages where he housed his three cars. These were a gift from British political officers and were carried in pieces

---

LIFE IN THE SUMMER PALACE

I was always happy to go to the Norbulingka. The Potala made me proud of our inheritance of culture and craftsmanship, but the Norbulingka was more like a home. It was really a series of small palaces, and chapels, built in a large and beautiful walled garden. ...The founder chose a very fertile spot. In the Norbulingka gardens we grew a radish weighing twenty pounds, and cabbages so large you could not put your arms around them.

...I played on the edge of the lake and twice nearly drowned myself. And there, also in the lake, I used to feed my fish, which would rise to the surface expectantly when they heard my footsteps. I do not know now what has happened to the historical marvels of the Norbulingka. Thinking about them, I sometimes wonder whether my fish were so unwise as to rise to the surface when they first heard the boots of Chinese soldiers in the Norbulingka. If they did, they have probably been eaten.

(My Land & My People, The Dalai Lama)

---

over the hills from India by yaks. Two of the cars are 1920s Baby Austins and the other is a 1931 Dodge. There's also the remains of a private zoo, housing a miserable bear and a collection of monkeys.

TRANSPORT

Four-wheel drive vehicles

Apart from using public bus or minibus the most popular mode of travel for overland travellers in Tibet is by rented truck or land cruiser. Vehicles are usually rented in Lhasa through officially sanctioned travel agents (ask at Banak Shol Hotel and Snowlands Hotel). It is also possible to strike a deal when you arrive in any other main town in Tibet.

You won't be permitted to hire a land cruiser on your own. Almost invariably, you will need to hire a driver and a guide through a travel agent.

Negotiating with an agent

● Make sure that you have worked out your itinerary, in writing, beforehand.
● The agreed price should include all travel, permits and guide fees.
● Generally try to pay half the total price as deposit and the final amount upon your return.
● Agree what you are going to do in the case of extra days, making the parameters clear if you are being charged by them.
● Agree what will happen if roads are impassable because of weather and/or the vehicle breaks down. For example if weather prevents completion of the full trip, you may need to agree that losses will be met 50:50 between you and the agency but for vehicle breakdown, all losses should be 100% covered by the agency and a backup vehicle should be provided.
● Check your driver's permits and insurance and make sure he is authorized to carry foreigners to the areas you have agreed to visit.
● Make sure you meet with the group and the driver before leaving and go through all of the final payment and itinerary details together.
● Try to view the vehicle before departure.
● Get all agreed points written up in a signed contract (make sure you receive a copy).
● Check everyone in the group is fully acclimatized before departing Lhasa (particularly critical for long trips out west to Mt Kailash and beyond).

Sample prices The cost fluctuates during the year (being much higher during peak tourist season in August and September). The price is generally calculated on the basis of kilometres travelled, as opposed to number of passengers or time taken. As a result, you can have as many stopovers as you want and this should not alter the price.

- Lhasa to Ganden   US$50-60   (2-3 hours each way)
- Lhasa to Nam Tso return   US$180-240   (2-3 days including Tsurphu)
- Lhasa to Yarlung Valley   US$300-350   (2-4 days, usually travel to Chongye
  return   via Samye and Tsetang)
- Lhasa to Nepal border   US$350-450   (2-3 days)
  (central route)
- Lhasa to Nepal border   US$600-750   (5-7 days including Yamdrok Tso, Gyantse,
                                                     Shigatse, Sakya and Mt Everest Base
                                                     Camp; price includes fee for land cruiser
                                                     entry into Everest National Park)

Mt Kailash The most difficult and expensive land cruiser trip to organize is from Lhasa to Mt Kailash. A typical 'long' trip could last 24 days – taking 13 days to reach Mt Kailash on the north road (via Ali) and five days to return to Lhasa on the south road. Most tours will include four days at Mt Kailash, completing a circumambulation of the sacred mountain, and one day visiting Lake Manasarovar.

Generally people get together in a group by putting up notices in Lhasa and meeting at places like Tashi's to chat and agree plans. Expect to pay around US$2500-3000 for a land cruiser or US$1200-2000 for a large truck (shared between 15 passengers).

The trip out west to Mt Kailash is difficult and land cruiser owners are usually reluctant to do it without support which means you will usually end up travelling in the back of a truck. Larger groups might negotiate a deal whereby they travel with a land cruiser and a truck. If that is the case, the fairest way to travel is to rotate passengers to give everyone a turn in the relative comfort of the land cruiser. Don't be surprised if the truck picks up a number of extra passengers en route and it starts to get a little bit crowded in your seating area – that's life in Tibet!

BUSES

There are three bus stations in Lhasa. The **main bus station** (south of the Norbulingka) has daily departures for Golmud, Shigatse, Gyantse, Tsetang and Damshung.

Lugu bus station (south-west of the Barkhor) has daily departures for Tsetang, Medrogungka, and Drigung Til monastery.

The **Eastern Suburbs bus station** (east of the Jokhang towards Lhasa Bridge) has departures for Medrogungka and Yangpachen.

More convenient are the private minibuses that depart each morning in front of Kirey Hotel for destinations such as Samye ferry crossing and Damshung. Also, there are regular 'pilgrim' buses for Ganden, Samye, Tsurphu and Tsetang leaving daily from just west of Barkhor square.

The airport bus departs three times daily from the courtyard in front of the CAAC building.

Around Lhasa

DREPUNG MONASTERY

Drepung monastery is an ideal first day-ride for cyclists from Lhasa. Even if you are not touring Tibet by cycle, it is worthwhile renting a Flying Pigeon from one of the hotels to cycle out to Drepung.

History

Drepung was founded in 1416 by a disciple of Tsongkhapa. Drepung means 'rice heap' and the name describes the appearance of the white jumble of buildings that are dotted on the hillside. It was once the largest and the wealthiest of the monasteries in Tibet and for many years its lamas were instrumental in the training of the Dalai Lamas. At its peak, the monastic town housed 9000 monks. There are officially no more than 500 living there at present although to a casual observer there would appear to be far fewer.

The monastery is separated into four colleges, each specializing in a different branch of Tantric knowledge. Each college had its own chanting hall, sleeping quarters and cooking buildings. The entire community would only come together for large festivals.

Visiting Drepung

The monks at Drepung are very friendly and will happily share a joke with you. Be careful if you discuss anything remotely political.

If you have time, it is worthwhile walking up along the hills to the west of the main monastic buildings. There are gentle grassy trails and across the river are a number of impressive rock paintings and carvings. Take a picnic or take the chance that you may be invited to join someone else's! It's nice to have something on you to contribute if this does happen. It is amazing how many hermitages still exist in this area and nuns and monks live all along the pathway in little caves and huts.

The large mountain behind Drepung is Gephal Ri (5200m), one of the highest and most sacred summits in the Lhasa area. It is important to Tibetans as a sacred site for the Saga Dawa festival.

Getting there

The monastery is 11km to the west of Barkhor Square and the road is flat all the way to the turn-off but ends with a climb up to the monastery. The road is generally in good condition and this trip is a good way to test your lungs on the high-altitude hills.

Drepung monastery and nearby Nechung (home of the Nechung oracle who currently resides in Dharamsala with the Dalai Lama) are nestled high on the hill to your right as you cycle from Lhasa. If you don't want to bike you may either take a taxi or the number 3 bus to Drepung. The road up to Drepung meanders through orchards and groves, which provide a welcome shade from the hot Lhasa sun.

SERA MONASTERY

'Sera, Sera, Sera': the cries of the minibus drivers in the Barkhor will ring in your ears long before you actually make the short journey up to Sera ('Rose Fence') monastery. The monastery is nestled in the hills north of Lhasa and provides magnificent views back across the city and the Potala. Once, it was a good 5km journey from Lhasa to Sera. Now, although it is still 5km from the Tibetan quarter to Sera, the city of Lhasa has crept right up to the monastery.

History
Founded in 1419 by another of Tsongkhapa's disciples, Sera is located at the base of Mt Purbuchok. Before it was established, Tsongkhapa and his students would study in the hills above in the hermitages of Sera Utse. You can still follow the paths up to Sera Utse although it is a fairly steep 1½ hour walk. It is worthwhile just to walk part of the way, as there are magnificent paintings on rocks along the mountain, similar to those at Drepung.

At its peak, Sera monastery housed between 5000 and 6000 monks. It was never quite as large as Drepung but it had fewer, larger colleges.

Visiting Sera
Two highlights of the site are the **Great Assembly Hall** (*tsokchen*) and the **debating courtyard** (*chora*), which is located at the front of the largest college, Sera Je Tratsang.

The debating courtyard is a lively place with much hand clapping and yelling of monks (usually from 15:00 daily). Watch from a courteous distance and do not interrupt the monks with questions or cameras. The debating forms an important part of the monks' studies and a high level of concentration is necessary.

Finally, there is a **pilgrimage route** that follows a clockwise circuit around each of the five Sera schools in the following sequence: Sera Me Tratsang, Ngakpa Tratsang, Sera Ja Tratsang, Hamdong Khangtsang, Tsokchen Assembly Hall and then on to Tsongkhapa's hermitage on Mt Purbuchok.

Getting there
Getting to Sera is easy. You can either board one of the many minibuses in the Barkhor – at any time of day although mornings and late afternoons are often best. Alternatively, you can easily cycle up there, following one of two routes from the Tibetan quarter. One route is to head east along the Chinese-named Beijing Shar Lam and turn left onto Ramoche Lam (this road will take you past Ramoche monastery). Follow Ramoche Lam to the end and at the crossroads continue north on Sera Lam. Sera Lam takes you straight past Drapchi Prison, on the right-hand side.

Following the other route, cycle out west towards the Potala and turn right (north) into Nyangdren Lho Lam. Follow that road directly north. Either way, the 5km cycle ride should take about 25 minutes. You can leave your cycle locked to a tree at the entrance, along the tree-lined pathway, and it should be safe enough.

OTHER SITES AROUND LHASA

There are hundreds of temples and sacred places within the Lhasa city limits. Some particularly important sites are found along the **Lingkor** (the outer pilgrim circuit of Lhasa). It is possible to either walk or cycle this route.

The Blue Buddha
Along the Lingkor (see Lhasa City map p50) is the Blue Buddha. To get there go past the south base of Chakpori to a staircase with rows of prayer flags. Further on from the staircase is a cliff face covered with religious paintings and carvings. Some date back over thousands of years and the largest is the Blue Buddha. This is described as the largest outdoor gallery of paintings in the world.

Lukhang Park and Temple

Situated behind the Potala, Lukhang Park was where the Tibetan aristocracy would come to picnic. On fine summer days some people still come for a picnic and to drink and play games. There are fish in the lake and bumper cars to ride in, under the shadow of the empty Potala.

Something of the past is preserved in the beautiful **Lukhang Temple** on an island in the middle of the lake. The tiny three-storey chapel is constructed in the form of a mandala and was used as a quiet retreat by a number of Dalai Lamas. There are at least two monks in residence in the temple. It is still a serene and spiritual place and the monks will quietly follow you round and offer information if you ask.

Kunduling monastery

Kunduling is directly behind Chakpori Hill, to the west of Lhasa. In the summer it's the venue for Tibetan operas, not quite as sanitized as those that are held in the nearby People's Opera House (opposite Lhasa Hotel). It is a pretty monastery with a large number of monks in residence. If you are fortunate enough to attend an opera at the monastery, you should take along a gift (usually of food) for your hosts.

ROUTE GUIDE 3

Lhasa to Ganden
and beyond

Not all who wander are lost
From *The Fellowship of the Rings*, **JRR Tolkien**

INTRODUCTION

Cycling a few hours out of Lhasa towards the south-east will take you to the valley of one of the greatest schools of Tibetan Buddhist teaching. In the counties of Taktse and Medrogongka is the 14th-century **monastery of Ganden**, which was the principal repository of Gelug teaching.

The road is largely paved and flat and it traverses fertile fields with the Kyi chu meandering alongside. It is a picturesque journey and a pleasant one-day cycle to the foot of the mountain on which Ganden is built. At the foot of the mountain the adventure begins: it's a long hard climb up to the monastery from the road. This is a good hill ride to undertake as preparation for the Friendship Highway. And rest assured that no other hill climb will ever seem as hard – partly because you will be acclimatizing and partly because it is just plain steep and the terrain is difficult! Once you reach the monastery you will forget the effort immediately. It is an inspiring sight.

Ganden monastery, albeit impressive (and painstakingly restored in recent years) is by no means the only reason to cycle in the region. The monasteries of the Gyama valley include several important **karmapa sites** of the 12th to 14th centuries, including the birthplace of Songtsen Gampo.

Culture aside, the area also offers some of the most interesting and accessible **trekking routes** in the region. From Ganden you can trek over to Samye monastery on the shore of the mighty Tsangpo. You can also visit the Uri Katsel – a 7th-century geomantic temple representing the religions of Tibet, India and China.

Alternatively, if you continue by bicycle towards Tibet's eastern border with China, you will reach the small **Dagpa monastery**, just after the Chinese town of Medrogongka. By turning off at Medrogongka itself, you can travel up to the distant sites of **Drigung Til** or **Tidrom**.

INFORMATION FOR CYCLISTS

Ganden monastery is close to Lhasa and an excellent cycle to 'break-in' you and your gear. Any faults in your bike (or you) can be fine-tuned upon returning to Lhasa before embarking on any more arduous rides.

Ganden has been a site of relatively recent political unrest. However, currently you do not require a permit to visit Ganden. There is a check-

Lhasa to Ganden and beyond

HIGHLIGHTS

Ganden monastery: founded by Tsongkhapa and the first of the great Gelugpa monasteries
Uri Katsel monastery: seventh-century geomantic temple representing the religions of Tibet, India and China

ROUTE INFORMATION – MAIN ROUTES

ROUTE	DISTANCE	TIME*	ROAD	CLIMB	PASSES
Lhasa to Ganden	53.5km	6-7hr	tarmac/dirt	620m ascent	none
Lhasa to Medrogongka	71.5km	6-8hr	tarmac/dirt	little	none

*ESTIMATED CYCLING TIME – DOES NOT INCLUDE STOPS FOR REST/FOOD OR SEVERE WEATHER

ROUTE INFORMATION – SIDE ROUTES

ROUTE	DISTANCE	TIME*	ROAD	CLIMB	PASSES
Road turn-off to Ganden	9.5km	2.5-3hr	dirt	550m ascent	none
Road turn-off to Katsel	2km	10min	dirt	none	none
Road turn-off to Dagpa	1.5km	10min	dirt	none	none

*ESTIMATED CYCLING TIME – DOES NOT INCLUDE STOPS FOR REST/FOOD OR SEVERE WEATHER

CHECKPOINTS

Between Lhasa and Medrogongka – 5km east of Lhasa bridge (on Sichuan-Tibet Highway)

SUGGESTED ITINERARY

Minimum (3-4 days)
Day 1: Cycle Lhasa – Ganden   Camp near Ganden or stay in guesthouse
Day 2: Cycle Ganden – Dagpa/Katsel   Stay at Dagpa or Katsel monastery
Day 3: Cycle Dagpa/Katsel – Lhasa   Option also to bus from Medrogongka to Lhasa

Maximum (4-5 days)
Ganden (one day trekking)

point 5km east of the Lhasa bridge. Be aware that there are a number of military areas along the early parts of this route so be careful and do not hang around and take photographs of sensitive areas.

LHASA TO GANDEN   [SEE MAP 1]

Lhasa bridge

The starting point for the route guide from Lhasa to Ganden is Lhasa bridge, 3km from Barkhor Square. To get there, go east along Beijing Shar Lam to a major intersection. Turn right (south) at the end of the road onto Lingyu Chang Lam and turn left onto Chingdrol Shar Lam. At the end of Chingdrol Shar Lam, turn right again and follow the road directly south across Lhasa bridge. Across the bridge is a large, foul smelling rubbish dump. Although the stench is incentive enough to move on quickly, it may interest you to know that the hill overlooking the rubbish dump and the south banks of the Lhasa chu is Bumpari (4300m). You will see the prayer flags fluttering from above.

Turn left across the bridge to go to Ganden monastery. If you turn right you will come to Drib military camp.

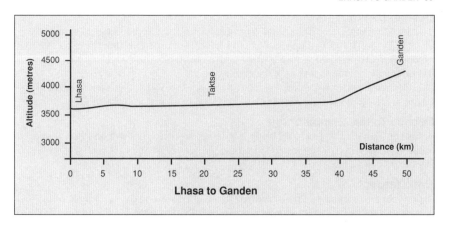

ROUTE GUIDE – LHASA to GANDEN AND BEYOND

CYCLO-METER (KM)	ROAD MARKER (KM)	ALTIMETER READING (M)	NOTES AND KEY POINTS OF INTEREST
0	#318	3600	Lhasa Bridge – 3km from Barkhor Square
	4632		*(cross bridge and turn left/east to Ganden)*
5			Checkpoint
20	4612		Taktse (Dechen Dzong) 🍴 ⅄
			(Dzong ruins on north spur overlooking village)
23	4615	3670	Dechen/Taktse bridge across Kyi chu
			(Don't cross bridge, continue east to Ganden)
30			Minor town
37			Rear of Ganden monastery visible
			(high on top of ridge to the right)
41	4591	3670	Turn-off for Ganden monastery is just before village – no sign!
			(take winding trail on right heading inland south)
		4220	Ganden monastery 🍴 ⅄ ⌂
			(9.5km steep ascent with many switchbacks!)
51	4581/2		Lamo monastery – west of village
55.2			Bridge
			(Don't cross, continue east to Medrogongka)
59.5			Deserted truck stop
68.5	4564	3800	Medrogongka Xian 🍴 ⅄ ⌂
			(Turn-off to Katsel monastery and Drigong Til)
73	4568/9		Dagpa monastery turn-off ⅄ ⌂
			(1.6km inland to monastery, camping possible)
88	4545		Balo 🍴 ⅄ *(turn-off south for 4.5km to Sephu also Takar la to Yon valley or Le la to Samye)*

Notes: 🍴 = Food, ⅄ = Water, ⌂ = Accommodation available*)

Dechen Dzong

Twenty kilometres along the road from Lhasa bridge toward Ganden monastery is Dechen Dzong, a fort that once protected Lhasa from invasion from the east. The ruin of this fort can be seen from the road and it overlooks Dechen Dzong (in Chinese Taktse Xian), a town that is now the county capital.

Dechen Dzong was once the seat of the Kyisho Depa, the ancient ruler of the Lhasa district and the ruin contains a Gelug temple known as Samdrubling.

Dechen/Taktse Zampa bridge

A further 3km east of Dechen Dzong is a large, modern, concrete and iron bridge. It leads to Drak Yerpa, a suggested side route. Do not cross the bridge if you are heading directly to Ganden.

Drak Yerpa

A possible return cycle to Lhasa would be to take the road on the north bank of the Kyi chu including the Drak Yerpa meditation caves (albeit on a more difficult road than the main road). You need to cross the large Taktse Zampa bridge. After you cross the bridge, you will reach Dromto village. From Dromto it is a further 2km to the next junction. At the junction, turn left for a further 11km and then turn right (north) for a further 7km, which will take you to Yerpa Da. The caves at Drak Yerpa are a three-hour walk from Yerpa Da.

Drak Yerpa is a limestone cave complex associated with King Songtsen Gampo, Guru Rinpoche (the enlightenment cave) and Atisha. All of these religious figures are believed to have meditated here at some time. In terms of religious significance, the site ranks with Samye Chimpu and Yarlung Sheldrak, these being the three principal cave retreats of Tibet. Each one has special geomantic qualities, and Drak Yerpa has more than 80 caves. It may be possible to stay inside one of the caves – but bring your own food and supplies.

From Yerpa Da it is 26km directly back to Lhasa, via two hydropower stations.

Ganden Namgyeling monastery

If you continue along the main road on the south of the river, directly to Ganden, the Ganden turn-off is a further 21km past Dechen Dzong. You will see the turn-off on your right-hand side, just before a small village (near the 4591km road marker). From the main road you will not be able to see Ganden monastery as it is nestled around the other side of the mountain above. Turn right onto the metal road from where it is a 9.5km ride up a difficult 550m ascent. The road has many switchbacks and creeps up to an altitude of 4220m. It is hard work, particularly if conditions are wet. The dirt road can get extremely muddy and the corners of the switchbacks in particular can bog down the tyre of the hardiest mountain bike. It is worth persevering with the road, even if you have to get off your bike at the steeper parts.

GANDEN MONASTERY

Ganden monastery was founded in 1409 by Je Tsongkhapa, who was also the founder of the Gelug school. The name 'Ganden' means 'Paradise of Maitreya'. Maitreya is 'The Joyful'.

Ganden was the first of the three great Gelug monasteries (the other two of which are Lhasa's Drepung and Sera). Ultimately, there were six great Yellow Hat monasteries. These were the original three. Shigatse's Tashilhunpo, the birthplace of Tsongkhapa, Kumbum (near Xining) and Labrang (near Lanzhou) followed. If you take the route from Xining to Lhasa/Shigatse, you will be able to visit all six sites on the way.

❏ **Je Tsongkhapa (1357-1419)**
Tsongkhapa, or Je Rinpoche, was born in 1357 in Amdo, eastern Tibet. He is believed to be a reincarnation of the young boy who offered the Buddha a clear crystal rosary and received a conch shell in return. The Buddha prophesied that the boy, born in Tibet, would found a great monastery, present a crown to the statue of the Buddha in Lhasa and go on to be instrumental in developing Tibetan Buddhism. In 1409 Tsongkhapa established the first Gelug monastery at Ganden and organized the first Great Prayer Festival (Monlam) in Lhasa. He provided 24 volumes of written Tibetan scripture in his lifetime and, after his death, the principle of *tulku* ('living Buddha') came into existence. The head abbots of the Gelug school were believed to be successive incarnations of the Bodhisattva Chenresi (the 'Protector of Tibet'). Tsongkhapa's successors were subsequently bestowed the universal title Dalai Lama ('Master Ocean of Wisdom').

Ganden is situated on the south-facing ridge of Gokpori. On the left-hand side of the ridge is the sacred Wangkuri. This natural amphitheatre was the site of the first ever Monlam festival. From Ganden there is a spectacular view of Kyi chu valley.

During its history, Ganden became a Mecca for the faithful followers of the Gelug sect. Prior to 1959, the Ganden abbot (Ganden Tripa) was responsible for the tutorship of the 14th Dalai Lama (jointly with leaders from Drepung and Sera). At Ganden, unlike at other monasteries, the position of abbot is neither a hereditary right nor a reincarnation. It is a position that resembles management or leadership roles in the West, whereby a learned monk is chosen for his ability and carries the position for a seven-year term. The abbots then became potential candidates for the regency, the effective rulers of Tibet during the absence or minority of reincarnate dalai lamas.

The year 1959 was not the first time that Ganden was involved in political upheaval. Throughout the 19th and 20th centuries, the monks of Ganden joined with their colleagues at Drepung and Sera and formed a reactionary political force that hindered the dramatic reforms that were introduced under the rule of the 13th Dalai Lama.

The monastery was severely ransacked by Red Guards in 1966 and during that period it came to represent a triumph of Mao's policies over Tibetan religion and history. However, by 1986, 16 of Ganden's temples had been rebuilt and approximately 200 monks have now returned to live and study at the site. It has never returned to its former glory at a time when between 2000 and 3000 monks resided at the monastery. As recent as 1996, Ganden monks were shot at during violent demonstrations against the banning of Dalai Lama pictures. The PLA fired on the protesting monks, killing two and arresting at least 100.

Services
Bus Buses to Ganden leave at 06:30 from the west side of the Barkhor. You can buy bus tickets from a small tin shed on the south-east corner of the Barkhor. The trip is approximately 2hr 30min and the bus will remain at the monastery until it makes a return trip to Lhasa in the afternoon, at around 14:00.

Accommodation It is possible to spend the night at Ganden: the basic *guesthouse* is on the left-hand side as you enter the Ganden gates. The accommodation block is a large building beside the parking area. Alternatively, there are places to *camp* if you climb up the hill a little, just before the entranceway to the monastery.

Food At the guesthouse *restaurant* you will be served simple meals such as noodles with steamed bread or vegetables. There is also plenty of hot water and tea. There is a small shop a little further along the road that sells a few provisions and sweets.

Ganden highlights

Bear in mind that most of the buildings and statues at Ganden are now reconstructed replicas. Some original statues and treasures are held in museums but most were destroyed.

● **Serdung Lhakhang** This is the red painted building with a large white stupa and the largest golden roof in the Ganden complex. It is the main assembly hall. Reconstruction work on it is almost complete. To get to it, simply follow the road around from the accommodation building past the Debating Courtyard. (There is often debating in the afternoons.)

● **Tongwa Donden** This is Tsonghapa's reliquary chorten (his tomb), and it is found on the first floor in the Yangpachen Khang Chapel. There is a cabinet to the left of the chorten, which contains relics of the great leader, including a tooth, begging bowl and vajra. Women are not allowed to enter protector temples (*gonkhang*) for fear that the wrathful appearances may upset them.

● **Sertrikhang** If you climb further up the hill from the Tongwa Donden, on the right-hand side you will find the Throne of Tsonghapa. This also served as the throne of successive abbots and is backed by large images of Tsongkhapa and his two foremost students. Near the throne is a cloth bag containing the 14th Dalai Lama's Yellow Hat.

Ganden kora

The Ganden kora is a one-hour walk, in a clockwise direction, starting from up behind the little shop in the Ganden complex. The walk takes you in a circle right around the top of the mountain upon which Ganden is built. It is well worthwhile, not only because it is an extremely sacred kora, but also because it offers a magnificent vista of the Lhasa valley (as well as an opportunity to liaise with the locals away from the watchful eyes at the monastery).

As you follow the kora, you will pass the site of Tsongkhapa's prostrations (at the summit) and the site of sky burials. Towards the end of the kora, just as Ganden monastery comes back into view, you will reach Tsongkhapa's hermitage Ozer/Waser Puk ('Cave of Light'), which is still the original building. A sweet monk guards the building and will point out the relief image of Tsongkhapa and the two Buddha images carved into the rock. The rocks around it are beautifully painted.

BEYOND GANDEN   [SEE MAP 1]

Gyamashing valley

If you continue on past the turn-off to Ganden, you will reach the Gyamashing valley situated in Ngonda county. The valley is approximately 18km east of the Ganden turn-off (and about 60km from Lhasa bridge).

Situated in the Gyamashing valley are the remains of three important Karmapa monasteries. The first, Gyama Trikhang, is located close to the highway, within a large walled enclosure that once belonged to influential nobility. The second monastery, Rinchen Gang, was founded in 1181 and the ruin of Dumburi can be seen nearby. The third monastery is the Gyelpo Khang monastery, located on the hillside east of Trikhang. This is a small temple, containing an image of the Emperor Songtsen Gampo, who is said to have been born in a village nearby.

Medrogongka valley

The next valley along as you continue to travel east is the Medrogongka valley. It is worth making the trip to Medrogongka as it provides a useful base for a number of important sites and has very good bus links back to Lhasa should you care to put your mountain bike on the roof and take the easy route back.

❑ **Trekking – Ganden to Samye**
Ganden provides an ideal opportunity for trekking in Tibet. The 80km Ganden to Samye trek takes four to five days and is one of the most popular treks in the country; the locals are well-equipped to help anyone who wishes to undertake it. This is a demanding trek, involving two high passes: it must be taken seriously. You'll need to take a tent.

The route will take you to the little village of Hebu, where the locals will negotiate yak and guide hire. You will not be permitted to take a yak without a guide and, to be honest, you will not want to.

The route follows a winding track, impossible to cross by bicycle, over the two mountain passes that divide the Kyi chu valley and the Tsangpo. The lush green hillsides of Ganden are a stark contrast to the desert-like sand dunes of Samye.

The alternative to organizing a guide at Hebu is to do so at Ganden. Ask around at the monastery hotel and they will introduce you to someone who can help. Apart from anything else, this gives you a great opportunity to meet the locals.

Medrogongka

The township of Medrogongka is 67km east of Lhasa and is a three-hour bus journey from the city. The fare is reasonable and the bus departs Lhasa daily at 10:00 from the Eastern Suburbs bus station and leaves Medrogongka for the return trip at 07:00.

Medrogongka is a very strongly Chinese-influenced town, based at the confluence of Medro Phu chu and Kyi chu rivers. It has a heavy PSB presence so it is wise not to hang around too long. There are good stores at which to stock up on supplies and the restaurants provide basic Chinese food. It is a popular stop for Chinese cadres travelling from the east to Lhasa so keep a reasonably low profile.

There is one *truck stop* that offers accommodation to foreigners. It is frankly not worth the stress and a *campsite* outside of the town is a far better option. Recommended spots to camp are in the nearby monasteries of Uri Katsel (2km) or Dagpa (5km).

Dagpa monastery

There is little information available about the small monastery at Dagpa. It has very few visitors but the monks in residence are delightful. The villagers in this region, or even the monks, may tolerate you choosing a campsite nearby. There are a lot of dogs though, so be careful when you step out of your tent in the dark.

Drigung Til monastery

Drigung Til monastery is a site that is more regularly visited by foreign travellers. It is a three-hour jeep journey by road, directly from Lhasa (130km north-east). Alternatively, it a 25km cycle or jeep-drive from Medrogongka to Drigung Qu (in a north-east direction). Drigung Qu is at the confluence of the Kyi chu and Zhorong rivers.

From Drigung Qu to Drigung Til it is a further 38km. The monastery is at 4300m, which is an ascent of 180m from the valley floor.

Zhoto Terdrom/Kadampa nunnery

Zhoto Terdrom hermitage is in a nearby side valley (Zho valley), which branches off from the main Zhorong Tsangpo valley. The hermitage is 16km to the north, before the base of Drigung Til. Near the hermitage is a Kadampa nunnery and a medicinal hot spring called Chutsen Chugang. Guru Rinpoche promised Tibetans that the water would cure all ailments. The main hot spring, with an average temperature of 40°C, is right at the nunnery. There are a few *guesthouses* at the site.

Lhasa to Nam Tso

In Tibet, the loftiest land on earth, even valleys run higher
than the summit of any mountain in Europe, Canada or the United States.
Sir Charles Bell

INTRODUCTION

Nam Tso (or *Tengri Nor* – 'Sky Lake') is one of the most beautiful spots in Tibet. It is a remote and isolated lake set high on the plateau, accessible only via a long and winding mountain pass. The Tashi Dor monastery is moulded out of the landscape with its temple and hermitage cut into a magnificent rock formation on the lakeside.

The arduous cycle journey from Lhasa to Nam Tso is unquestionably worth the effort. First, Nam Tso is completely off the beaten track, even for Tibet, and there is a surreal and ethereal quality about the place and its inhabitants. Secondly, the majority of the ride is on paved roads, which are in extremely good condition with plenty of little towns dotted along the way for supplies. Thirdly, approximately half way between Nam Tso and Lhasa is a hot pool complex, which is an unexpected and welcome treat for tired cyclists' legs.

The ride itself is divisible into two quite different sections. First is the ride from Lhasa to Damshung, which is along a paved road through picturesque villages and a spectacular gorge. Take plenty of film.

The second section is the difficult part of the ride. Once you turn off the main Lhasa to Golmud highway at Damshung there is a well-packed dirt track up to the bottom of the pass. The pass itself is long and steep but it can be done – despite what the locals will tell you. At the top, the view of Nam Tso is breathtaking. From there, the road is all either downhill or flat. That is, until you have to come back over the pass!

WARNINGS

High altitude

Tibet jealously guards jewels like Nam Tso, placing geographical barriers along the way. This ride is beautiful, but it is also difficult.

If you have just arrived in Lhasa, you'll need a few days to acclimatize properly before attempting to travel to Nam Tso. The pass itself is over 5000m and, once you reach the pass, it is only a 500m drop to the lake. Consequently, you will spend all of your time at the lake at an altitude of approximately 4700m. This altitude is higher than Ganden and over 1000m higher than Lhasa. It is not to be taken lightly – especially given that you will exert a lot of energy simply getting over the pass.

If you plan to spend longer than two nights at the lake, you will inevitably feel the effects of the altitude. As noted on p35-39, altitude affects people in different ways. The reason for an extra warning here is two-fold. First, many people will attempt this trip reasonably early into their visit to Tibet. At such time, you will only be beginning to get used to the altitude. More importantly, Nam Tso really is off the beaten track and if you do run into trouble it will be very difficult to find any assistance.

Unpredictable weather

Alpine conditions mean unpredictable weather and Nam Tso is certainly an alpine environment. Weather on the plateau surrounding the lake will vary from magnifi-

Lhasa to Nam Tso

HIGHLIGHTS

Nam Tso ('Sky Lake') – second largest salt-water lake in Tibet
Tashi Dor Hermitage – ancient and holy hermitage nestled in caves on the shore of Nam Tso
Yangpachen – highest swimming pool in the world, hot mineral bathing with altitude
Tsurphu monastery – leading monastery of the Karmapa sect of Tibetan Buddhism

ROUTE INFORMATION

ROUTE	DISTANCE	TIME*	ROAD	CLIMB	PASSES
Lhasa to Yangpachen	87km	8-9hr (6hr rtn)	sealed	660m ascent	none
Yangpachen to Damshung	77km	6.5-7.5hr	sealed	150m descent	4580m
Damshung to Largen la	25km	4-4.5hr (2hr rtn)	dirt	900m ascent	5160m
Largen la to Nam Tso	38km	5hr(6-6.5hr rtn)	dirt/grass	400m descent	none

*ESTIMATED CYCLING TIME – DOES NOT INCLUDE STOPS FOR REST/FOOD OR SEVERE WEATHER

CHECKPOINTS

Yangpachen (south side of village)
Toll gate (9km from Damshung towards Nam Tso)

SUGGESTED ITINERARY

Minimum (6 days)
Day 1: Lhasa – Damshung (bus/van)
Day 2: Campsite – over Largen la
Day 3: Campsite – Tashi Dor
Day 4: Tashi Dor – over Largen la
Day 5: Campsite – Yangpachen
Day 6: Yangpachen – Lhasa

camp 1hr ride beyond Damshung
camp near turn-off to Nam Tso Qu
Tashi Dor guesthouse
camp 1hr before/after Damshung
hotsprings guesthouse

Maximum (6-9 days)
Include cycling from Lhasa to Damshung (allow two days minimum)
Tashi Dor, Nam Tso (one day trekking)

cently clear hot sunny skies to hail and snow, sometimes within minutes. These variations will occur at any time of the year but particularly from late September, by which time the nomads have left the high plateau for the warmer pastures back over the pass. Remember the nights have alpine temperatures.

Shortage of drinking water

The lake is large and beautiful – but saline. There are no shops after Damshung until you reach Nam Tso. You need to carry as much water as you can but once you reach the lake there is a small store that will sell you boiled lake water.

ACCOMMODATION AND FOOD

Accommodation and food will not pose any significant problems on this route. The only concern is obtaining sufficient water between the bottom of the pass on the Nam Tso side and Tashi Dor. Careful planning will prevent any problems in this regard.

Between Lhasa and Damshung, there are plenty of little roadside stores so you will always be able to obtain Cokes and lemonade. The same stores have a plentiful supply of dried noodles and often you will also be able to buy fresh (or almost fresh) bread.

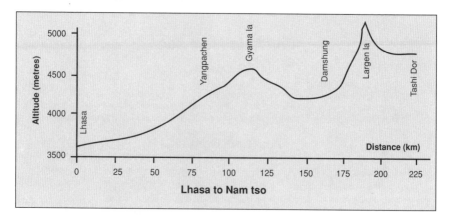

From Damshung to Nam Tso and Tashi Dor there is nothing except for numerous picturesque campsites and, near the bottom of the pass on both sides, running water.

In terms of food, you will need sufficient supplies to feed yourself from Damshung to Nam Tso **and back**, though you can buy hot noodles once you reach Nam Tso.

There is accommodation in Damshung, although it is probably less stressful to camp outside the township. Tashi Dor is a highlight and you can get accommodation and food at the guesthouses. At Nam Tso Qu (the local village) you will be able to find basic accommodation and there's a small shop/restaurant.

BUS TRAVEL

If you do not relish the thought of 'return' bike trips, you can quite easily catch a bus on the uphill part of this route (Lhasa to Damshung) and cycle back downhill to Lhasa (2-4 days).

Small white mini-buses depart from in front of the Kirey Hotel at 07:00. You will need to be reasonably forceful to get you and your bikes on the bus, given that they are usually quite crowded with locals. For a sum, you will ensure yourself a place.

The bus trip up to Damshung is crowded and bumpy. However, it will be one day instead of two to four days by bicycle and the best option if you have time restrictions.

The bus will continue north of Damshung and will not turn off towards Nam Tso. Therefore, from Damshung you are on your own, unless you can negotiate a ride over the pass (or just to the top) on a truck. Don't underestimate the difficulty of the 30km ride from the bottom of the pass to the monastery.

INFORMATION FOR CYCLISTS

This cycle ride is a return trip along the same road. You may choose to travel by bus or car one way and return by bicycle. If you do, remember that it is predominantly uphill from Lhasa to Nam Tso and almost all downhill back to Lhasa.

The ride to Nam Tso starts out along the main Lhasa to Golmud highway. If you entered Tibet and Lhasa from Golmud in the north, this ride will mean you will be retracing your steps for 150km back to Damshung (where your bus may have stopped for a toilet stop).

The ride from Lhasa up to Damshung will take from two to four days. It will be two long days if you do it that quickly – but it is possible. There are little villages along

ROUTE GUIDE – LHASA to DAMSHUNG

CYCLO-METER (KM)	ROAD MARKER (KM)	ALTIMETER READING (M)	NOTES AND KEY POINTS OF INTEREST
0	none	3600	Barkhor Square
			(head west towards Potala/turn left at Lhasa Hotel)
4.5	3638		Lhasa – main bus station
12			Road junction – **reset** cyclometer – 48min from Barkhor
			(veer right to Damshung and Nam Tso/veer left to Shigatse)
0	3879/80		'See You Again' sign
3			Officially leaving Lhasa – many shops 🍴 ⍭
			(Poplar tree-lined road for next 10km)
9.4			Replenish water bottles 🍴 ⍭
			(no other 'shops' for next 36km)
13.4	3866		Series of three slate quarries
15.6			Leave river
17.2			*(enter dry barren valley until rejoining river)*
19			Small monastery LHS – near large Chinese compound
19.5			Village
21			Village
22.9			Village
24.8	3855		White chorten marking end of the Lhasa valley
26.8	3853	3750	Iron bridge across river – Tsurphu monastery turn-off
			(monastery is 28km up valley at 4400m)
31.5	3848		Village with monastery
39.8	3840		Chinese mobile military camp
46.6	3833		Small village
52.5			Town 🍴 ⍭
			(valley narrows and road steepens for next 24km)
65			Stunning narrow gorge for next 10km
75	3804/5	4260	Yangpachen 🍴 ⍭ 🛏
76.8	3803/4		Turn-off for Yangpachen thermal station & hot spring – see billboard
			(turn left/west to town 2.5km and hot springs 7km and also
			for north Friendship Highway; go straight for Damshung)
83.7	3797		Artwork on road
102		4580	Gyama la
			(possible strong winds over next 23km)
130.3		4200	Possible campsite – amongst nomads
			(wide grassy valley on left, Nyenchen Thangla range behind)
133.6			Chinese memorial to Asian Games held in Beijing
			(the Games torch/baton passed here en route to Beijing)
133.7	3748		Truck stop with thermal swimming pool 🍴 ⍭
			(inside large compound on left)
142.3			Small hydro plant on left
145.1			Damshung visible in the distance
151.7	3729/30	4260	Damshung 🍴 ⍭ 🛏

Notes: 🍴 = Food, ⍭ = Water, 🛏 = Accommodation available

the way and plenty of places to camp. It is often easier to camp just outside the main townships and then pick up breakfast on your way through the next day, rather than try to find accommodation in the towns. Having said that, there are truck stops to stay at if you prefer.

It is worthwhile restocking supplies in Damshung and to have a good hot meal while you are there. There are a number of roadside 'cafes' which will offer you a range of meals from momos to fried rice and noodles. Take a little time to talk to the locals – but don't let them talk you out of cycling over the pass to Nam Tso. They might know the road better than you do but they are not fully versed in the capabilities of a modern mountain bike.

Once you turn off at Damshung for the pass, the road is no longer paved but it is tightly-packed dirt and easy to ride on up to the foot of the pass. The pass is a big ride and there are some really nice spots to camp at the foot of it on the Damshung side. If you get an early enough start, you will be able to get over the pass and to Tashi Dor in one day. That is, in one very long and difficult day. Alternatively, there are plenty of places to camp on the other side of the pass (although it is a lot more exposed than the Damshung side) and there is a creek for water.

From the top of the pass, if you look to your left you will see a large rock formation that looks a lot like Ayers Rock in Australia. Tashi Dor is built into this rock. If you are heading for the monastery, you need to follow the road towards the rock. However, because the lake has a large estuary that indents between the pass and the rock, you must be careful to cycle on the tracks closest to the mountain range away from the lake. This is sometimes confusing and difficult because there are a number of weaving roads and tracks and the one you are meant to be on often looks the least likely!

It is over 30km from the foot of the pass on the Nam Tso side to Tashi Dor; 30km may not seem like much but as the roads are difficult to follow, and often extremely muddy, it will be a long 30km. It might be flat but this part of the ride is still difficult.

Between the foot of the pass and Tashi Dor, you will not be able to get water. The odd filthy muddy trickle might run under your bicycle, but you will not want to drink it. You must carry enough water to reach Tashi Dor (and this should include enough for the night in case you get on the wrong track and do not make it before dark).

LHASA TO YANGPACHEN   [SEE MAPS 2 and 4]

It is 87 kilometres from Lhasa to Yangpachen village and just over seven kilometres to the Yangpachen hot springs. If you cycle directly to the hot springs, there is good *accommodation* near the pools and the opportunity to soak tired muscles at the highest swimming pool in the world (4250m).

Leave Lhasa via the road to Drepung. Head directly past the Drepung monastery and, when the road forks, veer right. The road to the left is the beginning of the Friendship Highway, leading in the direction of the airport and Shigatse. Head out under the 'See you again' sign marking the end of Lhasa and begin a pleasant ride along sealed and reasonably flat roads up to Tsurphu monastery. There is a lot of heavy traffic along this route including trucks, buses and mini vans, and it is constantly in need of repair. Wherever roadworks are underway, the route becomes extremely dusty and unpleasant.

There are several pleasant little Tibetan villages dotted along the roadside and the turn-off for one of the most important monasteries in the region, Tsurphu monastery, is about 39 kilometres from Lhasa at an iron bridge (road marker 3853).

Turn left up the dirt road at the beginning of the village for Tsurphu. If you are short of time, you could try to catch a lift up to the monastery on a truck. It is 28 kilo-

❑ **The 17th Karmapa**
The 17th Karmapa is a key religious figure for Tibetan Buddhists, both in Tibet and in exile. Until recently, he was the most senior Tibetan lama residing in Tibet who was equally recognized by the Chinese authorities and the Dalai Lama. In December 1999, he fled Tibet to join the Tibetan community in exile in India, causing enormous concern to Chinese officials in Tibet who had been grooming him as a leader of Tibetan Buddhism who could be controlled.

The search for the 17th Karmapa began after the death of the 16th in November 1981. Four senior lamas of the Karmapa-Kagyu tradition, Situ Rinpoche, Shamar Rinpoche, Jamgon Kongtrul and Gyaltsab Rinpoche, took on the role of regents and were responsible for collectively identifying the reincarnation of the Karmapa. In March 1992, Situ Rinpoche announced that he had discovered a prophetic letter from the 16th Karmapa which led him to identify the whereabouts of a boy in Eastern Tibet. When Jamgon Kongtrul, who had been charged with travelling to Tibet to find the candidate, was killed in a car crash in India, Shamar Rinpoche withdrew his support for Situ Rinpoche and his candidate, marking the beginnings of a dispute that has continued to the present.

On 7 June 1992 the Dalai Lama announced his official support for the candidate, having been consulted by Situ Rinpoche following the dispute amongst the regents. Situ Rinpoche also approached the Chinese authorities, who allowed a search team to travel to Eastern Tibet where they located the candidate, a nomad's son, Ugyen Trinley Dorje, and formally identified him as the 17th Karmapa. He was escorted to Lhasa on 13 June 1992 and the Chinese authorities announced their formal support for him on 27 June, on the same day that the boy conducted his first religious ceremony. An enthronement ceremony took place at Tsurphu monastery, the traditional seat of the Karmapa, on 27 September 1992, attended by Chinese officials who took this opportunity to claim that they had a historical and legal right to appoint religious leaders in Tibet.

Tibetans had been concerned for some time about Chinese attempts to manipulate the Karmapa and use him for their own political purposes such as undermining support for the Dalai Lama in Tibet. The Karmapa had already been taken on two tours of China and has met various Chinese leaders including Jiang Zemin. Less than a year before his departure from Tibet, after a meeting in Beijing with Chinese officials, including Li Ruihuan, Chairman of the Chinese People's Political Consultative Conference (CPPCC), he was quoted by the Beijing-based journal 'China's Tibet' as stating in a speech in Mandarin that he had 'received an education in patriotism' during the visit and that he would follow the instructions of Jiang Zemin and 'work hard for the unification of the motherland and national unity'.

The 17th Karmapa fled Tibet for the safety of exile in India on 28 December 1999, with a small party of monks in complete secrecy, his departure unknown even to his own family. He left his historic monastery, Tsurphu, north-west of Lhasa, and travelled with his party over the winter passes of the Himalayas to freedom. They arrived in Dharamsala, India, on January 5, 2000, where he was warmly welcomed by His Holiness the Dalai Lama. Since then, His Holiness Karmapa has been living temporarily at Gyuto Ramoche Temple near Dharamsala, where he receives training in Tibetan Buddhist studies and practices from masters of the Karmapa-Kagyu lineage.

metres from the road turn-off to the monastery and mostly uphill (climbing up to 4400m). If you do decide to make the detour by cycle, commit yourself to spending at least one night – although there are a number of villages in the valley so it shouldn't be difficult to find a place to stay.

Incidentally, buses leave the Barkhor at 7:30am most days to Tsurphu so you could either catch the bus in Lhasa or try to catch a lift up to the monastery from the turn-off (although these buses are fairly crowded).

Tsurphu monastery
Tsurphu monastery is the seat of the Karmapa (Black Hat) sect of Tibetan Buddhism. A lineage of seventeen reincarnate Karmapas has been enthroned at the monastery since it was founded in 1190 by Karmapa Dusum Khyenpa. Until the Cultural

Revolution, Tsurphu monastery was home to approximately 900 monks. It had four internal monasteries, which were set within a vast complex of buildings. One of those monasteries was the seat of the Goshir Gyaltsabpas, who traditionally represent the Karmapas between incarnations (in the same capacity as the Dalai Lama's regents).

Drupon Dechen Rinpoche, the current abbot of Tsurphu, was the former retreat master of Rumtek. Drupon Dechen Rinpoche fled from Tibet in 1959 together with His Holiness and the 16th Karmapa. They carried with them some of Tsurphu's primary relics and holy objects to the safety of Sikkim. Those relics are kept in the Rumtek treasury.

Some years later, the 16th Karmapa advised Drupon Dechen Rinpoche to return to Tsurphu to supervise the reconstruction of the monastery after its destruction by the Red Guards in the mid-20th century. He did so and the reconstructed monastery has become an important site of worship for Tibetans and a key tourist attraction.

The monastery is situated between the mountainous peaks of the To valley north-west of Lhasa. A river runs alongside the walled monastic complex, which is auspiciously located amidst the hills and valleys of the region. Tibetans believe that the spiritual powers and energy of the *vajrayana* mandala are concentrated in the neighbouring mountains.

The Kagyu lineage of Tibetan Buddhism originated from Sakyamuni Buddha through Marpa the Great Translator. Marpa travelled to India in order to return to Tibet with authentic Buddhist teachings and texts. His most famous student was Milarepa (see Milarepa Cave, pp124-5). Milarepa was the teacher of Gampopa who, in turn, passed the teachings on to the First Karmapa, Dusum Khyenpa. From that time, the Kagyu lineage has been headed by a succession of reincarnations of the Gyalwa Karmapa. The line is said to be 'self-announced', in that each incarnation leaves a letter predicting his next rebirth. All great Kagyu teachers regard His Holiness Karmapa as the embodiment and source of all of the blessings of the lineage.

Tsurphu Thangka Prior to the Cultural Revolution, every great monastery in Tibet possessed magnificent silk appliqué hangings, which were used for public display and worship. These banners were often huge and were among Tibet's greatest art treasures, due to their spiritual significance, size and intricacy of design. At Tsurphu, on the south bank of the river, in front of the monastery (now reconstructed), are the old steeply inclined steps upon which the gigantic thangka was traditionally displayed for a few hours each year.

The creation of such huge images, called *Ki-gu* (literally meaning 'Satin Image') was traditional throughout Tibet. They are constructed by sewing together a range of heavy brocades, silks and satins, using a technique called appliqué. The same process was used in traditional Tibetan tent designs as well and the Karmapas were renowned for their elaborate tent settlements.

Many of the thangkas in Tibet were destroyed during the Cultural Revolution, including the magnificent pieces at Tsurphu monastery. Between 1992 and 1994, Tibetan and Western experts worked to recreate a huge 23m by 35m silk/brocade appliqué banner of Sakyamuni for ceremonial display at Tsurphu.

Tsurphu turn-off to Yangpachen

The duration of the cycle from Lhasa to Yangpachen is approximately six hours. The Tsurphu turn-off is approximately halfway and you should reach this in under three hours. The next half of the journey to Yangpachen is uphill most of the way and will take a bit longer. However, this valley offers numerous great camping sites so if you have a tent and food supplies then make the most of the outdoors.

ROUTE GUIDE – DAMSHUNG to NAM TSO

CYCLO-METER (KM)	ROAD MARKER (KM)	ALTIMETER READING (M)	NOTES AND KEY POINTS OF INTEREST
0	3729/30	4260	Damshung 🍴 ⵂ ⏧
			(turn-off left towards bridge to Nam Tso & Tashi Dor)
0.3	no markers		Bridge – cross over river
0.4	.		Road forks – turn right at 'orange wall' *(main road leads to airstrip)*
1.3			Compound – with high wall on left
1.8			Two storey 'glass' school building
2.6			Fork – veer left to Nam Tso *(right branch heads to nearby village)*
4.5			Good spot to get bearings – weather permitting
			(head towards concrete 'toll' building in distance)
6.7			Concrete bridge *(continue towards 'toll' building)*
8.8			Chinese 'toll' building *(enter valley on left, Bakura village on right)*
9.7			Road veers away from river *(good campsites with fresh water)*
13.6		4500	Bridge (L-R) *(Steep 'well graded' rocky section for next 4km)*
15.2			Bridge (R-L)
16			River crossing, no bridge (L-R)
17.7			Switchbacks for next 7.5km
25.2		5160	Largen la pass
31.7			Road forks – veer left to Tashi Dor monastery
			(right branch leads to Nam Tso Qu 7km away)
32.2			Cross river and head towards crumbled building
			(need to check best crossing point)
32.7			Crumbling house *(if necessary camp inside to shelter from the wind)*
35.84			Dilapidated houses
38.34		4775	Nam Tso Qu village *(village is visible looking back from the track on the right, 7km away)*
40.8			Fork after river crossing
			(keep well left to avoid 'swamp' for next 13.5km!)
46.6			Follow grassy 'wall' on left for 3km *(formerly the Nam Tso shoreline)*
49.5			Leave 'wall' section
51.8			House ruins – first of five sites
53.6			Last house ruins
54.2			Road forks – turn right/north-west to Tashi Dor monastery
			(road runs parallel to lake edge)
63.2		4760	Tashi Dor monastery 🍴 ⵂ ⏧

Notes: 🍴 = Food, ⵂ = Water, ⏧ = Accommodation available

The gorge up through this area is magnificent. The villages are extremely pictur-esque and the prayer flag-laden footbridges make magnificent photo opportunities. The road is smooth and sealed but it is uphill so the return trip is far more enjoyable.

Yangpachen
Yangpachen township is 48-49km from the Tsurphu turn-off. It is the largest town along the route (prior to Damshung) and houses and little shops line both sides of the road

marking the outskirts of the town. The town centre is actually 2.5km from the main highway, structured around the thermal power station (where the steam rises from the left of the main road). The hot springs are near the power station but to get to them you need to continue along the main highway past the shop-lined part of the main road. The turn-off to the main part of the town and the hot springs is marked by a huge sign of a Chinese girl in a bikini (not that you will see many of those in the pool) on the left of the road. Turn off here onto the sealed road and cycle over the bridge and through the main village (2.5km from the turn-off). Just follow the road towards the steam (veering left all the way but not actually turning off) for 7km from the turn-off.

There is *accommodation* in a truck stop compound near the hot springs. A high-altitude dip costs around Y20. The owner of the restaurant inside the pool complex operates the truck stop accommodation. He is a helpful Chinese man who will cook you up a feast for dinner.

YANGPACHEN TO DAMSHUNG [SEE MAP 4]

From Yangpachen hot springs, the route comprises a combination of undulating road and small hills, with one fairly easy pass to Damshung. It is just less than 75km and with the pass en route it is still a long ride in one day. Strong winds can belt through the valley making it tough going in places.

There are a few interesting sites on the way. The pass, Gyama la, is marked by the traditional array of prayer flags fluttering in the wind, 27km from Yangpachen. It is then downhill for a way, although the road may not be in fantastic condition. At 57km from Yangpachen there is an intriguing monument erected to commemorate the site where the Asian Games torch/baton passed through en route to Beijing.

Damshung

Damshung is everything you would expect a Chinese truck stop town to be – with a few redeeming features. It offers *accommodation* – in ugly concrete truck stop buildings – and has plenty of **shops** for stocking up at as well as quite nice *restaurants*. A good eatery is at the northern end of the town, on the left-hand side. The delightful Tibetan family that runs the place will invite you into the kitchen to chose your ingredients and then sort you out a delicious big fry-up – just what you'll need to get over the pass to Nam Tso.

DAMSHUNG TO LARGEN LA [SEE MAP 4]

It is 25km from Damshung to Largen la (5160m) – the pass that marks the entry to Nam Tso. It is a long and difficult climb and if you have timed your day to reach Damshung towards the end of the day, it would pay to have a hot meal and then head out to camp as close as possible to the foot of the pass. It is a lovely valley and there are plenty of campsite options – all obscured from the road.

It is not entirely straightforward to get from Damshung to the pass so you will need to follow the route guide fairly carefully. The turn-off is the sealed road to your left as you enter Damshung from Lhasa. There is a large bridge to cross. On the other side of the bridge, you need to turn right and skirt along the front of the river-side village. Follow the dirt track up between two little villages, towards a multi-storey building that appears to be a school.

As you head past the school building, continue to follow the dirt track, which forks to the left at 800m from the school building. Stay on the left fork; at just under 2km from the fork a yellow concrete building will come into view. This is the Chinese

❏ **The marmot cabaret**
The great delight of camping in this area is the prevalence of marmots. These little guys will come and play near your tent and snuffle around for food. They are very timid but if you put some food out and sit very quietly, they will pop up and play around for you – fun evening entertainment.

The Himalayan marmot is one of the highest living mammals in the world. Himalayan marmots are found from 4000m to the upper edge of the vegetated zone (approximately 5500m) in the mountains of Nepal and parts of India and Tibet. A subspecies of the Himalayan marmot, *M. himalayana robusta*, is one of the largest marmots and may weigh over 6kg. Virtually nothing is known about this species, which goes by the common name 'Tibetan snow pig'.

'toll' bridge (which is still 4km away). Head for the toll building, crossing a concrete bridge about half-way towards it. Just head straight on quickly (unless someone stops you – in which case negotiate).

For the next 3-4km the metal road begins to climb as it follows the river towards the pass. There are pleasant and sheltered fields along here where you can camp for the night. The river is close for water and you will not need to detour very far from the road to find a good site. The ground is a little damp on the river side of the road so try to break camp on the left-hand side.

Largen la
Most passes in Tibet are hard work and Largen la is no exception. The road is covered in loose metal and crosses the river time and time again. It is a relatively steep incline, climbing about 900m from Damshung to the pass. A few trucks go past should you decide to hitch a lift but this pass is no harder than a lot of the ones of the Friendship Highway so it is worthwhile getting in some early practice. It is about 10km from the campsites to the top of the pass so even if you need to push your bike, you will be able to get over the pass and a good way down the other side in one day.

The view from Largen la is absolutely magnificent. Nam Tso is a beautiful lake and it nestles in a majestic circle of snow-capped peaks. The lake is huge and its vibrant view provides a striking backdrop to the brightly coloured flurry of prayer flags at the pass.

LARGEN LA TO NAM TSO   [SEE MAP 4]

The lake itself is the second largest saltwater lake in China (after Lake Kokonor near Xining). It is 70km long and 30km wide.

It will take approximately five hours to cycle the 38km from Largen la to Tashi Dor monastery. It is a long way and the roads are difficult to follow and very boggy in places. Head down the pass (unfortunately as Nam Tso is so high there is not much of a downhill from Largen la to Nam Tso) and take the fork heading left just past the little ruined building on the left-hand side of the road (heading towards Nam Tso). You will need to cross the river but it should be shallow enough to cycle across (quickly) without getting your feet wet.

Follow the dirt tracks along the middle of the plain (about equal distance away from the lake shore to your right and the mountain range to your left). There is a mound on the lake shore, which looks a lot like Ayers Rock in Australia. The key is to head for the mound but, if in doubt, keep left. If you get too close to the shore of the lake, you will get caught in the bog and possibly find yourself at the estuary inlet that runs out across the plain just before the rock.

It is a little bit disheartening as the road leads you closer and closer to the rock and then, apparently bypasses it and takes you to the shore of the lake around the other side. The road does actually circle back again and you enter the monastery via the lake shore from the other side of the rock. You could try to take a short-cut but these plains are full of peat bog and it is impossible to cycle on the roads in some places, let alone off-road. Stick to the road: any detour will ultimately cost you more time.

Tashi Dor

The road surface is nice and tightly packed as you get near the monastery. There are big fences and signposts in the surrounding fields so you will know you are on the right track. Tashi Dor is more a concentration of hermitage caves than a monastery (although there are temples built into the caves). Two enormous rocks (like short, fat obelisks) mark the entrance way and the road passes between the two – under the row of prayer flags that join the two rocks.

Immediately through the entranceway is the Tashi Dor monastery, built into the rock face. Just along the road a little, past the monastery, a woman runs a *guest house* and will offer you a real bed (of a sort), in four-bed rooms for around Y30 per person. A small store offers basic food. You could also camp closer to the lake sheltering near the base of the rock cliffs.

Tashi Dor is a magnificent site with an array of hermitage caves dotted around the rock, entered through the twin pillars which act as watchtowers for the complex. Most of the façades in the caves were destroyed during the Cultural Revolution, although with the recent return of several monks and nuns to the monastery, some of the main temples have been rebuilt. Years of burning hermit fires have left centuries of soot on the cave roofs, which are shiny like boot polish.

The main temple, **Shabdrung Phukpa**, is a small and recently restored Nyingmapa chapel and inside is a large image of Guru Rinpoche. On the right of him is Nyenchen Thanglha (in a wooden cabinet) and the throne of the Tashi Dor lama (who resides in Damshung) is on the left.

There are currently a few intrepid monks residing in the caves and they will welcome you in for a glimpse of their lonely lives. The beautiful and serene surroundings, and their faith, seem to make them very contented people. It is easy to see why.

There is a pleasant 30-minute walk up to the **summit** of the rock, approached from back towards the entrance to the complex. The views from the top are magnificent. It is also possible to circle the entire rock in 90 minutes, visiting the different caves along the way. Around the other side of the rock (directly across from the monastery) are two large white chortens and, close to the chortens, a children's sky burial site.

Nam Tso Qu

There is not a lot to see at Nam Tso Qu. The little village does give travellers an insight into rural life in Tibet where nomadic bartering traditions are controlled by a centralized administration, responsible for a heavy-handed and arbitrary taxing regime.

There's *accommodation* here in a rather tired hut. The rooms are located next to the small *shop/restaurant*. The shop does not sell bottled water, but will boil water for you. The local women will also provide you with fairly ordinary, but adequate, food. It is a good spot to head for if the weather catches you out or, despite your careful planning, supplies do run low.

To get to the village (located 7km from the main track), simply head back towards the lake (left) when you get back to the main road coming from Tashi Dor or, if you are heading there from the pass, continue straight ahead along the main road.

Lhasa to Yarlung Valley

Make a habit of turning around and looking behind you
the views and perspective can be more fantastic than those ahead.
Mary Lu Abbot

INTRODUCTION

The Yarlung is the Tibetan 'Cradle of Civilization', fed and nurtured by the mighty Tsangpo river. The Tsangpo is a river of great spiritual and environmental significance for Tibetans and the many other peoples living along its shores.

With an average altitude of 4000m, the Tsangpo is the highest river in the world. Its source is the Tamchok Khambab glacier (5040 metres) located 100km south-east of Mt Kailash in the Chemayungdung mountain range, in the far west of Tibet. From there, the Tsangpo flows for 2900km east, across most of southern Tibet. It sweeps around Mt Namche Barwa (7756m), which is the world's highest unclimbed mountain, and then miraculously cascades down into north-eastern India, descending 3000 metres within a mere 80km!

The Indians call the river the Brahmaputra (meaning 'son of Brahma' the Hindu God of Creation). Its final destination is the Indian Ocean at the Bay of Bengal. It was not until 1924 that British botanists (Captain Frank Kingdon Ford and Lord Cawdor) were able to confirm that the holy river of the Brahmaputra was in fact the Tsangpo in Tibet. However, even to this day, no-one is believed to have travelled the entire course of the river.

As the river meanders gently alongside the road you can see the signs of years of inhabitation and cultivation of the land. A smooth sealed road from Lhasa to Tsetang is the latest symbol of civilization, but the greatest beauty of the road is that it can carry you to the multitude of valleys that hide the secrets of years of worship by the Tibetan people.

The road leads to many important pilgrimages, one of the most significant of which is to Samye monastery, across the river. (Note that Samye is also accessible via a trekking route through the mountains from Ganden monastery – see p69). If you take the ferry to Samye, you will be able to enjoy the company of Tibetan pilgrims dressed in their finery for the journey.

❏ Om Mani Padme Hum

This incantation is inscribed on numerous mani stones throughout Tibet, Ladakh and Nepal. The verse originally derives from the Milarepa school of Buddhist thought and can be traced back to Buddha's birthplace in India. Literally transcribed it means 'Hail, jewel in the lotus', it carries a much deeper significance to those who utter the phrase.

Om is the most fundamental of all mantras. It is the sound of enlightenment.
Mani padme means 'jewel in the lotus' but these words represent the fusion of complementary opposites – not dissimilar to the Chinese Ying and Yang.
Hum is the sound of fulfilment.

Together these sacred six syllables form the mantra as uttered to Chenresi, the Bodhisattva of Compassion and the Protector of Tibet.

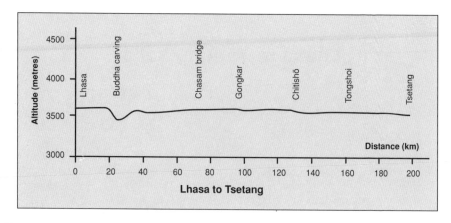

INFORMATION FOR CYCLISTS

The options for cycling excursions in the valley are numerous. This is an excellent route for building fitness whilst allowing your body to acclimatize. There are no high passes to deal with and the road remains below 3700 metres. It is level and sealed – and is in better condition than any other road in Tibet.

Tibet was ruled from the Yarlung valley up until the 9th century and Buddhism found a foothold along the banks of the Tsangpo. Consequently, there are many historic sites and monasteries located close to the fertile plains of the Tsangpo, which are easily accessible.

By way of practicalities, food, bottled water and accommodation are readily available. There are buses that travel daily from Lhasa to Tsetang (and vice versa) and will drop you anywhere in between.

The one disadvantage of travelling in this valley is that it is very heavily populated. Villagers tend to be more suspicious than in more remote areas of Tibet and there is a very strong Chinese presence, particularly in Tsetang. The road approaching Tsetang has become a dumping ground for the town's rubbish and is a sorry sight. It is not until you pass through the town and head up to Tsetang monastery (and the birthplace of Tibet, see p94) or further afield to Yumbulagang in the south that you will have an opportunity to interact with the Tibetans of the area and be able to absorb the historic significance of the region. Fortunately for the cyclist, cycling is the easiest way by which to do this.

Note that permits are required for Samye, Yumbulagang and the Kings' Tombs near Chongye. The PSB sometimes wait at the Samye ferry dock (on the south side of the river to check the bus when it stops to drop off pilgrims en route to Samye).

You do not need a permit to be in Tsetang itself, but this is a particularly difficult place to find 'approved' accommodation or eating-places. The Chinese authorities have a real stronghold over the local members of the hospitality industry, making life very difficult for budget travellers.

The only 'approved' accommodation is the crazily-priced Y900 Tsetang hotel (or a cheaper and nastier version at Y300-400 per double). The best alternative is to take a tent and camp outside the town. It is towards the south of the town that you will find the best options for camping, as there are loads of attractive fields to choose from.

Lhasa to Yarlung valley

HIGHLIGHTS

Gongkar Chöde monastery: spectacular collection of preserved Kyenri murals and artwork
(protected by a whitewash overcoat during the Cultural Revolution)
Mindroling monastery: most impressively renovated monastery in the Drachi valley
with a beautiful cobbled courtyard
Samye: ferry ride of a lifetime in a boat packed with pilgrims heading to Tibet's first monastery
Yumbulagang castle: site of reputedly the oldest temple in Tibet, dating back 2000 years
Kings' Tombs: ten tombs of the Tibetan kings, including the great first king, Songsten Gampo

ROUTE INFORMATION – MAIN ROUTE

ROUTE	DISTANCE	TIME*	ROAD	CLIMB	PASSES
Lhasa to Chaksam bridge	71km	3-4hr	sealed	35m descent	none
Chaksam bridge to Tsetang	123km	8-9hr	sealed	50m descent	none

*ESTIMATED CYCLING TIME – DOES NOT INCLUDE STOPS FOR REST/FOOD OR SEVERE WEATHER

ROUTE INFORMATION – SIDE ROUTES

ROUTE	DISTANCE	TIME*	ROAD	CLIMB	PASSES
Tsangpo (north bank) to Samye	1km	1hr	dirt/sand	50m ascent	none
Road turn-off to Mindroling	9km	45-60min	dirt	100m ascent	none
Road turn-off to Dranang	2km	10min	dirt	none	none
Tsetang to Yumbulagang	10.5km	50min	dirt	80m ascent	none
Tsetang to Chongye	28km	3hr	dirt	275m ascent	none

*ESTIMATED CYCLING TIME – DOES NOT INCLUDE STOPS FOR REST/FOOD OR SEVERE WEATHER

CHECKPOINTS

Tongshoi ferry depot: Samye permits checked
Tsetang – strong PSB presence
Chongye – Kings' Tombs permits checked

SUGGESTED ITINERARY

Minimum (5 days)

Day 1: Lhasa–Chaksam bridge	camp near bridge/Dagar guesthouse
Day 2: Chaksam Bridge–Mindroling	stay at Mindroling monastery
Day 3: Mindroling–Samye	camp near Tongshoi or Samye
Day 4: Samye–Yumbulagang	camp near/at Yumbulagang
Day 5: Yumbulagang/Chongye/Tsetang	return to Lhasa by bus

Maximum (6-7 days)
Samye Chimpu hermitage (half to one day trekking)

MAIN SIGHTS EN ROUTE

There are five major valleys branching off the Yarlung. All five are easily accessible from the south bank of the Tsangpo and they are located between Chaksam Bridge and Tsetang. The valleys are Gongkar, Namrab, Drib, Dranang, and Drachi. Each has its own claim to fame.

There is the opportunity to visit a few of the valleys on the north bank of the Tsangpo as well, via a ferry crossing (few such crossings exist in the desert-like plateau of Tibet) to both Drakyul and Samye valleys.

The most important religious sites in the area are affiliated to either the Sakya or Nyingma sects of Tibetan Buddhism.

The **Sakya monasteries** include Gongkar Chöde in the Gongkar valley, Dakpo Tratsang in the Namrab valley, Thubden Rawame in Rame, Dungpu Chökar near Chitishö, Dranang in the Dranang valley, and Tsongdu Tsokpa in the Drachi valley. All of the Sakya monasteries share a common characteristic in that many of their principal buildings auspiciously survived the Cultural Revolution of the 1960s. They survived because the local communities were quick-thinking enough to convert the buildings into grain stores or communist party offices. Given that the grain must be kept dry, the only damage that many of the murals in these buildings suffered was the superimposition of a layer of whitewash. The painstaking process of removing the layer of whitewash has been ongoing since the early 1980s. Gongkar Chöde monastery is of particular importance to art historians as it is considered to be the site at which the central Tibetan 'Kyenri' art style originated.

The valleys branching off the Yarlung also nurse two of the most important **Nyingma monasteries**. These are Dorje Drak in the Drakyul valley and Mindroling in the Drachi valley. Mindroling is particularly well restored and is absolutely beautiful. These monasteries are a little more difficult to reach than the Sakya ones (which are often on the roadside) but, as a result, they are somehow more worthwhile.

Dranang valley is the birthplace of several prominent **Nyingma masters**, including Longchenpa, who was the patriarch of the Nyingma sect, Orgyen Lingpa, who was one of the greatest 'treasure finders' (tertöns) of Tibet, and Minling Terchen, who was the founder of the Nyingma Mindroling monastery.

The area also contains two of Guru Rinpoche's 'Five most important **meditation sanctuaries**'. These are Drak Yongdzong and Samye Chimpu – both of which can be visited.

Finally, two of the four **sacred mountains** of central Tibet are in the valley, namely, Chuwori, which is near Chaksam Bridge and Hepori, which is near Samye. Samye itself holds the auspicious honour of being the oldest monastery in Tibet and is worth visiting for that reason alone.

Lhasa to Chaksam bridge [See Map 2]

The first leg of this journey is a pleasant, flat ride along the Lhasa river. This is the first 80km of the Friendship Highway and the route details are on pp96-99. It is possible to take a taxi or bus to Chaksam bridge should you wish to cycle either the Central or Southern Friendship Highway to Nepal.

Chaksam bridge Chaksam bridge means 'Iron Bridge' and this is the original iron suspension bridge across the Lhasa river, built approximately 600 years ago by Tangton Gyalpo. Known as Tibet's master bridge builder, Tangton Gualpo built more than 100 bridges throughout Tibet.

The bridge that traffic now uses to cross the river is the Chinese constructed concrete bridge 100m down the road at Dagar. Soldiers guard both ends of the new bridge and although they can be a little unnerving as they brandish their weapons, they should let you pass by without any difficulty.

After you cross the bridge, turn left towards Tsetang (the road to the right heads to Yamdrok, along the Southern Friendship Highway). Directly in front is Mount Chuwori.

Chuwori Chuwori (5962m) is one of four sacred mountains in central Tibet (along with Chakpori in Lhasa, Hepori next to Samye and Gongpori near Tsetang). The confluence of the Kyichu and Tsangpo rivers is considered an auspicious site for meditation and, according to tradition, the mountain contained 108 holy springs and 108 hermitages, Guru Rinpoche built one of his principal meditation caves, at Namkading

ROUTE GUIDE – LHASA to YARLUNG VALLEY

CYCLO-METER (KM)	ROAD MARKER (KM)	ALTIMETER READING (M)	NOTES AND KEY POINTS OF INTEREST
0	none	3600	Barkhor Square *(go west towards Potala/turn left at Lhasa Hotel)*
71	4704 old	3565	Chaksam bridge – **reset** cyclometer – start on north side
	66 new		*(200m across bridge then turn east towards Tsetang)*
1.5			Mt Chuwori (5962m) *(towering behind south side of bridge)*
15	81		Gongkar Dzong ruins *(high on the ridge with large chorten)*
18	84		Gongkar Chöde monastery *(about 200m south of the main road)*
25.7	91		Gongkar village ⑩ Ⴧ ⤵
28	93	3590	Gongkar Airport turn-off
35			Namrab valley entrance *(turn-off 5km south to Dakpo Tratsang monastery)*
37			Rame town (Gonggar Xian) ⑩ Ⴧ ⤵
44/45	110		Possible campsite
47.2	112/113		Dorje Drak ferry crossing
			(next to small Tibetan restaurant – monastery visible across river)
53	118		Chitishö town ⑩ Ⴧ
			(Dungpu Chökar monastery – 300m south of town on right)
57.3	122		Join Tsangpo river again
62			Drakda village *(seen on north bank of Tsangpo)*
66			Gaktsa town *(ferry to Drakda)*
72.5/73	137		Possible campsite
75	140		Yangkyur town ⑩ Ⴧ
77	142		Dratang village ⑩ Ⴧ *(entrance to Dranang valley)*
			Dranang monastery and Dranang town (Zhatang Xian) ⑩ Ⴧ ⤵
			(2km south of Dratang)
			Jampaling Kumbum *(1km south-east of Dranang monastery)*
82.2	146/147		Turn off to Mindroling monastery ⑩ Ⴧ ⤵
			(8.5km inland to monastery – 1hr ride in/40min return)
84	149		Tsongdu Tsokpa monastery
			(250m from road – a 13th-century, four-storey, Sakya monastery)
90.6	155		Tongshoi village ⑩ Ⴧ ⤵
			(Samye ferry depot)
			Samye monastery ⑩ Ⴧ ⤵
			(1hr cycle, 11km from north bank of Tsangpo near Surkar village)
97.5	162		Namseling manor *(seven-storey building visible 3km to south)*
99	163/164		Small sheltered campsite
106	171		Jing valley *(look across to giant sand dunes on eastern side of valley)*
121/122	186/187		Tsetang outskirts *(veer left at fork intersection after petrol station)*
124	189/90	3515	Tsetang town centre (Zetang Xian) ⑩ Ⴧ ⤵
			(traffic circle with bronze 'monkey sculpture')
129/30			Tandruk monastery
132/3			Turn off to Chongye valley
			(turn right/west to Chongye 20km, straight on for Yumbulagang)
135/6		3595	Turn off to Yumbulagang *(Yumbulagang high above road)*
(28 km ex Tsetang)		3800	Chongye ⑩ Ⴧ ⤵
			(Kings Tombs accessible from Chongye by foot – approx 1hr)

Notes: ⑩ = Food, Ⴧ = Water, ⤵ = Accommodation available

near the summit, which has been recently restored and can be visited. Pilgrims circumambulate Chuwori, in around four hours, via Phab la (4250m).

Gongkar valley

Gongkar Dzong The sealed and flat road along the river runs for 15km to the ruins of Gongkar Dzong (high on the ridge to the west of the Gongkar valley). Formerly, seat of the Lord of Gongkar, the fort was strategically important during the Sakya ascendancy. The commanding site was also one of the two final choices considered by the 5th Dalai Lama for building the Potala Palace.

Gongkar Chöde monastery Gongkar Chöde monastery is 3km further towards Tsetang. The monastery is only 200m south of the main road and well worth a visit (just before marker 84).

Gongkar Chöde monastery was founded in 1464 by Kunga Namgyel (1432-96) of the Sakya school. The main monastery building remains more or less intact. As noted above, the murals on the ground floor of the monastery were whitewashed during the Cultural Revolution in the 1960s. They were subsequently restored in the 1980s.

The monastery's founder, Kunga Namgyel, was a renowned master of Tantric ritual. The complex is the site of the 16th-century 'Kyenri' style of Tibetan painting, created by Jamyang Kyentse (born 1524), and many other original works are preserved here. Kyenri painting is less symmetrically rigid than the traditional 'menri' style found throughout most temples in central Tibet. It is possible to visit the building directly north of the main courtyard where the young monks learn to paint Buddhist statues from the elder masters of the art. There are about 40 resident monks (compared to the 160-odd who resided at the complex prior to 1949).

The **highlights** of the Gongkar Chöde monastery are:
● The original Kyenri murals of the 'Five Founders of Sakya' (Kunga Nyingpo, the patriarch, Drakpa Gyaltsen, Sonam Tsemo, Sakya Pandita, Pakpa) – inside the main assembly hall flanking the entrance to the inner chapel;
● The unusual depictions of 'sky burials' on the inside gönkhang at the front left of main assembly hall;
● The mural depicting the original monastery layout on the second floor chapel; and
● The paintings of principal tantric deities (yidams) of the Sakya tradition on the second floor of the Yidam chapel.

Dechen Chökhor Dechen Chökhor is 4km further inland from Gongkar Chöde. It is situated 150m above the road on the eastern side of the Gongkar valley (approximately one-hour's walk from the road).

Dechen Chökhor has a 13th-century hermitage and the monastery belongs to the Drukpa Kagyu school of Tibetan Buddhism. Only one chapel has been restored, following the destruction in the mid-20th century. At its peak, the monastery's head abbots served the kings of Ladakh.

Gongkar airport (in Chinese Gonggar) Gongkar village is 18km further along the road and the turn-off to Gongkar airport is 2km past the village. There is food and *accommodation* available at the airport and also in the village. Buses stop in the village and you may catch a ride from here to Lhasa or to Tsetang.

Namrab valley   [See Map 2]

Dakpo Tratsang monastery The Namrab valley entranceway opens up to the south, 5km past Gongkar valley (past marker 100). The monastery, at the entrance to the valley, was founded by Tashi Mangyel (1398-1459) of the Sakya school in the 15th century.

This is the second Sakya monastery in Yarlung that has managed to keep the majority of its magnificent structure intact. The recently renovated main assembly hall retains some of its original murals as well as a central image of Sakya Pandita. The monastery founder, Tashi Mangyel, was a teacher of Sonam Gyatso and a favourite disciple of Rongtonpo (1367-1449). Tashi Mangyel wrote more than 300 different works and was considered to be one of the 'six jewels of Tibet' by the Sakya sect.

Rame (in Chinese Gonggar Xian) Rame is the district prefecture town, located 18km east of Gongkar Chöde. You will be able to stay in the *truck stop*, situated about halfway down the main street (which is the road full of shops to your left, ie north). It is perfectly adequate, although on balance, the best option is to replenish supplies in this town, have some lunch in one of the *Tibetan restaurants*, and move on.

Approximately 250m down the main street (which runs north) is the dilapidated Thupten Rawame monastery. The monastery was founded by Rawalepa (1138-1210). This is another Sakya monastery, which now has a large transmission aerial on the roof and is surrounded by government buildings.

Drakyul valley [See Map 2]

Dorje Drak monastery Dorje Drak monastery is, like the great Samye, on the north side of the river. There is a ferry crossing to the monastery next to a small *Tibetan restaurant* on the north side of the road (between road markers 112 and 113).

The ferry ride across the Tsangpo is approximately one hour each way. The Tibetan restaurant staff will assist you to locate the boat and operator. It is possible to *camp* near the monastery beside the riverbank (or alternatively you could try inside the monastery). It is tempting to try to cycle from Dorje Drak to Samye – given that they are on the same side of the river – but this is not recommended as the 'trail' proceeds over low ridge spurs and is a mixture of sandy dunes and stony flood plains.

Dorje Drak monastery itself is at the bottom of a ridge. It is one of two principal Nyingma monasteries in Central Tibet (the other being Mindroling) and was founded on this site early in the 16th century by Tashi Tobgyel, a third incarnation of Rigdzin Chempo Ngodrub Gyeltsen (1337-1409).

The celebrated Nyingma lineage was established by Ngodrub Gyeltsen, the tertön who discovered the 'northern treasure' (Jangter) of the Nyingma tradition in Western Tsang. The religious instruction at Dorje Drak stems from this lineage. The fourth incarnation of Ngodrub Gyeltsen, Pema Trinle (1641-1717) developed the lineage further and led to the discovery of the major Dorje Purba texts in one of Guru Rinpoches 'five principal meditation sanctuaries' at Drak Yongdzong (about 12km further up the valley near Kur la). Drak Yongdzong is a labyrinth of interconnecting limestone passages and natural caverns.

The monastery was destroyed by the Dzungar Mongols in 1717. It was rebuilt then destroyed again by the Red Guards in the 1960s. The existing structure was gradually rebuilt and restored from the mid-1980s. Up until the Cultural Revolution in 1959, approximately 400 monks studied at Dorje Drak.

The **highlights** at Dorje Drak are:
● The large image of Guru Rinpoche inside the main assembly hall;
● The murals depicting 'Eight Manifestations of Guru Rinpoche' and Ngodrub Gyeltsen, inside the main assembly hall;
● The dorje and bell of Pema Trinle, a 'treasure chest' and detailed plan of the original monastery inside the large temple to the right of the main assembly hall; and
● The trek up to the Drak Yongdzong hermitage.

Drib valley [See Map 3]

Chitishö Back on the south side of the river, 16km east of Rame is Chitishö. Chitishö was formerly an important trading town, situated on the ancient caravan route between Lhasa and Bhutan/India.

The ruins of Chitishö Dzong can be made out on an eastern ridge high above the town. Chitishö is known for its manufacture of woollen cloth, particularly colourfully striped aprons (panden) made with dyes sourced from Bhutan. The best quality aprons are made from up to 20 different colours.

Today, there are a few *shops* in the village and a small *restaurant*.

Chitishö may be used as a base and starting point for a three- to four-day trek, via Drib la (5296m), to the eastern arm of Yamdrok Tso.

Dungpu Chökar monastery On the right side of the dirt road, approximately 300m south of Chitishö, is Dungpu Chökar monastery. Chitishö township may not warrant a stop (except for supplies) but the monastery certainly does.

Dungpu Chökar is a Sakya monastery founded in the 15th century by a disciple of Rongtonpa (a contemporary of Tsongkhapa). Another 'granary monastery', the three-storey main temple building has been preserved with many murals still in good repair.

The monastery contains a room where the present 14th Dalai Lama briefly stayed during his flight to India in March 1959. After he left the Norbulingka, the Dalai Lama crossed the Kyi chu river and approached the Tsangpo via Che la. He crossed by coracle to Chitishö and he and his entourage continued to make their way south over the Drib la to Lhodrak, before veering east to Chayul and finally down into Assam, India.

The **highlights** at Dungpu Chökar monastery are:
- The paintings of the 'Wheel of Life' and 'Buddhist cosmology' in the main assembly hall entrance porch;
- The murals of the '12 Deeds of Sakyamuni Buddha' on the left wall inside the main assembly hall; and
- The 14th Dalai Lama chamber on the third floor of the main assembly hall.

Dranang valley [See Map 3]

Commonly known as the 'Valley of 13 Buddha-Lamas', Dranang valley has a rich mix of archaeology, art and religion. This is where some of Tibet's best-known religious masters were born, including Longchempa (patriarch of the Nyingma school), Orgyen Lingpa who was one of greatest Nyingma 'treasure finders', Minlin Terchen (founder of Mindroling monastery) and Drapa Ngonshe (founder of Dranang monastery).

Dratang At the entrance to the Dranang valley, 24km east of Chitishö, is Dratang village. The village is immediately past a large, modern intermediate school.

You will find a Tibetan *restaurant* and *teahouse* alongside the road.

Dranang monastery Dranang monastery is approximately 2km down the flat dirt road (which turns south of the main road). It is in the district prefecture town of Dranang (Zhatang Xian). The road leading to the monastery is lined with Chinese-constructed concrete blocks.

Dranang monastery was founded in 1081 by Drapa Ngonshe (1012-90), a Nyingma lama. Control of the monastery was later usurped by the Sakya school during the 13th century.

Drapa Ngonshe was responsible for building many religious sites in central Tibet but Dranang was the most important of his projects. He was also a renowned Nyingma tertön who recovered the 'Four Medical Tantras,' which continue to be studied today by all doctors of Tibetan medicine.

The monastery's original architecture was based on a mandala design and is similar in style to Samye. However, it is most celebrated for its original murals, which are a synthesis of the Pala art style (which flourished in eastern India in the 9th-11th centuries) and Central Asia (Xixia) influences. The extant paintings are said to be both the oldest and only surviving ones of their kind in Tibet. The 'Pala-Xixia' mural is inside the inner sanctuary chapel (entrance at the rear of the main assembly hall).

Jampaling Kumbum Jampaling Kumbum is 1km further inland from Dranang monastery, located approximately 50m above the dirt road on the eastern side of the valley.

To reach the impressive ruins of the Jampaling Kumbum, continue past Dranang monastery and turn left at the fork past two large government compounds, which flank the dirt road.

The monastery was built in the 14th century and the 13-storey stupa was formerly the largest of its type in Tibet (exceeding even the impressive Gyantse Kumbum). The structure was destroyed during the Cultural Revolution.

Drachi valley [See Map 3]

This valley contains some of the most impressive treasure houses of the Yarlung valley and is a must see.

Mindroling monastery Perhaps the most impressively renovated building in the valley is Mindroling monastery, which is 8.5km south of the entrance to Drachi valley (turn-off 5km east of Dratang between markers 146/147km). It is approximately one-hour's cycle ride to Mindroling from the turn-off. The return trip is downhill (slightly) so it is about 40 minutes back.

The undulating dirt road rises gently after it passes through a small village and continues to rise until you reach a second village (Mondrub). There is then a slightly steeper gradient for the final one to two kilometres up to the monastery complex (which you enter from the south gate). You cannot actually see Mindroling monastery (which is situated on the east-facing side valley) until you reach the village of Mondrub.

Mindroling is the largest and, along with Dorje Drak, the most celebrated Nyingma monastery in central Tibet and originally covered a 100,000sq km area. In the 10th century, Lumé Tsultrim Shenrab (who spearheaded the Second Diffusion of Buddhism into Tibet together with Atisha and others), built a modest Kadampa chapel on the site. This was greatly expanded by Terdak Lingpa Gyurme Dorje (950-1025). Terdak Lingpa is the tertön who discovered those key texts that form the basis of the 'southern treasure' (Lhoter) of the Nyingma tradition. Terdak Lingpa was renowned for having compiled the 13-volume *Nyingma Kama* (an exposition of Guru Rinpoche's methods of attaining enlightenment).

As with Dorje Drak, most of the Mindroling complex was destroyed in 1718 by Dzungar Mongols. It was rebuilt and destroyed again by the Chinese in the 1960s. The 13-storey kumbum, which was completely flattened, is now being rebuilt below the main monastic complex.

The **highlights** at Mindroling monastery are:
● The exceptional 'brown stone' masonry on the outside of the large temple;
● The 1.5m statue of Terdak Lingpa, in a glass case inside the main assembly hall;
● The murals depicting the entire Nyingma lineage, inside Lama Lhakhang on the third floor of the large temple;

- The rooftop view across Drachi valley; and
- The hermitages, high up both sides of the valley.

Mindroling monastery is an excellent place to spend a night and explore the surroundings. There is *accommodation* (converted monks' quarters) on the north side of the main courtyard. The rate is modest and the monks are very hospitable. A small *shop* is located immediately outside the monastery entrance.

Tongshoi (Samye ferry depot)
The ferry crossing to Samye monastery is located at Tongshoi, 13km east of Dratang (road marker 155km). Tongshoi village is a small collection of buildings including a little *guesthouse*, **shop** and *restaurant*, operated by a very friendly Tibetan family.

On the north bank, both Surkar village and Samye monastery offer guesthouse *accommodation* to foreigners.

Beware of strict PSB officers who lurk around Tongshoi – especially when the buses stop. They will fine foreigners who do not hold valid permits for Samye monastery. The fine applies to everyone, including those travellers who trek to Samye from Ganden. It is best to arrive at the ferry crossing early in the morning (08:00 to 09:00) before the first Lhasa buses (and first PSB officers) arrive. If you do arrive when the PSB is present, you may want to casually cycle on towards Tsetang and return to Tongshoi later in the morning.

The **ferry** across the Tsangpo from Tongshoi is a relaxing 90-minute trip across to Surkar (only 45 minutes to get back). There are no fixed departure times and there is no extra charge for bicycles. The boat zigzags its way between the Tsangpo sand banks and the pilgrims sharing the boat will spend the journey blessing themselves with the sacred Tsangpo waters. This ferry trip is well worth it just for the experience of being so close to these devout pilgrims making a trip of a lifetime.

Samye valley   [See Map 3]
Surkardo village Once you are across and on the north bank of the Tsangpo, the roads are very sandy and difficult to cycle on – but not impossible. From the ferry 'terminal' on the Tsangpo's north bank it is a couple of kilometres to Surkardo village and 11km to Samye monastery.

It takes about one hour to cycle to Samye, a gentle climb over a mix of flood plain and soft sandy trails. This route would be impossible to cycle in wet weather. One option is to take a day trip on foot and leave the bike in a dormitory room at Tongshoi. There are trucks on the north bank that will take you (and your bike if you have it) to Samye monastery for a negotiable fee.

Surkardo chortens As you head in the direction of Samye, you will see above the road, about 4km from the Tsangpo, five white chortens that have been built out of the granite boulders. The chortens were reputedly constructed to mark the location where King Trisong Detsen first met Guru Rinpoche. According to tradition, the King waited for the Guru to pay homage but instead the Guru raised his hand and fire sprang from his fingers. The King bowed in terror and subsequently ordered that the chortens be built in an attempt to restore some merit.

This is a nice place to stop for a break and to look out over the sand dunes and the mighty Tsangpo.

Samye monastery
The entranceway to Samye monastery is at the north gate of the round perimeter wall. Samye's political and religious importance to Tibetans overall makes it as significant to pilgrims in the Yarlung-Tsangpo region as the Jokhang is to those in Lhasa.

Samye ('Forest of Monasteries') was the first monastery built in Tibet and was instrumental in the establishment of Buddhism in the country. There are older temples in Tibet (such as the Jokhang) but monks were neither trained nor ordained at these temples. The monastery was completed in 779 under the patronage of King Trisong Detsen (742-97), who was born 6km up the valley at Drakmar. The King invited the renowned Indian Buddhist scholar, Shantaraksita (700-760), to formally establish Buddhist monasticism in Tibet (he also became Samye's first abbot).

At the time there was strong opposition to Buddhism in the region (primarily from aristocratic families who supported the indigenous Bön religion) and the king asked the Indian Tantric master Guru Rinpoche, known for his mystical powers, to subdue the hostile spiritual forces in Tibet. It is believed that Guru Rinpoche defeated the local Bön demons from the summit of Mount Hepori and consecrated the site upon which Samye was built. Following the completion of Samye, Tibet's first group of monks were ordained by Shantaraksita.

King Trisong Detsen commissioned Indian and Chinese scholars to translate the principal Buddhist texts into Tibetan. However, a conflict arose regarding doctrinal interpretation and in 792 the King called for a public debate between Karmalashila (an Indian *Mahayana* proponent of the 'graduated path to Buddhahood', which emphasizes scholarly study and moral discipline) and Hoshang (a Chinese *Zen* proponent of the 'instantaneous path to Buddhahood', which emphasizes meditation and inaction). Karmalashila is reported to have won the debate and this is heralded as a crucial juncture for the direction of Buddhism in Tibet. Nonetheless, elements of both principles are still present in Tibetan Buddhism today.

Although Samye was originally associated with the Nyingma tradition (due to Guru Rinpoche's involvement), both the Sakya and, more recently Gelug, schools have presided over the monastery throughout its history. This multi-denominational rule has enabled Samye to become a national symbol for Tibetans, which binds together all 1200 years of their Buddhist heritage.

Samye mandala Samye was built as a three-dimensional mandala representing the Buddhist universe. It was modelled on the plan of the Odantapuri monastery in Bihar, India. The central temple (called the Ütse) represents Mount Meru, the mythical mountain at the centre of the cosmos, which is surrounded symmetrically by temples representing the sun and moon, oceans, four continents and eight sub-continents of Buddhist cosmology. There are four stupas (each a different colour – red, black, green, white) at the corners of the Ütse. The entire monastery complex is contained within a circular perimeter wall, topped by 1008 smaller stupas.

According to the cosmography from *Ta Tang His Yu Chi* (records of the Western world – compiled during the Tang dynasty AD618-907):

The mountain called Sumeru stands up in the midst of a great sea firmly fixed on a circle of gold, around which mountain the sun and moon revolve. This mountain is perfected by four precious substances and is the abode of the Devas (gods). Around this are seven mountain ranges and seven seas.

Samye has been destroyed at least four times in its tumultuous history. The first time was when the original building was burnt down in 986 and the most recent destruction was by the Red Guards during the Cultural Revolution. At the time of the Cultural Revolution, the Chinese encouraged the local villagers to farm pigs and other animals inside the monastery.

From 1984, extensive renovation work has been carried out at Samye and, consequently, the perimeter wall and four stupas have been entirely rebuilt. Most of the smaller temples are still dilapidated and inside they feel somewhat depressing.

The unusually high number of dogs inhabiting Samye monastery is unnerving (I have a photograph in front of the Ütse that has a total of 21 dogs). Bicycles seem to make them particularly upset so hop off and push your bike into the main monastery courtyard. The cycle will provide you with a useful barrier to place between you and their canine jaws. Incidentally, to deter these dogs the Tibetans just yell at them. Try it!

Ütse The three-storey Ütse is renowned for its mix of architectural styles that exist in no other building in Tibet. The ground floor design is Tibetan/Khotanese, the second floor is Chinese and the third is Indian. The gilded roof, which can be seen from the Tsangpo, was restored in 1989. The Ütse is without doubt the highlight of Samye.

To the left of the entrance into the Ütse there is a stone obelisk (*doring*) dating from the original construction of the monastery. The obelisk was commissioned in 779 by King Trisong Detsen and its purpose was to officially proclaim Buddhism as the state religion of Tibet.

The **highlights** at Ütse monastery are:
● The 92m mural depicting the history of Tibet (Yarlung Period to the 9th Dalai Lama) in the middle gallery on the inner perimeter wall;
● The statue of Guru Rinpoche, on the second floor at the centre of the main chapel;
● The mandala paintings on the ceiling of the inner sanctum (Jowokhang), entered from the main assembly hall;
● The large murals depicting the life of Guru Rinpoche on the second floor on the left (south) wall gallery; and
● The exquisite mural of the original Samye Mandala (protected by a silk cover) in the Dalai Lama's throne room on the second floor on the left side of the main chapel.

Accommodation at Samye *Samye Monastery Hotel* has a reasonably clean dormitory and double rooms. There is a *restaurant* at the hotel and a couple of stores next door. An alternative is to *camp* south-west of Samye, well away from the monastery complex. This may be more pleasant.

Trekking near Samye The first trekking option is the climb up to Mount Hepori. Hepori is the hill directly east of Samye (the 60m climb takes less than an hour). Mount Hepori is the site where Guru Rinpoche defeated the local spirits and converted them to Buddhism. This is one of the four sacred mountains in central Tibet. The climb up is a worthwhile break from the temples and provides you with a brilliant 'bird's-eye view' of the Samye mandala.

The second trekking option is to Samye Chimpu hermitage, which is at an altitude of approximately 4500m (about 600m above Samye). It is 15km north-east of Samye. It takes approximately four hours by foot to reach the hermitage and the same to return. Along with Drak Yongdzong (above Dorje Drak), Samye Chimpu is one of Guru Rinpoche's 'five principal mediation sanctuaries' in Tibet. The site is a collection of caves set in a natural amphitheatre.

Since the mid-1980s the hermitage has once again become a vibrant retreat site and many of the caves have become occupied. Up to 100 dedicated yogis may reside in the caves at any one time. The principal cave is called Drakmar Ketsang, which was said to be the chief sanctuary of Guru Rinpoche and the site where he instructed his main disciples. A two-storey temple has recently been constructed around the cave.

To get to Samye Chimpu, head north from Samye skirting the north end of Hapori until you reach the mouth of the next valley lying to the east (Chimpu valley). Turn left (north) across the desert plain of this valley and follow the clear tracks to the caves. It is a long day's walk (so take plenty of water). You may prefer to take your tent with you and camp overnight at the hermitage.

TSETANG AND ITS SURROUNDINGS   [SEE MAP 3]

Namseling Manor

Back on the south bank of the river, directly across from Samye monastery and just before the spur leading into the Jing valley is a tall seven-storey building, 3km south of the main road (near road marker 163km). This is Namseling Manor, which was built in the 15th century by a feudal lord. Namseling Manor is one of the tallest estate buildings in Tibet.

As it winds past Namseling, the road turns into the small Jing valley. Here you will see a series of impressive, giant sand dunes on the eastern side of the valley. From here, cyclists may relax and cruise over the next 20km of gently undulating, smooth road and look out for the triangular Mount Gongpori at the approach to Tsetang.

The rubbish carelessly strewn on the sides of the road (including the familiar broken blue glass and white tiles) mark the outer reaches of Tsetang. When you reach the first major fork in the road (near an absent marker 187km) veer left and continue for a couple of kilometres (all lined with buildings) towards the centre of Tsetang. At the centre there is a junction with a large traffic circle (with an unusual bronze 'monkey sculpture' in the middle).

Tsetang (Zetang Xian)

Given the magnificent sights along the duration of the Yarlung valley, you may be forgiven for believing that Tsetang will be the jewel in the region's crown. Unfortunately it is not. Tsetang is an important administrative centre and army base for the Chinese government. Little, if anything, is left of the former grandeur of this town that was the capital of the vastly beautiful Yarlung valley.

Tsetang is the fourth largest town in Tibet and is at a relatively comfortable altitude of 3515m. It has a regular bus and minibus service to and from Lhasa. The buses depart Tsetang daily from the main bus station, which is back along the road that you entered the town by (before turning at the monkey statue). The journey takes up to three hours. The bus from Lhasa to Tsetang leaves from the main bus station in Lhasa from 09:00 daily.

Accommodation options in Tsetang are limited. This town is firmly within the tight grasp of Chinese law enforcement and most hotels and restaurants will simply refuse to serve you. There are, however, two alternatives in the town; both are located on the street heading south from the junction with the monkey statue, on the right-hand side of the road. The first option is *Tsetang Hotel* (a hopelessly overpriced, outdated and run-down Chinese-built 'luxury' tourist hotel), which has big gardens and fences outside. The second option, *Shannon Hotel*, is cheaper, but still grossly overpriced. These hotels are not great but they do have showers and Western toilets (without seats). There is no service for foreigners in any other hotel in Tsetang (which is extremely frustrating when you see the tariffs and vacancies advertised all along the main street).

You may well prefer to stay in your tent: if you head further south down the main street, towards Yumbulagang, you will find a *campsite*.

Three sites in the area make up for the disappointment of the township itself. These are Tsetang monastery, Yumbulagang and the Kings' Tombs.

Tsetang monastery

The monastery is in the Tibetan quarter of Tsetang, which is directly down the main road (after turning right at the monkey statue) about midway down through all the Chinese shops and hotels. It is on the left-hand side and rests beneath the sacred mountain, Gangpori.

Tsetang monastery is a 14th-century institution that was originally founded by the Kagyu sect. It was taken over by the Gelug in the 18th century and then destroyed by the Red Guards.

There is a very important kora from Tsetang monastery up to the neighbouring Ngacho monastery. Head north (back towards the town) along the hill from Tsetang monastery. The walk is the most interesting part of this trip as you pass magnificent displays of mani stones and a number of cheerful pilgrims making the kora. The path follows the base of Gangpori and heads up to the mani stones and prayer flags. You can also reach Sang-ngag Zimche nunnery if you follow the track down from Ngacho.

Gangpori

Gangpori is an extremely auspicious site. It is the summit of a 4130m mountain, the legendary birthplace of the Tibetan people. See p186 for a description of the Bodhisattva of Compassion's descent from the heavens in the form of a monkey and his union with the white demoness, leading to the birth of the Tibetan people. This act is believed to have taken place right here at Gangpori.

It is a long walk up to the summit (a full day there and back) but there will be plenty of company.

YARLUNG VALLEY   [SEE MAP 3]

This section is described as Yarlung valley but, officially, the Yarlung valley is actually the side valley entered into through Tsetang. It is a long, wide and fertile plain, with many very ancient and very important historic Tibetan sites.

There are two roads down the valley from Tsetang. The first is a continuation of the main street of Tsetang past the turn-off to Tsetang monastery. If you keep heading down that road it will narrow into a smaller metal road and lead you to Trandruk monastery and Yumbulagang.

Trandruk monastery

Trandruk monastery is a bit over halfway between Tsetang and Yumbulagang, so it makes a nice stopping point for a drink and rest. Trandruk is one of the earliest monasteries in Tibet, dating back to the 7th century. It is one of the temples that Tsongsten

---

❏ **Useful Tibetan words relating to monasteries**

gompa	monastery
dukhang	main assembly hall
lhakhang	chapel
tsangkhang	inner chapel/sanctuary
gönkhang	chapel with 'protective deities' of the monastery
yidams	principal deities
barkhang	second floor
khang	house
trapa	novice/student monk
dorje	diamond sceptre – hand-held ritual object
lashing	tree
sangkhang	hearth
tsuklakhang	large temple
lungta	prayer flags

Gampo ordered built to subdue the demoness (along with Katsel monastery near Medrogongka).

Trandruk is 7km south of Tsetang. Take the southern road that runs past Tsetang monastery on the east side of the river.

The monastery was destroyed during the Cultural Revolution but restoration commenced in 1988. Given its history, it is no surprise that Trandruk is very similar to the Jokhang in its layout. Through the entrance there is a courtyard with the large temple building behind. In the centre of the building is the main assembly hall with a series of smaller chapels along the sides.

This is an important pilgrimage site for Tibetans and a pleasant place to visit, especially as you are going to pass it anyway en route to the magnificent Yumbulagang.

Yumbulagang

This beautiful and ancient temple is located 10.5km due south of Tsetang. Yumbulagang is said to be the oldest building in Tibet – dating back to the first king. Archaeologists have suggested that the foundations are as old as 2000 years (although there is some dispute about this).

The building was originally designed as a fortress, although it has subsequently been restored as a chapel. Sadly, the building was totally destroyed during the Cultural Revolution and has been completely rebuilt in the last 20 years.

The tower is 11m high and there is a delightful walk you can take up the four levels. The ceilings are low and the rooms are tiny and dark, giving a real medieval sense to the surroundings. The smell of burning butter lamps permeates throughout. The view from the upper floors down into the ground floor chapel that dominates the entire core of the building is quite spectacular. The door is often locked so befriend one of the resident monks to be allowed in. They are wonderfully hospitable so this should not be a problem.

It is possible spend the night in a spare bunk inside the *temple*, which would be more pleasant than any of the options in town. It takes approximately 50 minutes to cycle to the temple from Tsetang.

Kings' tombs

The tombs of Songsten Gampo and his heirs are found in Chongye valley, 28km south of Tsetang. Unfortunately, from Yumbulagang you will need to backtrack to Tsetang to get to Chongye. For Chongye, take the south road out of town that is on the west side of the river – the sealed road. Be aware that if the local PSB get wind of where you are heading, they will want to see permits.

It is possible to spend the night in a basic *guesthouse* in Chongye but try to camp outside the village. The tombs are an easy walking (or cycling) distance from the town. These comprise a collection of ten little burial mounds to the south of Chongye – not too exciting to look at but a very important place in Tibetan history. The largest tomb is that of Songsten Gampo and it has a small Nyingmapa temple erected on its summit.

To reach King Trisong Detsen's tomb, it is a one-hour walk to the summit of Mt Mura. The summit does provide good views of the valley.

Friendship Highway
Lhasa to Kathmandu
(via Southern Friendship Highway)

*A journey of a thousand miles
starts in front of your feet.*
Lao-tzu

INTRODUCTION

The journey from Lhasa to Kathmandu is spectacular. To decide to undertake it overland is to embark on a thrilling adventure. Many visitors to Tibet, particularly cyclists, will have it as their primary goal. And it is not difficult to see why. This incredible route is arguably the best high-altitude overland tour in the world.

Starting and finishing in two of Asia's most exotic cities, on the journey from Lhasa to Kathmandu, in around 1000km over 13-20 days you cross six major passes, traverse the backbone of the Himalayas and complete the world's longest downhill run (from a high point of just under 5000m at Lalung la to below 800m in Nepal – around 4200m in just over 160km of heart-stopping descent). If you add a further five to six days and 170km you can even cycle to Mt Everest Base Camp.

Mountain biking on the highest roads in the world is a physically and mentally demanding challenge and the journey from Lhasa to Kathmandu is long and hard. But the rewards are extraordinary. Difficult and often exhausting conditions combine to test your internal and external fortitude. But the view of the world from the dizzying heights of Tibet and the long, lonely expanse of solitude that envelops you is a humbling experience. Inevitably, your view of the world and of yourself will never be the same again.

The secret, jealously guarded by the few travellers who have already mountain biked in the region, is the experience of living with the Tibetan people and discovering the 'old Tibet', and nowhere is this more so than on the Friendship Highway.

On most days it is impossible to cover the distance from one open town to the next by bike. Accordingly, cyclists are forced into the situation where they must camp with

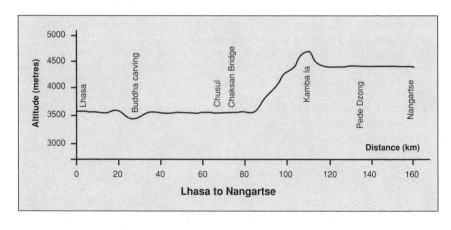

ROUTE GUIDE – LHASA to NANGARTSE

CYCLO-METER (KM)	ROAD MARKER (KM)	ALTIMETER READING (M)	NOTES AND KEY POINTS OF INTEREST
0	none	3600	Barkhor square
			(head west towards Potala/turn left at Lhasa Hotel)
3.5	4638	3595	Lhasa – main bus station
12.3	4646	3590	Road junction – **reset** cyclometer – 48min from Barkhor
			(veer right to Golmud/ left to Shigatse and Kathmandu)
2.7	4648/9	3600	Dongkar bridge *(turn-off to Zhongpa Lhachung pond)*
9.5	4655	3500	Bridge to Shugseb nunnery *(on left-hand side of Kyi chu river)*
10.7	4656/7	3500	Buddha rock carving
17	62/3 new	3570	Nethang monastery ⦿ Ɣ *(new road markers start)*
17.8	63/64		Ratö monastery turn-off *(follow red pipeline on right)*
26.7	72/73	3550	Grove on left-hand side of road *(nice spot for camping or lunch)*
27.7	73/74	3555	Bridge over Kyi chu
29.8	76	3555	Nam village
40	85/86	3560	Sakyaling monastery
49	94/95	3560	'Quxu County' sign *('next to school)*
51	96/97	3565	Chüsül town (Quxu Xian) ⦿ Ɣ ↲
			(at confluence of Kyi chu and Tsangpo rivers)
58.3		3565	Dagar village ⦿ Ɣ ↲
			(turn left for Gyantse, straight for Central Friendship Highway)
58.5	4704 old	3565	Chaksam bridge
	66 new		*(cross bridge – turn west to Gyantse, east to Tsetang)*
62.5		3565	Jangtang village ⦿ Ɣ *(mixed road surface)*
70		3580	Road fork – 'no signage'
			(turn-off left onto dirt road to Kampa la)
70.5			Excellent campsite *(right-hand side – 50m past turn-off on terraced land)*
70.7	78		First new road marker seen since Chaksam bridge
74.7	82		Last group of houses before Kampa la
			(road gets steeper from here!)
78.7	86	4040	Ford river *(chance to refill water bottles)*
82.3	89/90	4270	Ford river *(refill bottles again, switchback road steepens further!)*
93.8	100/101	4700	Kampa la pass (summit stone reads 4794m)
			(excellent views over Yamdrok Tso)
98			Tamalung village ⦿ Ɣ
			(edge of Yamdrok Tso, near hydroelectric dam tunnel)
101	108		Ferry crossing depot *(possible campsites for next 7km)*
108.2	115		Excellent campsite
118.5	125	4395	Pede Dzong village ⦿ Ɣ *(quite large fishing village)*
126.5	133	4400	Road fork (Yarsik) – go left around inlet to Nangartse
			(right road leads west to Rinpung Dzong)
127/128	134	4400	Good flat campsite with views over lake on right-hand side
	151/152		Turn-off to Samding monastery – 50m before Nangartse
			(1hr ride, 8.8km – with 1.2km steep climb, trail OK if dry)
144	152	4405	Nangartse Dzong ⦿ Ɣ ↲– **reset** cyclometer

Notes: ⦿ = Food, Ɣ = Water, ↲ = Accommodation available

CYCLING TIMES – LHASA to NANGARTSE

Barkhor to Lhasa outskirts (marker 4646) – 30-45min
Lhasa to Chaksam bridge (marker 4703) – 3-4hr
Chaksam bridge to Ganda campsite – 30-60min
Ganda campsite to Kampa la – 3-5hr
Kampa la to Pede Dzong – 1-2hr
Pede Dzong to Nangartse – 90min-2hr 30min

ESTIMATED CYCLING TIMES – NOT INCLUDING STOPS

---

nomads or negotiate accommodation at local villages or monasteries. That exercise leads to an extraordinary insight into nomadic, village and monastic life, which would be impossible to achieve if you were rapidly passing on an organized and tightly scheduled vehicle tour. There are three roads out of Lhasa towards Nepal: the Southern, Central and Northern Friendship Highways respectively. Most traffic (goods trucks and military vehicles) will take the newly sealed central road. However, it is the unsealed Southern Friendship Highway that is the most popular route for cyclists and overlanders in Tibet. It is indisputably the most magnificent and picturesque route from Lhasa to Shigatse. Though not the easiest route, with careful planning any reasonably fit and well-acclimatized cyclist can complete the trip. (For the Central and Northern Friendship Highways see pp128-130).

DAYS 1–2: LHASA TO PEDE DZONG   [SEE MAP 2]

Day 1: Lhasa to foot of Kampa la

On both the Southern and Central routes, the first day out of Lhasa is the same – a long flat cycle from Lhasa to Chüsül bridge. It is a pleasant way to commence the long and arduous trip to Kathmandu. The road is fast, flat and sealed as it winds alongside the Lhasa River. The cost of the excellent road condition is that the traffic is relatively heavy (or at least heavy for Tibet). Thereafter, regardless of the route you take, you will rarely see another piece of similar tarmac until you reach Nepal.

There are some amazing sights along the route and it is worth leaving Lhasa early in the morning so you can take a little time to stop off at a monastery or two and even take your picnic lunch with the local ferrymen at the side of the river. There are places to buy cold drinks along the way as well.

The first important landmark is only 23km from Bharkor square. The landmark is the beautiful relief rock painting of the Blue Buddha, serenely sitting in a little grotto overlooking a deep green pond. He is on the right-hand side of the road and you cannot miss him as you cycle past: there will probably be pilgrims at the site and you will see the prayer flags fluttering on the pass above.

The turn-off for Tashigang monastery is only a short way before Nethang Drölma Lhakang, one of the most important and best-preserved monasteries in Tibet. If you only have time to stop at one (and there is still a long ride ahead to the foot of Kampa la) stop at Nethang.

Tashigang monastery Tashigang monastery is 15km from Lhasa, and it is a detour from the main road. It has been renovated recently and approximately 20 monks are in residence.

Nethang Drölma Lhakang Conveniently situated a little way back from the main road, this monastery is 17km from Lhasa. It contains relics and paintings dating back to the 11th century. The great Bengali Buddhist master, Atisha, helped resurrect Buddhism in Tibet and died at the monastery in 1054. During the Cultural Revolution the monastery was protected from damage because of a direct request from East Pakistan (now Bangladesh). The Chinese Premier, Zhou Enlai, personally intervened in order to protect the chapel and, consequently, it stands today in its former glory. The tale goes to show that the pillaging of Tibet's great history during the Cultural Revolution was an event that was not entirely out of the government's control, as suggested in contemporary Chinese literature.

The little chapel may be entered through double doors into a courtyard. It is a little overgrown but very sweet. In the centre of the main courtyard is a stone used by the dalai lamas to dismount. Next to it is a grinder where Tibet's original physician, Yutok Yönten Gönpo, ground his medicines.

Inside the chapel are two clay guardian kings and Atisha's robes. A large white chörten dominates the centre of the chapel and contains relics that were handmade by Atisha and even an old clay portrait of the man himself.

There are many precious items in this little, unassuming place, including a conch shell used by Atisha, thangkas and a number of relics brought with him from India. If you take a little time, the resident monks will show you all of their precious secrets.

Ratö Ratö monastery is an hour-long side trip up a dirt road, which turns off the main road about 800m from Nethang. It was also founded in the 11th century and is now a Gelug monastery with about 40 monks.

Nam village The road continues to meander along past a Chinese-built school and a number of buildings and compounds that were erected for goodness knows what purpose. Nam is not particularly exciting but from Nam you can take a three-day trek over to Tsurphu monastery.

Sakyaling monastery At 40km from Lhasa is a small and sad looking little monastery on the left of the road, which is near the village of Tsepanang.

Chüsül Chüsül is a heavily militarized Chinese town with very few Tibetans in sight. The town is equipped with a large tannoy that blares out military marching music across the street. It is so forceful that it is tempting to march in an exaggerated military style down the road.

In contrast to the heavy military atmosphere in this little junction town there are pool tables lining the roadside. Despite being a rather unpleasant place, you'll be able to get hot Chinese *food* here so it is an option for an early dinner before heading for your campsite at the foot of Kampa la. If you do not have camping equipment, you can stay in a two-storeyed *guesthouse* at Dagar (which also has a restaurant), but it is extremely noisy and you will have a much better sleep and more beneficial starting point the next day if you can camp further on.

Chaksam Bridge is on the left-hand side just past Dagar. There is a watchtower for an armed guard but it is often empty. Move on reasonably promptly and do not draw attention to yourself unnecessarily by taking photographs of the watchtower or other military positions in the area.

Across the bridge, turn right (the road to the left leads to the airport and the Yarlung Valley). The junction is clearly signposted. Follow the road south, with the river now running along to your right.

You need to pitch your tent as near as possible to the foot of the pass so that you can make an early start on day two. There is a delightful, protected and private little spot to *camp* in amongst the willow trees on the right-hand side of the metal road that you turn into at the start on your way up the pass. It is easy to miss the turn-off and find yourself in the nearby township. To avoid that, keep a careful eye out for a small metal road on your left-hand side soon after the white chortens in the fields and on the hill at approximately 11.5km from Chaksam Bridge.

Day 2: Kampa la

Kampa la – ooh la la! This is the big one – very big. Be ready for it.

A key reason for taking a little bit of time in Lhasa (apart from the fact that you need time to take in all there is to see) is that you need to be properly acclimatized before you undertake the second day of the Southern Friendship Highway.

Kampa la pass is 4700m high – a steep, continuous 23km climb up more than 1100m. The road up is very long and winding and the surface is variable, ranging from deep, soft sand at many of the steep corners to relatively tightly-packed dirt on the straight stretches. There is not a lot to do along the way except put all of your energy into getting to the top. Kampa la is probably the most taxing climb for cyclists on the entire journey from Lhasa to Kathmandu – so if you conquer that pass, everything else will pale in comparison.

It takes at least five to seven hours just to reach the top with full panniers (depending upon how many times you need to stop to refuel or rest). There are water taps at some of the complexes along the roadside and where the stream runs across or under the road at several places there are places to collect running water. As always, if you wish to drink the water from the streams or taps, you will need to purify it first.

This day is long and difficult: the best idea is to get over the pass in one day – because 4500m and above is really too high to be sleeping overnight, especially so early into the long trip to Kathmandu.

The effort is worth it – the view that awaits you at the top of the pass makes it so. The lake, Yamdrok Tso, is a magnificent sight laid before you from the top of the pass. It might be the thin mountain air at 4500m but the sight below of the exquisite lake will really and truly take your breath away. As you stand beneath the prayer flags (secure in the knowledge that there will be no more uphill for at least two days) you really do feel as if you are on the top of the world. Himalayan snow-covered peaks are what you come to expect along this route, but the gold and turquoise glory of this sight is something special.

Unfortunately, you will need to descend again quickly to find a place to spend the night. Ideally, making camp on the side of the lake is the best plan. If it does take longer than you thought and you are just too cold and exhausted to erect a tent and put together a meal, there is a small town, Tamalung, on the roadside just before the road meets Yamdrok Tso. If you make some inquiries at the buildings nearest to the roadside you may well find someone who is prepared to give you shelter for the night, but for a price!

Yamdrok Tso – The Scorpion Lake Yamdrok Tso (4408m) is named the Scorpion Lake because of its scorpion-like shape. It is one of the four holiest lakes in Tibet. (The other three are Nam Tso, Manasarova, near Kailash, and Lama Lhatso, near Tsetang.)

There is a second, smaller lake enclosed in the arms of Yamdrok called Jem Tso (Devil Lake), which is 15km by 5km.

If possible, try to cycle a further 10km alongside the lake close to Pede Dzong on this second day. There are loads of fantastic *campsites* along the way and it is a nicer experience than staying in Tamalung village.

DAYS 3-6: PEDE DZONG TO GYANTSE   [SEE MAP 5]

Day 3: Pede Dzong to Nangartse

Pede Dzong is a fishing village and its fortress ruins run alongside the lake. Just after the village is a rock cluster painted red, which is the site of a shrine to a local deity. It is a place where Tibetan water burials take place – unusual given the prevalence of the sky burial traditions in Tibet.

❑ **Chinese hydroelectric projects**
In September 1988, the Chinese government announced the commencement of a hydroelectric project at Yamdrok. The plan was to drop the water from Yamdrok by a height of 846m down to a hydroelectric pump station located near the Tsangpo river.

Yamdrok is the third largest lake on the Tibetan plateau and is sacred to Tibetans. It is also a dead lake (no perennial source of water) and Tibetans claim the project will dry up the lake within a few decades. By 1993, Beijing announced that Yamdrok Tso would be followed by construction of an even larger dam – the Zhikong hydroelectric project, located 96km from Lhasa on the Lhasa River. In October 1994, Chinese engineers completed a 9.5km tunnel linking the lake to the Tsangpo River below and, by 1997, China reported that the generation of electricity had commenced.

Whether you set out from Tamalung or Pede Dzong, you will have a long but relatively easy day's cycle to Nangartse. You will almost cycle over the Yamdrok dam project as you leave Tamalung. This is a huge development that has caused enormous angst to the Tibetan people. The road circles the lake, which is deceptively large with inlets at a number of bends. There are many little coracles (yak-skin boats) en route, carrying pilgrims across to the other side of the lake. This is real Tibetan countryside and the lake is extremely holy so it is not unusual to see nomadic families prostrating themselves alongside the road. Continue around the lake towards the magnificent Himalayan mountain range and eventually Nangartse Dzong will come into view on the right-hand side of the road. The remains of the fort are still quite impressive as they loom over the road and the lake. The town locals will probably not take a lot of interest in you. By way of history, Nangartse was a small feudal state, the princess of which married into the aristocratic leaders of Yarlung and went on to give birth to the 5th Dalai Lama in 1617.

Now the town has a heavy Chinese presence, which does mean that there are quite a few decent options for restaurant food. Given the enormous population of seemingly homeless dogs, it might be a good idea to avoid red meat in this town.

Accommodation and food There are a number of accommodation options, all of which come with a complimentary symphony of high volume tannoy (there is a disco in town which cranks up the volume at night) and dogs. Lots of dogs. Do not go walking late at night. You can choose whether or not you eat them – don't offer them any opportunity for a reciprocal choice.

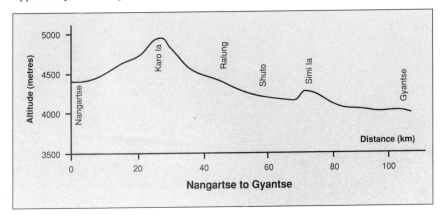

Most of the truck-stop *guesthouse*-type options do not have English names. The tour groups tend to use a place with a 'Hotel for Foreigners' sign but no other English name. As you pass through the town, past the main restaurants, turn left at the relatively major intersection, heading towards the school.

The *People's Guesthouse* is signposted on the right-hand side, about five buildings along. The rooms here are upstairs and are slightly more peaceful at night than the other options. The restaurant below had dog carcasses hanging in the backyard (unless they were four-legged chickens) so it might be an idea to pass on the meat momos. Otherwise, the food seemed OK.

Alternatively, if you have a tent you can either *camp* at Samding monastery or try to cycle up to the base of Karo la and camp there – although it is a bit cold and damp in the bottom of the valley entrance to Karo la.

There are a number of *restaurants* along the main street including one on the ground floor of the *Grain Guesthouse*, which serves particularly good Sichuan chicken – but be sure it is chicken and not pork (they tend to sneak a bit of pork in if you're not looking).

Day 4: optional side-trip from Nangartse to Samding monastery

The short cycle from Nangartse to Samding is highly recommended. First, it gives you the opportunity to cycle back through the town and you may see things that you missed when you dragged yourself in the night before – such as the friendly faces peering out at you from the older parts of town.

If you are cycling in October and November, it is harvest season and all the Tibetans will be out in the fields hulling the barley (which is used for tsampa – the staple of the Tibetan diet).

To get to Samding, head back towards the fort along the road you came in on. There is a dirt road turn-off on the right-hand side, which is a little muddy in the wet

---

❏ Sows at Samding

There are a few facts about Samding that make it an interesting place and a highlight of the region. Legend has it that Samding was built on its current site to assure that the water from Yamdrok did not flood into the rest of Tibet.

It is the only Tibetan Buddhist monastery that has a woman as its head lama (or abbess), Dorje Phagmo. The monastery now accepts both men and women. In 1716, in defence of the invasion by the Mongols, the female head lama was supposed to have turned herself and her nuns into sows. The Mongol army entered the monastery by force and its commander was overcome when the sows turned themselves back into nuns and, rather than destroy the monastery, he made offerings instead.

The monastery is considered to have been founded in the 13th century by Khetsun Zhonnu Drub. A sub-sect of Buddhism, the Bodong sect was initially taught at the monastery but it died out with the rise of the Gelug school. The abbess is considered to be a reincarnate of Bodong Chokle Namgyal (1306-86), the founder of the Bodong sect. Bodong was practised at Samding until the Cultural Revolution. Unfortunately, the sow trick did not work in the 1960s and the monastery was all but destroyed by the Red Guards. The walls were dynamited. Much of it has been rebuilt and a thriving little monastic community has developed.

Interestingly, inside the monastery is a large black and white photograph, depicting the head lamas who remained in Tibet after the Dalai Lama fled in 1959. In place of honour in this photograph is the monastery's own abbess, in her present incarnation. The monastery is fairly well maintained and supplies are delivered from Lhasa, where the head lama visits on occasion.

At the same time, the learning and preservation of art and artist skills in the little community is extraordinary, and you could sit for hours looking at beautiful books and watching the monks paint their statue icons.

ROUTE GUIDE – NANGARTSE to GYANTSE

CYCLO-METER (KM)	ROAD MARKER (KM)	ALTIMETER READING (M)	NOTES AND KEY POINTS OF INTEREST
1	153	4410	First road marker out of Nangartse
7.9	160		Road fork – go right to Karo la *(left road goes to Taklung monastery, 17km)*
13.5	165/166	4550	Possible campsite next to river *(past Langla village and around spur into narrow valley)*
15.7	167/168	4655	Good campsite 30m on left after small bridge *(water available from stream)*
17	169		Start climb proper to Karo la
22.3	174	4750	Last Tibetan house before pass *(road steepens and leaves riverside above here, very windy)*
24/29		4850	Awesome views of nearby glaciers/mountains *(Mt Nojin Kangtsang at 7190m to the north, Mt Jetsung Chusang at 6235m to the south-east)*
29.3	181/182	4960	Karo la pass
37.2	189	4575	Namru chu Valley on right side *(trail north leads to Rong valley and Rinpung Dzong)*
37.7	189/90	4600	Sign indicating turn-off to Ralung monastery (4/5km) *(main road veers south-west across plain – possible camp)*
47.8	199/200	4355	Ralung village *(across bridge over Nyeru chu)*
59	211	4240	Lungma village 🍴 ⟁ ⤴ *(valley leads north to Rong valley and Rinpung Dzong)*
60	212	4200	Shuto village
68.9	220/221	4360	Road forks by Kangwang village – possible camp by river *(Turn right uphill to Gyantse, Nyeru Tsangpo valley to left leads south to Bhutan)*
72.3	223	4275	Simi la *(approximately 15-25min climb)*
73/74			Large hydro-electric project in Nyerulung Valley below *(stay on the high road – some new roads lead down to valley)*
75.1			Road goes between gap in rock – a strong wind tunnel! *(clearly created by explosives)*
78.6		4140	Large 'sombre' Chinese cadre village 🍴 ⟁ ⤴ *(checkpoint at far end of village – look confident!)*
90/100		4025	Distant views of Gyantse Dzong *(road is tree-lined and flat but dusty, loose metal)*
102.4		3990	Edge of Gyantse – at start of sealed road
103.9	254	3985	Gyantse 🍴 ⟁ ⤴ – **reset** cyclometer *(main traffic intersection)*

Notes: 🍴 = Food, ⟁ = Water, ⤴ = Accommodation available

but fine to bike on in the dry season. The locals will point out the road if you get lost but it is not difficult to find given that you can see the monastery from the roadside.

It is a very pleasant cycle through traditional Tibetan villages to the foot of the hill where the monastery is built. The hill itself is hard work and you may need to push your bike some of the way. You can either leave your bike at the chorten and walk the last part, or take your bike right up to the monastery gates. There are two entrances. Take the road up to the back entrance if you are taking your bike. Otherwise, there is a shortcut directly up to the front door. Ask someone to show you around the monastery. The views from the rooftops are magnificent.

Day 5: Nangartse to Lungma village

On Day 5, supported cyclists continue right through to Gyantse. If you are super-fit, you may be able to do this in a day carrying gear, but it will be hard work and you will not have any time to enjoy the scenery or the people along the route. You will also be shattered the next day because there are two mountain passes between Nangartse and Gyantse (although the first is a lot harder and higher than the second).

Leaving Nangartse via the same main street out of town toward the lake, turn right as the road meets the fields (instead of left which is the direction of the fort). The road heads out past a school (on the right-hand side) and forks at 7.9km from Nangartse. Take the right fork (the left will lead around the southern side of the lake). The right fork heads away from the lake towards Karo la, which is the next pass en route to Gyantse.

The road follows the plain right up to the valley entrance. A heavily flowing river comes out of the valley and the road to Karo la begins to follow that river at the valley entrance. Once again, the surroundings are sensational but completely different to anywhere else in Tibet. Magnificent glaciers almost touch the road and the harsh wind beats down the valley. Hardy souls live in tiny ramshackle lodgings en route – so there may be some assistance in a weather emergency but it would be unwise to count on it.

Karo la Be prepared for a soul-destroying headwind as you head up Karo la. The pass itself is a steady and reasonably gentle climb but the icy wind whips down from the glacier and makes it hard going. Leave early because this is not a pleasant place to be caught out for the night. The few Tibetans that live in the valley have been forced to load heavy stones onto the tin roofs of their shacks to stop them blowing away.

Unbelievably, monks make the trip across Karo la from Ralung monastery (on the northern side of the pass) to Nangartse – you may meet a few on their Flying Pigeons bicycles. Don't be surprised if they pass you, or at least keep up, on the uphill. You will leave them eating your dust coming down the other side!

The top of the pass is cold and exposed but with amazing views in both directions. The downhill is superb. The road is tightly-packed gravel and dirt so it is great fun to cycle down. It winds its way through a magnificent granite canyon and the sun plays bizarre tricks above. Just as you come down the pass and start to get to the canyon-like area, look up and you may see a formation similar to the Northern Lights – where a collected concentration of coloured light sparkle and twinkle from a certain spot high above the canyon walls. Or maybe we were just a little heady from the altitude.

Keep control of your speed down here – although a full-scale assault is tempting – because the river near the bottom does wash away the road in the rainy season.

Namru chu valley Eventually you will come out of the canyon and onto the wide-open plains of Namru chu Valley. This is a reddish brown plain and looks different again to anywhere else in Tibet. The Ralung monastery turn-off is on the left-hand side and well signposted. It is a long cycle from the road to the monastery but, if you have time, you could spend the night there and continue to Gyantse the next day.

Otherwise, continue on for a couple more hours and get closer to the foot of the final pass between here and Gyantse (and in fact the final pass between here and Shigatse). There are plenty of places to camp alongside the river that flows through the valley. The little village of Ralung is one option for board across the bridge over the Nyeru chu river. Bear in mind that the locals in this valley see jeeps go by daily but do not often have overnight visits from travellers. They will be very friendly and welcoming but also extremely curious – don't expect to get a lot of sleep if you stay in or near a village.

Lungma village We cycled on to the next village of Lungma and were granted permission to set up our tent in the little court-yard where the tsampa is roasted in a huge clay oven. It was extremely warm and we were offered delicious potato casse-role and rice for dinner with the entire village.

CYCLING TIMES – NANGARTSE to GYANTSE
Nangartse to Samding monastery (side route) – 1hr
Nangartse to Karo la – 2hr 30min-3hr 30min
Karo la to Lungma – 2-3hr
Lungma to Simi la – 45min
Simi la to Gyantse – 2hr 30min-3hr 30min
ESTIMATED CYCLING TIMES – NOT INCLUDING STOPS

We negotiated a camping rate; they seemed happy and we were happy to pay it for the shelter from the wind, the warmth of the fire and a hot meal. We could boil our own water in the tsampa oven as well which saved on kerosene in our own cooker. That evening was one of our most memorable nights in Tibet. Several of the village children joined us in the enclosure (and the rest all crowded over the walls for a look). In the morning we woke to the sound of the women singing as they carried on with the barley roasting. The smell was delicious and the kids picked out the burst pieces for us to eat with them – popcorn, Tibetan style!

As you continue down the valley, in the autumn season everyone is out harvest-ing the barley crops. It is a busy time of year where all the members of each village pool their efforts to prepare for the onslaught of winter.

Day 6: Lungma to Gyantse
Kangwang village The village of Kangwang is a little place near the foot of Simi la. The road forks at the village; the road to the right heads up Simi la to Gyantse. The road to the left heads through a valley to the south, leading eventually to Bhutan.

Simi la
Simi la is a nice pass as passes go. It is a welcome relief in that it is well sealed, has a good gradient and is not too long. You ought to be able to cycle to the top within 30 minutes and it is a lovely view from the top.

From the top of Simi la, you can see the enormous hydroelectric project that is being undertaken in the Nyerulung valley below (in an abortive attempt to try to redi-rect water into Yamdrok as it is being simultaneously drained off from the other end). As a result of that project the road has been completely rerouted. Keep on the high road, which traverses along the ridge – with a pleasant downhill on a good sealed sur-face – to the top of the dam construction site. (Previously the road dropped straight into the valley and continued along the flat to Gyantse.)

It is a steeper descent into a village that just appeared on the map overnight, a vil-lage built for the Chinese immigrants working on the hydroelectric project. There is a heavy military presence here, but also food, water and *accommodation*. It is not a pret-ty village and probably not a place to hang around in – particularly if you plan to col-lect a cycling permit in Shigatse.

There is a toll bar on the road leaving the town but the guard should raise it and let you pass through without any difficulty. This road may be completely changed again once the dam is filled but if you just follow the high part of the road you will end up in Gyantse.

As you leave the new Chinese village at the dam site, you meander through a val-ley and, approximately 10km along the road, you will start to get your first glimpse of Gyantse Dzong. It is a magnificent sight on the horizon and a great marker as you get closer and closer to the village. We covered this ground very quickly, despite the loose gravel road surface. The thought of a hot shower and nice meal in Gyantse was a big motivator!

Gyantse

Gyantse is a pretty magnificent place. For the overlander, it has the advantage of being a main stop for jeeps en route from Kathmandu to Lhasa so it has excellent food and accommodation options. You can enjoy the luxury of a three-star hotel or rough it in a hostel (rats compliments of the house). There are plenty of restaurants and a little place in particular, called Tashi, which is reminiscent of its namesake in Lhasa.

Although the site has been inhabited for centuries, at the end of the 9th century the castle on the hill was founded by the heir to the kingdom, Palkhorstan. The castle was named 'Crystal Castle on the Peak' and was used as the heir's residence at a time in which political turmoil meant he could not exercise his birthright and rule central Tibet.

The line of powerful Gyantse princes started with the Phagpa Pal Sangpo (1318-1370), a great scholar who became closely connected with the rising power of the Sakya sect from southern Tibet, appointed at the age of 25.

Interestingly, the Chinese emperor directly appointed the Gyantse princes, which had the effect of giving the Ming Dynasty a system for controlling the country. The alliance between Tibet and the Ming emperors is evident in the art in Gyantse, as reflected in the Kumbum structure. What makes this so interesting is the manner in which contemporary Chinese leaders in the region have managed to create a Chinese and Tibetan community that is far more assimilated than the communities of other Tibetan towns. There is still a distinctive older Tibetan quarter in the town, with the typical cubic Tibetan houses running in uniformed style along the little streets near the fort. But in the town centre, which contains many modern, Chinese blocks, the Chinese and Tibetans operate their businesses side by side.

Gyantse, unlike most other Tibetan communities, has developed an historic 'common enemy', which is exploited to the extreme by the Chinese tourism industry. The common enemy is none other than the British, and more particularly Francis Younghusband (see box opposite), who has an entire museum dedicated to the atrocities that he committed against the Tibetan people in 1904.

The principal historic structures in Gyantse are the castle on the ridge overlooking the town and the walled monastery complex with its massive temple of Palkhor Chode and the great Kumbum chapel. These main sights can be visited in a day.

Gyantse Dzong   Quite apart from the brief (and destructive) visit from Younghusband, the Gyantse fort (dzong) is an interesting place. It was built in the 14th century and some of the buildings inside can be visited.

The interior of the fort is not really comparable to the magnificent views that can be had from the top. It is worthwhile to trek (or cycle) up to the fort for the view. Decide when you get there whether or not to pay the entry fee to see the Younghusband museum and the old and musty rooms inside. The view is free.

Gyantse Kumbum   The Kumbum is, unlike the fort, unforgettable both inside and out. It was built before the fort, in the 13th century, and is essentially a great multi-chapel chorten with an interior of amazing little shrines that you can visit as you spiral your way six floors up to the top.

The name *Kumbum* literally translates as '100,000 images' and all 100,000 can be viewed inside the many little chapels as you make the clockwise kora up and around the structure. Many of the chapels and statues were damaged during the Cultural

Revolution (and not the Younghusband invasion), but they have been recently restored.

The primary reason for much of the recent refurbishment work is the close proximity of Gyantse monastery to Tashilhunpo monastery in Shigatse. Tashilhunpo is the base for the Chinese appointed Panchen Lama (the second most important religious leader in Tibet after the Dalai Lama) see p112-114.

The nine-storey (including the base) Kumbum has 75 chapels inside. The journey around the chapels takes you through a progressive hierarchy of three-dimensional mandalas (which were outlined in the Sakyapa compilation *Drubtob Gyatsa*). The chorten incorporates the entire spiritual path and gradation of the tantras.

The entrance way is at the south side of the first floor – the side facing you as you walk through the monastery entrance-gate. Two or three monks man the entrance and are usually very friendly.

On the first floor of the Kumbum are staircases in each of the four cardinal directions, each leading up to the chapels on the second floor.

On the second floor there are 20 chapels – one of which is the staircase. The staircase to the third floor is the 18th chapel (as you circumambulate the chapels). To see chapels 19 and 20 you need to go past the stairway and, in theory, you must then walk clockwise around the chapels again to return to the stairway at number 18.

There are 16 chapels on the third floor, including the White Tara at chapel 12.

There are 20 chapels on the fourth floor (the stairs between the third and fourth are in the third floor chapel number 16). In the twentieth chapel on the

---

❏ **Younghusband – Gyantse's Public Enemy No. 1**

In 1904, the British army moved troops into Gyantse, amid fears of the threat of a Russian invasion from the north. There is no evidence to suggest that the Russians were taking over Tibet from the north in 1904 and there is little tangible evidence to justify the invasion on these grounds. Nevertheless, Younghusband led his heavily armed troops on a four-month journey from India to Gyantse. The Tibetan army responded with a mismatch of assorted weaponry, including swords, stones and some antiquated firearms. Most importantly, each man was armed with the Dalai Lama's mark – a charm sealed by the 13th Dalai Lama in person.

The protection of the charm did not stave off the British bullets and 700 Tibetans were killed in a very short period of time. When the British entered the fort, it was empty of all troops and the British established their base on the outskirts of the town. Two months later, a subsequent battle ensued on Karo la as Younghusband endeavoured to lead his army into Lhasa and the British troops returned to Gyantse to retake the fort that had been reoccupied by Tibetan troops in the interim. When the fort fell a second time, the Tibetans no longer opposed the British invasion and Younghusband and his troops marched into Lhasa a short time later. The British remained in Lhasa for a period of approximately one month, established trade ties with the regent (in the absence of the Dalai Lama) and left.

The most interesting thing about visiting the fort at Gyantse is actually seeing for yourself how impenetrable the structure is from the outside. The fort is built on the summit of a long and narrow ridge, with a sheer face at the front. The British assaulted the fort by creating a diversion in the north-east – where the road is now and attacked from the south-west, up the front of the fort. The British shelled the walls and managed to destroy the Tibetan ammunition dump, taking the fort in one day (with hundreds of Tibetans and four British dead).

The Chinese have generously dedicated an entire museum (Anti-British Imperialists Museum) at the fort to the memory of the evil deeds of the British Younghusband and his troops. You can witness the Chinese version of the destruction of the Tibetan people and Tibetan culture in Gyantse, whilst the Tibetans fought to 'safeguard the motherland' – China. It is always a good defence strategy to create common enemies.

fourth floor are murals of the eight stupas and the stairway to the fifth floor.

On the fifth floor there are 12 chapels, each depicting the lineage holders of Buddhism in Tibet, starting with Atisha at the first chapel, Songsten Gampo and the royal family at chapel eight and the ascending staircase and murals of the Dashakrodha kings at the final, twelfth chapel.

On the sixth floor (the 'bowl'), there are four chapels representing the Yogatantra deities.

On the seventh floor ('lower spire'), entered by a wooden ladder, is a single chapel with ten mandalas of the Father Class of Unsurpassed Yogatantras.

On the eighth floor ('upper spire) is another single chapel, which shows the 11 mandalas of the Mother Class of Unsurpassed Yogatantras.

On the ninth floor ('pinnacle') is one chapel with a magnificent copper-gilded image of Vajradhara Buddha – this alone is worth the trip to the top to see.

Pelkhor Chode The Pelkhor Chode is in fact the entire monastic complex at Gyantse, within which the Kumbum is located. The main temple is the Tsuklakhang, built by the Gyanste prince, Rabten Kunzang Phak in the 13th century. By the end of the 17th century, there were 16 Tantric colleges in Pelkhor Chode, representing three different schools of Buddhism: Gelug, Sakya and Zhalu.

The main temple contains several important 15th-century murals. The temple is not always open in the afternoons (although the Kumbum does seem to be). Try to visit in the mornings to avoid any problems. Most importantly, the inner sanctum contains murals of scenes from the Sutra of the Auspicious Aeon in its corridor and inside the sanctum are images of the Buddhas of the Three Times.

There is also a royal chapel on the ground floor, containing clay statues of the ancient kings of Tibet including Songsten Gampo, Trisong Detsen and Tri Ralpachen. There are many beautiful images on the upper floors as well, including the foremost medicinal deities on the top floor and images of Jowo, Tara, Tsongkhapa and others.

After the harvest and at the end of autumn (November) the monks may be undertaking a little DIY work at the monastery. During our visits, the entire monastic community was out in force on the front walls of the monastic compound – repainting them with the familiar reddish-brown paint of Tibet. There was not a spray gun or paintbrush in sight. The monks at the bottom of the wall would send buckets of paint up to the monks on the top of the wall using a series of rope pulley systems. When the buckets reached the top of the wall, the monks would simply tip the paint down the walls. Not the quickest way to paint such an enormous surface area but they certainly seemed to be having fun.

Accommodation and food There are two extremes for accommodation in Gyantse. There is *Gyantse Hotel* – a flash Chinese tourist hotel with hot showers and sheets (at over Y500 per night) or a couple of mid-priced Chinese-run guesthouses. The two 'older' Tibetan-style hostels (Hostel of Gyantse Town Furniture Factory and Hotel of Nationality Clothing Company) are currently closed to foreigners.

The popular *Wutse Hotel*, located on the main south road, has pleasant rooms and showers Alternatively the more pricey *Canda Hotel*, located after the buildings north of Wutse Hotel, is also comfortable and clean.

Happily, the food situation in Gyantse is far more encouraging. A highlight has to be *Tashi Restaurant*, opposite the Hotel of Nationality Clothing Company. The restaurant is signposted, and is upstairs behind a Tibetan door curtain. The food is tasty.

Do explore a little with the restaurants in Gyantse – there are some nice places hidden away.

DAY 7: GYANTSE TO SHIGATSE [SEE MAP 6]

This ride can be done in a day – albeit a long one. The road is flat from Gyantse all the way to Shigatse and, despite the uneven and unsealed surface, it is a pleasantly easy trip.

Shalu monastery There are a number of interesting sights along the way, including the Shalu monastery, which is the location of the so-called flying monks of *Magic and Mystery in Tibet*, by Alexandra David-Neel. The Shalu monastery is actually quite famous in Tibet – being one of the earliest temples following the reintroduction of Buddhism in the 11th century. The monastery has a significant collection of 14th-century Newari-style murals, created by generations of artists, and it played an important role in the development of Tibetan art.

Riphuk The Riphuk cave hermitage is a 75-minute walk from Shalu.

Other places of interest Other monasteries along the way include Drongtse monastery – founded in 1442 – at 21.5km and Tsi Nesar monastery, which is a south-facing white building located 100m from the road on the left-hand side, just over 27km from Gyantse.

There is one village constructed by the Chinese, which sells soft drinks and has cheap Chinese and Tibetan restaurants. The town is called Penam Xian and is situated 43.5km from Gyantse, almost halfway, making it an ideal lunch stop.

Shigatse
This is the last opportunity for luxury for the Lhasa to Kathmandu cyclist, at least until you hit the Nepalese border. Make the most of the facilities and the Western companionship!

If you are coming by road from Gyantse, you will enter the town from the south. You will actually see the Shigatse fort and the remains of the enormous thangka wall, high along the ridge, well before your reach the town.

Cyclists need to be a little bit wary as they approach Shigatse: the children are particularly naughty and use their slingshots to send rocks flying, very hard, at passing

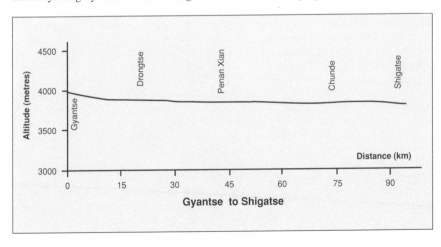

ROUTE GUIDE – GYANTSE to SHIGATSE

CYCLO-METER (KM)	ROAD MARKER (KM)	ALTIMETER READING (M)	NOTES AND KEY POINTS OF INTEREST
0		3985	Gyantse – main traffic intersection
2.1			'T' intersection – following south-west road out of Gyantse (turn north/right to Shigatse, south to Chumbi valley & Bhutan)
2.8			Turn-off west to 'Pala manor' (1km) and Changra
3.2	89		Start of new road markers to Shigatse (road follows left bank of Nyang chu)
5.2	87		Tsechen monastery ruins (seen left on top of hill)
21.5	71/70	3900	Drongtse monastery, founded in 1442 (up a hill on left side of road)
27.4	65		Tsi Nesar monastery (south-facing white building 100m from left of road)
30	62	3880	Small village ⦿ Ⲩ
40.5	52/51	3865	Concrete bridge
43.5	49/48	3860	Penam Xian ⦿ Ⲩ
			(a few Chinese Tibetan restaurants – a good place for lunch!)
52/62		3850	Arid valley road inland from Nyang chu
72.8	20/21	3830	Small town ⦿ Ⲩ
74.5	19/18	3840	Chunde village – turn-off left to Shalu monastery (3930m) ⦿ Ⲩ ⌇
			(25min ride, 4km south, gompa visible from main road)
77/80	15/12	3845	Large thangka wall of Tashilhunpo monastery seen in distance
87	6	3845	Concrete bridge over Sha Chu
89	4	3845	Cobblestone road – outskirts of Shigatse
92.5		3825	Shigatse (in Chinese Xigase) main bus stn ⦿ Ⲩ ⌇ – **reset** cyclometer

Notes: ⦿ = Food, Ⲩ = Water, ⌇ = Accommodation available

cyclists. If possible, try to ride past here during school hours, ie before 5pm. If you can't get there before this, just keep your head down and cycle fast.

Shigatse itself is now a big and booming Chinese city. As you cycle in from the south you will wonder if you are still in Tibet at all. There are big multi-storey buildings everywhere (concrete blocks with blue glass windows) and very little suggestion of traditional Tibetan lifestyle. Heading directly through the town via the main street, towards the north is the Tibetan quarter. It is the second largest city in the TAR (after Lhasa) and is at a slightly higher altitude than Lhasa. It can be quite cold in Shigatse, with temperatures averaging 16°C in summer and –5°C in winter.

Historically, power struggles have ensued between the rulers of Shigatse and the rulers of Lhasa. The head lama of the Shigatse monastery, Tashilhunpo, is the Panchen Lama. He is the second highest religious leader in Tibet and, like the Dalai Lama, of the Gelug (Yellow Hat) sect. In the 16th century, Shigatse became the capital of Tibet as the then leader, Karma Tseten, took power. He was executed and his son succeeded him, only to form an alliance with the Mongols and capture Lhasa in 1605. The Shigatse fort (a model for Lhasa's Potala) was built in the early 17th century but was completely destroyed by the Red Guard in the mid-20th century.

From 1642, Shigatse lost its central political power over Tibet to the stronger powers from Lhasa and, although Shigatse remained the seat of power for the province of Tsang and the residence of the Panchen Lamas, Lhasa remained in overall control of Tibet from that time until 1950.

Accommodation and food

There are two hostel-type options (one Tibetan and one Chinese) and also some newer 'concrete' hotels.

Tenzin Guesthouse in the Tibetan quarter is easily the most popular spot for budget

> ### CYCLING TIMES – GYANTSE to SHIGATSE
> Gyantse to Penam Xian – 2hr 30min-3hr 30min
> Penam Xian to Shigatse – 2hr 30min-3hr 30min
> Chunde to Shalu monastery (side route) – 30min
> ESTIMATED CYCLING TIMES – NOT INCLUDING STOPS

travellers. To get to Tenzin Guesthouse from the south of town, head up the main street past the People's Hospital and take the fourth road on your left. The guesthouse is about 500m further on (and the Tibetan open market is on the right) up that street. The entrance is at the front, next to the restaurant.

The joy of the guesthouse is the ability to take a shower. Don't get too excited – the water is heated by staff cranking up an enormous water boiler. It will be hot from 20:00, so first in first served until the water runs out. This creates great camaraderie in the guesthouse and gives you an opportunity to get to know some new people!

Gang Gyen Fruit Orchard Hotel is a Chinese-style establishment (situated opposite the entrance to Tashilhunpo monastery). It is an option if Tenzin Guesthouse is booked up.

Shigatse Hotel is the mandatory 'tourist group' hotel though it is located a little further from the action. It is back on the main road as you first come into the town from Gyantse and is next to the main Bank of China. It has great shops for things like film but is expensive and unfriendly.

Food in the Tibetan quarter of Shigatse is quite fun. If you are staying at Tenzin Guesthouse, there is a good *restaurant* down below and the Tibetan quarter is close by.

Alternatively, if you take the first road south, heading east from Tenzin Guesthouse, you will see a variety of restaurants along the street. Take a look, experiment a little. Some look very clean and very good – others less so.

There are a couple of **Internet cafés** in Shigatse.

Tibetan markets The Tibetan open markets are on the same street as Tenzin Guesthouse. This will be your last chance to buy little Tibetan souvenirs before Nepal.

There are also a number of **department stores** and **supermarkets** where you can stock up on overland supplies.

Shigatse authorities Much is said about Shigatse being more relaxed than Lhasa when it comes to visas, permits and the general approachability of the authorities. This is true to a degree, but don't rely on it.

In 2001, two cyclists arranged a jeep tour (with several others) from Kathmandu to Lhasa. They breached the conditions of their visas and permits by escaping the tour guides in Dingri. The cyclists gave little thought to the safety of their Tibetan guides who were left to explain to the Chinese authorities how they had managed to lose two foreign travellers en route. Think about the repercussions of your actions for others if you are going to try something like this. In any event, the cyclists were caught up with in Shigatse, where they were staying at Tenzin Guesthouse.

Having said that, if you stay within the rules you may find the authorities in Shigatse surprisingly accommodating. If you arrive in Shigatse from Lhasa without a permit you will be able to get one for the rest of the journey from the PSB in Shigatse.

The Shigatse **PSB** (open Monday to Friday) is on the road between Tenzin Guesthouse and Tashilhunpo monastery. It is on the right-hand side of the road (heading towards Tashilhunpo) and is the building after the Intermediate Court and

❏ **Politics of the Panchen Lama**
The Honourable 10th The Tibetan Government-in-Exile put out an interesting publication in 1996 called *The Panchen Lama Lineage, How Reincarnation is Being Reinvented as a Political Tool*. It is an interesting read but starts from the misplaced premise that the reincarnation of Panchen Lamas needed to be reinvented to assume a political purpose. The fact is that the Panchen Lama lineage has been affected by politics since the first Panchen Lama in the 15th century. Nonetheless, it is fair to say that the two most recent panchen lamas have been key factors in China's bid to wrestle religious control of Tibetan people from the grasp of the exiled Dalai Lama.

The 9th Panchen Lama died in 1937 and the Tibetan Government and Tashilhunpo monastery leaders immediately organized the search for his reincarnation. Two candidates were found, one in Kham and one in Amdo. The Amdo candidate was recognized by pro-Chinese members of Tashilhunpo in 1941, prior to the official recognition by the Dalai Lama. That official recognition did not come until 1952 but, in the interim, the Chinese authorities began to exploit the young reincarnate in an effort to obtain political power in Tibet. In 1949, the 11-year old 10th Panchen Lama was said to have sent a letter to Mao Zedong requesting the 'liberation of Tibet'. The letter was organized by a local member of the People's Liberation Army and is still cited as the justification for China's interference in Tibetan politics.

In 1951 the Panchen Lama was invited to Peking and forced to participate in the '17-point agreement on measures for peaceful liberation in Tibet', the document that sealed the future of Tibet. After the Dalai Lama fled from Lhasa in 1959, the Chinese pressured the Panchen Lama to assume the Dalai Lama's position as political leader of Tibet and to publicly denounce him as reactionary. The Panchen Lama refused to do so and became increasingly recalcitrant toward the Chinese authorities.

In 1961, he was invited to Peking to attend the 12th National Day Celebration and there he presented to Mao Zedong a 70,000-character petition detailing the conditions in Tibet. In the petition, he demanded more food, an end to persecution, care for the aged and infirm, a genuine acceptance of religious freedom and a cessation of mass arrests.

In October 1964, the Chinese officials gave the Panchen Lama the opportunity to rectify his 'errors' and repent but, instead, he publicly declared his loyalty to the Dalai Lama and voiced support for Tibetan independence. Consequently, he was imprisoned in Beijing for a term of ten years and was released in February 1981.

From the time of his release, the Panchen Lama maintained an uneasy peace with the Chinese authorities. He was called to be present at major public events and was considered by some to be a Chinese 'chopstick' (or puppet). When he passed away in Shigatse, on 28 January 1989, controversy and speculation continued regarding the cause of his death. The Chinese authorities reported a heart attack – he was 51 years of age at the time. *(cont'd opposite)*

Procurate. Head up the stairs and you will be given a form to complete. Once you have filled in the form, the usually friendly PSB officer in charge will take you into his little office, chat away with you in excellent English, and fill in your Aliens' Travel Permit (ATP). Check out all the photographs of cyclists under the glass top on his desk.

It will cost about Y50 for a permit from Shigatse to Dram (in Chinese Zhangmu); Y100 if you want to be permitted to cycle. It is not clear if there is any advantage in having the cyclists' permit (which simply states that you are permitted to ride your bike or travel by truck, jeep or bus). No one paid much attention to our permits, except at the turn-off trips to Sakya monastery and Everest. At both of those places they made sure we had a permit but did not pay any attention to the fact that our ATP 'permitted' cycling.

Make sure that you list **every** main town between Shigatse and Dram on your permit, including Sakya and Everest.

Tashilhunpo monastery The highlight of Shigatse, and the one thing that you must see if you pass through the town, is Tashilhunpo monastery. This is a truly magnificent sight and much work has gone into recent renovation work.

❏ **Politics of the Panchen Lama (cont'd)**
Controversial Selection of the 11th Immediately, on 1 February 1989, the Chinese Premier Liu demanded that the Tibetan Government-in-Exile not take part in the selection of the reincarnate 11th Panchen Lama. At the time, Kalon Tashi Wangdu, a member of the Dalai Lama's exiled cabinet, said:

An authentic reincarnation will be discovered by the Tibetan lamas only, not by the Chinese. That means it does not need anyone's approval. There are very well established procedures.. that have to be followed. Political appointment of the Panchen Lama is not at all appropriate; such an appointment will not be acceptable to Tibetans.

The Tibetan leaders did participate in the process for the recognition of the 11th Panchen Lama and the Dalai Lama announced in May 1995 that six-year old Gendun Choekyi Nyima was the reincarnation of the 10th Panchen Lama.

The Chinese government did not accept the Dalai Lama's recognition of the reincarnate Panchen Lama and, in December 1995, announced the name of a different six-year old child, Gyaltsen Norbu. The announcement came after a carefully structured Chinese selection ceremony was held, which directly contradicted the choice made seven months earlier by the Dalai Lama and disregarded many ancient Tibetan religious traditions.

The Tashilhunpo abbot, Chadrel Rinpoche, headed the original Panchen Lama search group and the Chinese authorities accused him of secretly colluding with His Holiness in the proclamation of Gendun Choekyi Nyima as the reincarnation of the Panchen Lama. He was arrested along with 60 others by the Chinese authorities. In February 2002, it was reported that Chadrel Rinpoche had been released from prison but remained under house arrest in Shigatse.

The safety of Gendun Choekyi Nyima and his parents has been a matter of international concern since he was taken from his home in late 1995. At the time, the authorities made public statements that denounced the boy, claiming that he 'once drowned a dog', describing his parents as 'notorious for speculation, deceit and scrambling fame and profit', and declaring that the family's attempts to 'cheat the Buddha would not be allowed by all ordinary pious Tibetans'.

The Chinese Government have consistently denied requests for access to Gedhun Choekyi Nyima and his family, claiming that he is leading a normal life and did not want to be disturbed. In September 2000, during a round of EU/China human rights dialogue in Beijing, Chinese officials unexpectedly produced two photos they claimed to be of Gedhun Choekyi Nyima.

In spite of the international outcry for Gedhun Choekyi Nyima's release, the boy has not been seen in public since he was abducted.

Tashilhunpo is the seat of the Panchen Lama and was founded in 1447 by the first Dalai Lama, a disciple of Tsongkhapa. The Gelug seat of power was Lhasa until the balance was tilted when the 5th Dalai Lama named his teacher as the reincarnation of an important Buddha (Amitabha). His teacher happened to be the abbot of Tashilhunpo at the time and the declaration commenced the lineage of Panchen Lamas (Panchen meaning 'great scholar'). From that point on there was to be a recurring struggle for power between the line of Panchen Lamas and the Dalai Lamas. The second Panchen Lama was coveted by the Chinese and declared by the Chinese to be leader of Tsang and western Tibet.

The same autonomy battle that is being waged today between the Dalai Lama and Tibetans on the one-hand, and China on the other, was emulated in a lesser way in the early 20th century between Shigatse and Lhasa. The 9th Panchen Lama was involved in a dispute with the 13th Dalai Lama over Tashilhunpo's autonomy and, in particular, taxes. He fled to China and his successor, the 10th Panchen Lama, was raised by Beijing authorities and used as a pawn in the power struggle between Beijing and the

Dalai Lama from the 1950s until his death in 1989. The controversial appointment of the 11th Panchen Lama continues to create tension between the sects.

The good news about the Panchen Lamas finding favour with the Chinese is that it has meant that the magnificent Tashilhunpo monastery remained largely intact during the Cultural Revolution. The monastery is in excellent condition and on a sunny day the sun gleams majestically on the gilded rooftops.

The monks at Tashilhunpo have had a bad press with many travellers. This is not entirely fair. Travellers have reported them to be rude but the reality is that they are simply more vigilant about collecting entrance fees than monks at many other monasteries. The reason is not that they are greedy – they are heavily monitored by the Chinese authorities and risk the consequences if they do not enforce the appropriate policies. If you unbegrudgingly pay your entrance fee and take your time, and are respectful about the places you are entering, your good manners will be reciprocated. These monks get a huge number of visitors and a fair share of those try to skip through without paying – it creates a bit of tension. Be nice, show your ticket when asked, and you will have a lovely time.

The monastery itself comprises several important chapels as well as the tombs of the Panchen Lamas. The most impressive building is the **Chapel of the Maitreya**, which houses the 26m gold-gilded Future Buddha statue built during the reign of the 9th Panchen Lama. The Chapel of the Maitreya is the first chapel on the left as you walk into the monastery.

The **Palace of the Panchen Lamas** is the large white building in the centre of the complex, which was the residence of the Panchen Lamas. It is closed to the public although you can enter the chapels around it. The 10th Panchen Lama's tomb is the large white chorten in front of the palace, which has his image at the front. The 4th Panchen Lama's tomb is also in the monastery – a gold and silver chorten.

The **Kelsang temple** is the main assembly hall at the monastery and is a hive of activity. Young and old monks go about their business in the courtyard and inside, prayers take place daily. There are a number of chapels inside and several beautiful statues and paintings. The tombs of the 5th to 9th Panchen Lamas are inside the temple.

The Tashilhunpo kora (circuit) is a one-hour walk around the back of the monastic complex. The views are spectacular.

Shigatse Dzong The fort, which you would have seen on the approach from Gyantse, is pretty much destroyed. It was once the palace of the Gyantse kings but was destroyed during the Cultural Revolution. Heinrich Harrer's second book, *Return to Tibet*, has a photograph of the palace pre-1959 and it bears a remarkable resemblance to the Potala.

DAYS 8-10: SHIGATSE TO LHATSE [SEE MAPS 6 & 7]
Overview

It is not so easy to leave Shigatse and begin the long and isolated ride to Kathmandu. Shigatse is abuzz with travellers, many of whom will be travelling from Kathmandu, and stories about impossible passes will be rife.

Be reassured that, no matter what the travellers coming from the other direction may tell you, none of the passes that you will cycle over will be any more difficult than Kampa la – the very first pass en route to Yamdrok Tso. However, the factor to bear in mind is that if you are cycling in or around October/November, it is going to get colder and colder and this factor will make life harder on the passes.

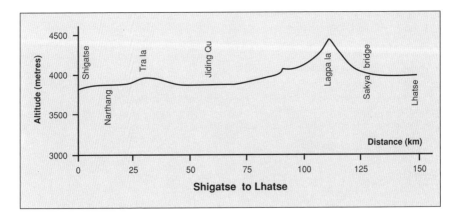

Shigatse to Lhatse

The 150km from Shigatse to Lhatse will involve at least two nights and possibly three. If you decide to make the side-trip to Sakya monastery (which is highly recommended) you need to add at least one extra day and night.

Day 8: To Lagpa la

Leaving Shigatse the road climbs gently past Narthang monastery (the end point of a three-day trek from Shalu via Chak la) and over the minor Tra la (3975m). From the pass it is an enjoyable 27km to a large bridge and deserved lunch break.

The village of **Chemo**, situated around 57km from Shigatse, has accommodation and restaurants. Just before the town there starts a teasingly short run on a beautifully-sealed road. It finishes just across the other side of town. Over the bridge, one of the first shops on the right-hand side of the road is a *restaurant* with great egg fried rice and chips. They have *accommodation* upstairs but you are better off trying to get a bit closer to the foot of the next pass – Lagpa la. We had a large lunch of hot potato chips and took a plastic bag filled with egg fried rice with us for our dinner. It stayed warm enough to enjoy that night, once we had our tent sorted, and saved us having to cook.

Day 9: Lagpa la to Sakya/Lhatse

Lagpa la is a further 35km from the compound, although you can camp anywhere between there and the foot of the pass (essentially the closer the better). It is a pleasant undulating road but the surface is not great – except for the odd sections that are smoothly paved. The pass itself could be worse! It is actually a surprisingly tolerable uphill (although a bit steep in places) and the downhill on the other side is fantastic. Now you realise you are definitely travelling in the right direction. (It was about here that we met a rather flabbergasted Japanese cyclist who told us that he has been climbing hills ever since he left Kathmandu.)

CYCLING TIMES – SHIGATSE to LHATSE
Shigatse to Jiding Qu – 4hr-4hr 30min
Jiding Qu to Lagpa la (1hr climb up pass) – 3hr 30min-5hr 30min
Lagpa la to Sakya Bridge – 45min-1hr
Sakya Bridge to Lhatse – 90min-2hr
Sakya Bridge to Sakya monastery (side route) – 2hr-2hr 30min
ESTIMATED CYCLING TIMES – NOT INCLUDING STOPS

It is a bit windy up on the pass and probably a good idea to get down quickly. On the other side you have several options. It is easily possible to cycle from the top of Lagpa la to Lhatse in about three hours (as it is all either downhill or flat). However, the turn-off to Sakya monastery is 13km before Lhatse. From the turn-off to the monastery is a 26km side trip.

You could cycle directly to Sakya and spend the night in the *accommodation* in the monastery village or cycle as far as the turn-off and spend the night in the *guest-house compound* at the intersection (which is perfectly adequate, and the resident family is very kind), cycling to Sakya the next day.

Day 10: Optional side trip to Sakya
The road from the turn-off to Sakya is unsealed but reasonably tightly packed so not too difficult to ride on. It is clearly marked so you will not get lost. The kids in the villages along the way can be unpleasant but not as violent as kids in other areas! The road has a slight incline but no taxing hill climbs.

At Sakya, there are a number of very basic accommodation options. The best is probably the *Tibetan-run guesthouse* just north of the main entry gates to the monastery. It has dormitory rooms and a fairly good restaurant out front.

Sakya
The distinctive buildings of the villages in the town and monastery of Sakya (and the entire valley), with their uniformed red, white and grey stripes, make a striking contrast to the whitewashed buildings elsewhere in Tibet. The colour scheme is unique to the Sakya sect.

Sakya monastery
The monastery is extremely old and was once the seat of power in Tibet. It was founded in 1073 and the Kagyu sect of Buddhism was founded nearby by Milarepa and his followers and, subsequently, the Sakya sect was formed in the 11th century. The abbots are not selected by reincarnation but, instead, through a line of succession through sons of the ruling family. The close proximity of the monastic community to India meant that it was a great scholarly base and the place where many important Buddhist texts were composed.

A key aspect of the Sakya monastery's history was the relationship between the monastery's lamas and the Mongols. In the 13th century, the Mongols assumed the role of patrons to the monastery leaders and that 'overlord' relationship has been retrospectively construed by Chinese publicists to be the basis for the 'unified motherland' argument. In the event, the relationship was relatively short-lived and certainly did not suggest any form of centralized Mongolian rule.

From the 14th century Sakya continued as an important political seat, and the controlling centre of the Ü region, which remained relatively independent from Shigatse.

The monastery itself is set down in a valley and it feels quite cool and damp near the front entrance. The main assembly hall is the huge structure in the centre of the building and is magnificently decorated. There are a number of smaller chapels inside, including the Purkhan Chapel which contains images of Sakyamuni and Manjushri and paintings of Tara and the Medicine Buddha and others.

Take a little time to walk around the monastery and chat with the monks. The monastery's relative isolation from the main road and larger Chinese towns means that people are a little more relaxed with travellers, although there is still a sense of being watched in the area.

Permits
If you are heading off the main road into Sakya you do need a permit. In particular, if you intend to hitch in or out on a truck, for the sake of you and your driv-

ROUTE GUIDE – SHIGATSE to LHATSE

CYCLO-METER (KM)	ROAD MARKER (KM)	ALTIMETER READING (M)	NOTES AND KEY POINTS OF INTEREST
0	4903/4904	3825	Tashilhunpo monastery, outside main entrance
			(sealed road heads west out of Shigatse)
2.5		3850	Join main road – dirt road from here
3.9	4907	3870	First road marker out of Shigatse *(road climbs gently along 'dry' landscape)*
10	4913	3870	Road fork – turn right to Lhatse
			(left road leads to Ngor monastery over 15km away)
14	4917	3870	Narthang monastery *(on right side of road behind village)*
29.7	4932/33	3975	Tra la (short climb)
32.7	4935/36	3950	Turn-off to Ganchen monastery – 2km north of main road
			(gompa can be seen from the road)
52	4954	3870	Join Sha chu near Ne village
54.1	4956/57	3870	Section of asphalt road starts – bliss!
56.7		3875	Large bridge crosses Sha chu
57.3	4960	3875	Jiding Qu (Chemo) 🍽 ⟁ ⤴
		"	*(ruins of fort on ridge, north valley leads to the Tsangpo, possible checkpoint)*
58.8	4961/62	"	Asphalt ends (4.6km in total)
65.4	4968	"	Compound – possible accommodation
70	4972	"	Dilong
75.2	4978	3900	Turn-off on right leads to the Tsangpo and Pindsoling monastery
			(main road enters new valley around to left – river on right)
75-79		3925	Possible sheltered campsites for next 4km – near river
79.3	4982	3950	Road climbs away from river
82.5-91.1	4985	4050	Asphalt road starts – a nice surprise and easy riding
			(road follows river through gorge for next 10km)
97.7	5000	4115	Shrine on hill next to small village (road can be broken up badly here)
101.4	5003/04	4155	Bridge over river
102.5	5004/05	4170	Asphalt ends – can see Lagpa la in the distance
			(wide open valley past some houses 🍽 ⟁ to base of pass)
108	5010	4230	Jungbe village at foot of pass
112.2	5014	4450	Lagpa la (Tsuo la/Tropu la) *(road condition good, around 1hr climb)*
114		4360	Compound – with '4500m' sign
			(windy downhill for 7km, road condition good if dry)
127	5028/29	4040	Sakya bridge 🍽 ⟁ ⤴ *(Clean guesthouse in left compound or try small 'hotel' on right-hand side)*
			Sakya monastery – turn-off left just after Sakya bridge *(26km on mixed road, 2hr 30 min cycle with 180m climb, permit required)*
129.3	5031	*4005*	First road marker past Sakya bridge
138.3	5040	3980	Turn-off right to hot springs – sign in Chinese/Tibetan
			(400m from main road in green-roofed white building)
149.3	5051	3975	Dirt road on right leads 10km to Lhatse Dzong
150.8	5052	3990	Lhatse (Lhaze Xian) 🍽 ⟁ ⤴ – **reset** cyclometer

Notes: 🍽 = Food, ⟁ = Water, ⤴ = Accommodation available

er you **must** have a permit. In the little village just before the monastery, there is a **checkpoint** and a bar across the road. It may be that the day you travel through the bar is unmanned. However, there is often a heavy Chinese presence here and you will not be permitted to continue without a permit.

Make sure that Sakya is one of the places listed on your ATP that you obtain in Shigatse. If it is, you will have no problems at the checkpoint. Permits are rarely checked once you reach Sakya.

Day 10: Sakya to Lhatse
The 13km from the Sakya turn-off to Lhatse are fairly pleasant and uneventful. There is a delightful sign near Lhatse Dzong saying 'Tourist Reporting Point.' It is a military compound and no, it is not wise to report there. A little further up the road, on the right-hand side, are some **hot springs**. Not the booming business of the hot springs up near Nam Tso, but hot springs nevertheless. You could try and see if they are open when you go past or, alternatively, you may prefer to keep moving and get to Lhatse.

Lhatse will not set your world on fire. It is actually a very sad-looking jumble of concrete block, purpose-built complexes with the ubiquitous blue reflective glass. There are **shops** that sell woollen gear (including long johns, gloves and hats) and plenty of places to stock up on food.

Accommodation options are not great. Your choice is one of the few Chinese concrete block hotels on the road front or a bed in a dormitory in a compound behind the Chinese hotel fronts. The toilets are not worth the visit – wait for darkness to fall and go behind the buildings. There are no showers but there are hot water flasks and washbowls in the rooms.

The restaurant *food* will give you the necessary sustenance to get you to the next village but it is no great culinary experience. Lhatse – not a highlight of the trip.

DAYS 11-13: LHATSE TO DINGRI   [SEE MAPS 7 & 8]
Again, this leg may be broken up by a side trip that should prove to be one of the highlights of the journey – Rongphu monastery and Everest Base Camp. The Everest Base Camp side trip is dealt with on pp131-137.

Day 11: To the base of Gyatso la
As with most of the other sections of the Friendship Highway, this part may be tackled in a number of different ways. Some of your choices will depend on how far you cycled the day before.

Gyatso la is the pass that stands between you and Dingri and it is high. This is also the first of the two big passes that stand between you and Kathmandu (except for the pass in Nepal on the last day which is at 800m and you will feel as if you can fly at that height after weeks above 4000m!). However, Gyatso la, at 5105m, is not to be taken lightly. It is a climb of over 1100m from Lhatse so this is a big altitude gain in one day. You really do want to make sure you get over it and down to a decent level on the other side. One suggestion is that you tackle it over two days to avoid getting stuck at the top of the pass where you will be extremely exposed and cold.

One option for doing so is to eat in Lhatse but not actually spend the night there – you won't miss a lot! That way, you can keep going towards the pass and camp in the valley near the bottom. Unfortunately, the wind whips through here and it is extremely exposed even in the valley.

An alternative option is to spend the night in Lhatse and then take it easy the next day and cycle a bit further up the pass to about 4500m and camp wherever you can find some shelter.

To get to Gyatso la from Lhatse, head south along the Friendship Highway. At 5.7km from town the road forks; the right-hand fork heads to Kailash (some 800km away – see pp158-171). To get to Kathmandu, take the left-hand fork into the valley leading up

CYCLING TIMES – LHATSE to DINGRI

Lhatse to Gyatso la – 4-5hr

Gyatso la to Shekar turn-off – 3-4hr

Shekar turn-off to Mt Everest turn-off – 45min

Mt Everest turn-off to Dingri – 4-5hr

ESTIMATED CYCLING TIMES – NOT INCLUDING STOPS

to the pass. There may be accommodation options at the fork – there are a few buildings including a shop there but you do not gain enough distance from Lhatse to make it worthwhile.

Day 12: Gyatso la

The road up the valley is reasonably well sheltered and runs parallel to a river. During the autumn season, you will cross the river up to eight times – usually fording water of about 15-25mm without getting your feet wet. In the rainy season, these rivers flood and can become virtually impossible to cross.

The road meanders along at a gradual climb and steepens near the compound at 25km and then levels out again. It is a pleasant ride and you are never alone for long. Trucks regularly travel along the route and very near the top of the pass is a group of Chinese buildings in a large compound. If you did get stuck with weather difficulties you may be able to get help here. The Chinese compound is on the right, and directly opposite is a hardy Tibetan village.

The pass itself is quite spectacular and lays before you your first glimpse of the magnificent Himalayan ranges with Mount Everest taking pride of place above the other peaks. There is a sign marking the mountains on the range and a spectacular array of prayer flags on this particular pass. It is a truly magnificent sight – but very cold and very exposed. Once you reach this point it will be with some jubilation that you will realise it is just one more pass to Kathmandu (unless you are cycling to Base Camp – but that's a whole new adventure).

Coming down the pass the road is long, winding and the slope is fairly gradual. There are no breathtaking descents to be had here, unfortunately. Do not underestimate

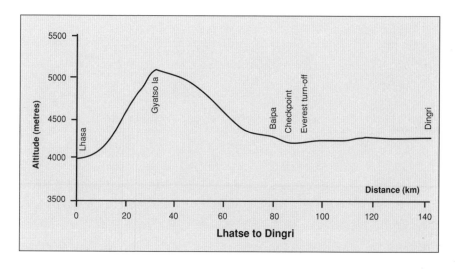

how long it will take to get down this pass. The decline is not steep and the winds are strong – headwinds. There are places to camp; try to get along as far as possible to avoid camping at too high an altitude.

After an hour or two the road eventually descends into a much warmer valley and there are villages where you might be able to find accommodation. The whitewashed huts in this pleasant valley shine in the sun and complement the magnificent glow of the Himalayas. It is a pleasant place to ride and a lovely reprieve from some difficult cycling.

Day 13: To Shekar/Chay/Dingri

The next town is **Baipa**, near Shekar, and you will find basic *accommodation* and a couple of good restaurants. Alternatively, if you camp before Shekar, you can cycle all the way to the turn-off to Everest Base Camp or to Dingri in one day. Baipa is where you must purchase (Y65) a permit for the Qomolangma Nature Preserve. Make sure you ask for the 10-day pass.

If you do not wish to cycle to Everest, but want to hitch a ride up or hire a jeep, a good place to find a vehicle is Shekar. **Shekar** township and fort are 7km up a side road to the right as you head towards Dingri. The distinctive fort ruins are worth a visit if you have time.

[Optional side trip to Everest Base Camp – see pp131-137.]

Dingri

Dingri as a town is never going to set your world on fire, but it is well known for its magnificent views of Everest, being the gateway to the final pass en route to the border. These factors make it an enjoyable place to visit.

There are a few **accommodation** options in Dingri, most of which are large compounds on the right-hand side of the road with dormitory-type rooms around a large courtyard.

The first option is *Everest Snow Leopard Hotel*, which is popular with tourist groups. It is a bit pricey but the rooms are clean. The next compound, just after the bridge, is called *Everest View Hotel* and is quite sufficient. The *restaurant* directly in front makes great egg fried rice and can do something reasonably tasty with potatoes. Stock up on carbohydrates as there is not much to eat between here and Nyalam.

The sights in Dingri are sparse. By the end of November the ice settles on the ponds on the way out of town and the nomad children have a tremendous time ice skating (well, sliding around on their shoes and knees or pieces of old sacking).

On the plains between Shekar and Dingri are dotted the ruins of many buildings destroyed in an 18th-century Nepalese invasion and the town is overlooked by the

---

❑ Prayer flags

Throughout Tibet the many mountain passes are adorned with stone cairns and prayer flags called *lungta* (meaning 'windhorse') so the wind may continuously distribute the multiple blessings written on them. Whenever Tibetans cross over passes by foot or other means of transport they will invariably add a new stone or tie some more *lungta* as an offering to the spirit of the mountain. Tibetans in buses will sometimes throw paper *lungta* out the window while shouting out a blessing.

Lungta are blue, white, red, green and yellow (arranged in that order) symbolizing the five elements space, water, fire, air and earth respectively with varying mantra printed on them.

ROUTE GUIDE – LHATSE to DINGRI

CYCLO-METER (KM)	ROAD MARKER (KM)	ALTIMETER READING (M)	NOTES AND KEY POINTS OF INTEREST
0	5052	3990	Lhatse Hotel ⚇ Ⴤ ↵ *(continue west to Shekar and Kathmandu)*
0.7	5053	"	First road marker out of Lhatse
3.3	5055/56	"	Asphalt ends
5.7	5058	4005	Road forks – turn south (left) to Shekar
			(checkpoint and turn-off right to Mt Kailash 798km away)
7	5059	4025	Small village
			(road steepens but surface condition good)
8	5060/61	4080	Road joins Lola chu
14.7	5067	4325	Compound – no houses until next compound 10km away
15/17	5068/70	4405	Possible campsite
25	5077/78		Compound – road becomes 'slightly' steeper!
31.3	5083/84	5105	Gyatso la (or Jia Tsuo/Maphu/Jachor la)
			(summit stone marker reads 5220m)
48.3	5100/01	4930	Compound – possible campsite
			(low gradient descent, about eight river crossings since pass)
59/60	5111/12	4580	Distant views of Mt Everest
			(road steepens after about road marker 5107)
63	5115	4475	Village *(possible campsite about 1km before village)*
69/70	5121/22	4360	Hot springs by roadside – not suitable for bathing
			(look for sulphur marks/smells near far side of Lolo chu)
71+		4330	Road levels out
81.5	5133/34	4250	Baipa village ⚇ Ⴤ ↵ *(Turn-off right to Qomolangma Hotel and Shekar Dzong 7km, good accommodation/food at 4370m heading towards Shekar just before new hotel complex)*
83.6	5135	4225	Turn-off left to Tingche Xian
87.8	5139/40	4190	Major checkpoint – show passports ⚇ Ⴤ ↵
90	5142	4200	Asphalt ends
93	5145	4220	Small concrete bridge
93.3	5145/46	4225	Turn-off south (left) to Rongphu monastery/Mt Everest
			(look for sign 'Qomolangma National Level Nature Preserve')
108	5160	"	Amazing 'moonlike' landscape – Tzipri range on right
			(road surface fine metal – slippery and quite tough)
110	5162	4250	Small village
118	5170	4255	Tsakor village
135	5187	4230	Hermitage cave halfway up hill on left
139.5	5191/92	4250	Asphalt road starts
			(Everest Snow Leopard Hotel in large compound on right)
139.9	5192	"	Small concrete bridge
			(turn-off south for trekkers to Ra chu valley and Mt Everest)
141.4		"	Large concrete bridge *(old town seen over to the south)*
141.7	5193/94	4250	Dingri (Tingri) ⚇ Ⴤ ↵ – **reset** cyclometer

Notes: ⚇ = Food, Ⴤ = Water, ↵ = Accommodation available

ruins of the large fort. If the weather is clear you will be treated to awe-inspiring views of both Everest and nearby Cho Oyu.

DAYS 14-16: DINGRI TO DRAM   [SEE MAP 10]

Day 14: Dingri to foot of Lalung la
This is it – the last leg to the border. One more pass (although it is a double pass so be ready) and then it is all downhill to Nepal. The world's longest downhill awaits.

Try to get an early start from Dingri and cycle to the bottom of Lalung la. The pass is tough going, especially once the cold weather has set in.

There are a number of reasonably pleasant sights along the way as you follow the course of the river through the valley. As you stop for your picnic lunch, local herdsmen might sit down and join you.

The village of **Gutso**, an important military point, is about halfway to the foot of the pass and you can get *food* or, if necessary, *accommodation* here.

As you keep cycling past Gutso, you turn left (south) into a valley, which looks like a gorge. This is a surreal-looking place with high cavern walls and a deep and fast-moving river running through it. There are a few little villages dotted in the cool shadow of the canyon walls and some pretty impressive bridges running across the river.

At 60.5km from Dingri there is a small *hotel* on the right-hand side of the road, just before the village of Sumo. You will be able to get accommodation here and, if you are lucky, food. There is a lovely warm fire in the middle of the restaurant and nightly entertainment from passing truck drivers.

Our visit coincided with the ritual killing of the winter season's supplies. As we cycled up to the hotel, about ten Tibetan men were slaughtering a yak on the front stairs. All evening we watched the restaurant owner trying to make mince with a very, very blunt knife. Better than a night at home with the *Pulp Fiction* video.

First thing the next morning, keep cycling south through the gorge. It opens out before too long and you can see the ruins of the very early settlement (the ruins resulting from Nepalese invasions in the 18th century).

Day 15: Lalung la
It is 12km from the hotel to the foot of Lalung la. The bottom of the pass opens out into a new valley (which forks south-west towards Kyirong – the village that Heinrich

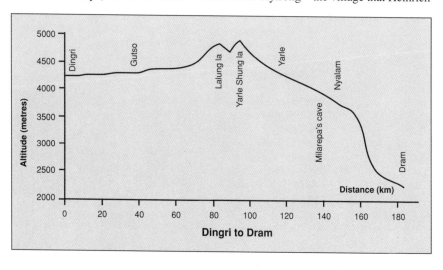

ROUTE GUIDE – DINGRI to DRAM

CYCLO-METER (KM)	ROAD MARKER (KM)	ALTIMETER READING (M)	NOTES AND KEY POINTS OF INTEREST
0	5193/94	4250	Dingri ⦿ Ⓨ ↩ *(continue west to Nyalam and Kathmandu)*
11.5	5205	4265	Tsamda village – a trail leads south 12km to Langkor monastery
12.7	5206	4265	Turn-off to hot springs ⦿ Ⓨ ↩ – 500m on left by white building *(great spot to soak tired limbs)*
17.1		4275	Guesthouse on right side of road ⦿ Ⓨ ↩ *(fortress ruins built during Nepalese invasion for next 20km)*
22.5	5216	4285	Pass through school buildings *(village to left with gompa visible 2km away)*
39.1	5232/33	4320	Gutso village ⦿ Ⓨ ↩ *(large military camp and hospital)*
43.8	5237/38	4350	Turn-off to Menkhab Me on north bank of Men chu *(road climbs gradually from here into headwind)*
50.4	5244/45	4375	Village
57.7		"	Turn-off over bridge to Takoya village with distinctive ruins
59	5253	4405	Two large meditation caves above road on right 100m away
60.5	5254/55	4415	Small hotel on right side of road ⦿ Ⓨ ↩
62.1	5256	4430	Sumo village ⦿ Ⓨ ↩
68/71	5262/65	4450	Possible campsites but limited wind cover *(views of Mt Shishapangma, 8012m)*
71.9	5265/66	4495	Turn-off right to Kyirong and Saga short-cut *(road surface good but start of steep 'switchbacks')*
78.6	5272/73	4785	Road flattens
82.8	5276/77	4845	Lalung la *(first pass across the Himalayas)*
88	5282	4700	Bridge on right ⦿ Ⓨ ↩ *(after road descends for 5km)*
95.7	5289/90	4945	Yarle Shung la *(second pass, Mt Shishapangma largest peak on right)*
96	5290	4840	First marker after pass – road surface good
109	5303	4425	Dulung village ⦿ Ⓨ ↩ *(approx 45min cycling from pass, road flattens)*
117	5311	4265	Yarle village ⦿ Ⓨ ↩ *(guesthouse/restaurant sometimes closed)*
124.1	5318	4195	Turn-off to Ngoru village and south-east face of Mt Shishapangma *(undulating 'sandy' road climb over next 10km)*
132.9	5326/27	4045	Concrete bridge over Pö chu
136.3	5330	3980	Nesar village *(minor climb out of Nesar over next 4km)*
140.7	5334/35	3945	Phegyeling monastery and Milarepa's cave Ⓨ ↩ *(look out for large white chorten 50m from left side of road)*
151.5	5345/46	3700	Nyalam (Nyelam Xian) ⦿ Ⓨ ↩ *(bridge/toll gate before town)*
153.8	5347/48	3700	Prayers flags mark entrance to Pö chu gorge *(road now descends 1470m in only 33km – have fun!)*
159+	5353+		Scenery changes – spectacular waterfalls and lush green forest *(excellent views of upper peaks of Nepal's Langtang valley)*
160.9	5354/55	3405	Steel bridge across Pö chu
164.3	5357/58		Chusang Hotel – near Chusang hot springs *(can accommodate travellers when the road is blocked)*
168	5361/62	2555	Tunnel – possible landslides around this area
172	5365/66		Final government compound
182	5376		Checkpoint before Dram
184.6	5378/79	2230	Dram *(ch* Zhangmu, *nep* Khasa) ⦿ Ⓨ ↩ *(outside the first Bank of China)*
185.8		2230	Chinese customs/immigration checkpost – **reset** cyclometer

Notes: ⦿ = Food, Ⓨ = Water, ↩ = Accommodation available

CYCLING TIMES – DINGRI to DRAM

Dingri to Gutso – 3-4hr

Gutso to Kyirong turn-off (marker 5265) – 2hr 30min-3hr 30min

Kyirong turn-off to Yarle Shung la – 2hr 30min-3hr 30min

Yarle Shung la to Nyalam – 3hr 30min-4hr 30min

Nyalam to Dram – 90min-2hr 30min

ESTIMATED CYCLING TIMES – NOT INCLUDING STOPS

Harrer described as the 'Valley of Happiness'). This area is now heavily militarized and you will not ingratiate yourself with the Chinese army if you try to enter it. There is a large grassy area at the foot of Lalung la. The road now starts a steady series of switchbacks to the top. It is cold, windy, exposed and hard work but stick with it – it is not as far as you think. At the top, the wind and snow is shockingly cold and the exposure is extreme. But this is a small price to pay for riding across the top of the highest mountain range in the world – the Himalayas. It is 14km from the top of the first pass to the second. In between the two is a small *restaurant compound*, the owners of which would no doubt provide you with shelter if the weather or nightfall caught you out.

From the top of the second pass – which is a magnificent spread of prayer flags and a sensational vista of Mt Shishapangma (8012m) – it is all downhill to the border. Head down, put your tail back and go for it. You've deserved this!

It is a long way to Nyalam in one day (90km with the double pass to boot) and it is probably a better idea to stop and camp about halfway. One option is the *guesthouse* in **Yarle Village**. The guesthouse may be locked up but someone will help you out. If you don't make it that far, there is a compound higher up the pass that offers accommodation as well.

Alternatively, if you can keep going, there is a little village called **Nesar**, which is 19km from Yarle. The local villagers will probably let you erect your *tent* in a stable (to shelter from the bitter wind). If you make it this far, and have enough light, consider cycling on to Milarepa's cave. The cave monastery complex has a *guesthouse* and the monks will heat some water for you.

Day 16: Milarepa's cave to Dram

Even if you don't stay at Milarepa's cave for the night, do call in for a visit. It is the last

---

❏ **Milarepa of Tibet**

Milarepa is one of the most widely known Tibetan saints. In a superhuman effort, he rose above the miseries of his younger life and with the help of his Guru, Marpa the Translator, took to a solitary life of meditation until he had achieved the pinnacle of the enlightened state, never to be born again into the Samsara (whirlpool of life and death) of worldly existence.

Milarepa is revered in Tibet for his retreat into the cave near Nyalam, robed in cotton cloth, where he subsisted on nettle soup (and is reputed to have turned green as a consequence).

Out of compassion for humanity, he undertook the most rigid asceticism to reach the Buddhist state of enlightenment and to pass his accomplishments on to the rest of humanity. His spiritual lineage was passed along to his chief disciples, Gambopa and Rechung. It was Rechung who recorded in detail the incidents of Milarepa's life for posterity. The narrative of his life has thus been passed down through almost a millennium to become an integral part of Tibetan culture.

Milarepa extemporaneously composed innumerable songs throughout his life relevant to the dramatic turns of events of himself and his disciples in accordance with an art form that was in practice at the time. These songs have been widely sung and studied in Tibet ever since and have been recorded as the Hundred Thousand Songs of Milarepa. He has many faithful followers and students to this day, including Westerners as well as Tibetans.

monastery that you will visit in Tibet and one of the oldest religious sites in the country.

The caves are on the left-hand side of the road (the same side as the river) as you head down the valley towards Dram. They are 23km from Yarle and marked by a large white chorten. If you reach the village after the chorten you have gone too far.

You can lock your bike up on the side of the road (hide it down in a ditch) and walk down to the monastery across the fields. There are a few steps to get down there but it is worth it to see the craggy monastery perched on the rock face.

It is practically all downhill from here (and definitely straight down from Nyalam) so you will make it to Dram (in Chinese Zhangmu) easily in one day. Enjoy the sights!

From Milarepa's cave to Nyalam it is a gentle undulating slope. Actually this part is a little bit annoying because you are desperately waiting for the long-promised downhill to commence but, in fact, you will have to wait until Nyalam.

Nyalam

There is not a lot to say about Nyalam except that it offers adequate **accommodation** and plenty of **food** options. Actually the food options are good – just call into any of the restaurants on the left-hand side of the road as you enter the town from Lalung la. The people are pleasant enough and a little more accustomed to foreigners than many other villagers in Tibet. There is a heavy Chinese presence in the town and a some-times strict checkpoint after the bridge into town.

Nyalam is 3700m above sea level. You are about to cycle to Dram, which is 2230m above sea level. **The drop is just under 1500m, achieved within a distance of 33km – you're going to FLY!**

This really is a mountain biking highlight, not of the trip but of your life! We had heavy snow at the top but by Dram we were getting sunburnt. And the trip down took less than two hours (with photo stops all the way). It really is a spectacular thrill. Be a little bit careful. There are lots of trucks and jeeps using this route and there is a nasty drop to the gorge below. But to go all out really is irresistible.

Dram

Dram is a Wild West border town perched precariously on the face of a rather steep hill, high in the Nepalese rainforests. The contrast in the vegetation and climate is absolutely unbelievable.

Dram has a surprisingly good choice of **food** and **accommodation**. We had the most spectacular hot pot of fried-up chicken and things with soup and rice from a nameless little place with a pink lace curtain on the right-hand side of the street.

The town is laid out along a series of switchbacks. As you go down the first few switchbacks you will reach the heart of the town and the concentration of guesthouses and restaurants. There is a choice of places to stay with hot showers and clean sheets.

DAYS 17-18: DRAM TO KATHMANDU [SEE MAP 10]

You've made it to the Nepalese border. But don't stop now – it is two days of fantas-tic, tropical (and mostly downhill) cycling from Dram to Kathmandu.

Day 17: Dram to Dolalghat village

Leave Dram by cycling down the remaining switchbacks to the Chinese border check-point at the bottom. The checkpoint opens at 09:00 (although sometimes not till 10:00) and then it is a 30-minute cycle down 'no-man's land' to the Friendship Bridge and the customs entry-point into Nepal at Kodari. The switchbacks are still good fun through here but pretty steep so you need to be careful of trucks and pedestrians.

The Friendship Bridge is a little bit glum in the morning shadows but as you emerge across it into Nepalese territory the whole environment just feels nicer. The

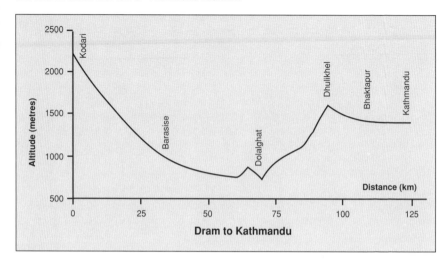

Nepalese customs officers will check your visa (you can normally obtain a Nepalese visa at the border but it may be safer to arrange one in Lhasa) and help you out with money exchange. Don't forget to put your watch back 2¼ hours, and welcome to Nepal!

Soon after Kodari is the hot spring town of **Tatopani** where you can stop for a thermal dip. There are little *guesthouses* all the way along the route from here to Kathmandu so don't worry about accommodation options.

It is possible to cycle all the way to Dolalghat, which is at the base of the final pass into Kathmandu. **Barabise**, en route, is a great place to stop for lunch. There are brilliant *food* options in **Dolalghat** as well. The first thing you will notice when you eat is the choice and the second thing is the price. It is surprisingly cheap after the prices in Tibet.

You can get accommodation on the rooftop of the little *guesthouse* in Dolalghat (directly in front of you after you cross the bridge into the town). The rooms have sweet little French doors that open to a view across the river – quite luxurious really. No shower though – that will have to wait until Kathmandu.

Day 18: Dolalghat to Kathmandu

The final day. There is one more pass but, although it is a climb of 1200m, you are starting from 600m above sea level – a lung-fillingly low altitude. No matter how tired you think you are, it is unbelievable how much energy you will have at this altitude in comparison to up on the Tibetan plateau. The ride is very pleasant. It is a big day but there are so many new and wonderful things to look at and enjoy. As you enter Kathmandu, near the turn-off to Bhaktapur, the road becomes busy and dangerous. Once you reach Kathmandu airport it is a further 7km to Thamel and a hot shower.

When you are clean again the tourist buzz and selection of delicacies will send you reeling. Be careful about what you eat after the poor diet in Tibet; the rich tastes of Kathmandu can upset your stomach, although a few chocolate bars to celebrate are certainly deserved!

CYCLING TIMES – DRAM to KATHMANDU

Dram to Friendship Bridge – 35min
Friendship Bridge to Dolalghat – 4hr-4hr 30min
Dolalghat to Dhulikhel – 2hr 30min-3hr
Dhulikhel to Kathmandu – 3-5hr

ESTIMATED CYCLING TIMES – NOT INCLUDING STOPS

ROUTE GUIDE – DRAM to KATHMANDU

CYCLO-METER (KM)	ROAD MARKER (KM)	ALTIMETER READING (M)	NOTES AND KEY POINTS OF INTEREST
0	5379/80	2230	Dram (*ch* Zhangmu, *nep* Khasa) 🍽 ⵏ ⌫
			(from Chinese customs/immigration checkpoint)
8.6	New system	1785	Friendship Bridge – Tibet/Nepal border
	starts 116km		*('no man's land' descends 530m in just over 8km)*
9.0	116	1785	Kodari village 🍽 ⵏ ⌫
			(remember put watch back 2¹/₂hr and cycle on left side of road!)
14	111		Tatopani village – hotsprings 🍽 ⵏ ⌫ *(Nepali immigration checkpoint)*
20.3			Landslide area for 1km
21.3	102		Lhaku bridge
23.3	100		Start of minor climb for 1.5km
25.4			Landslide area for 200m
27.2	97/96	1100	Turn-off to 'Borderland' hotel/resort *(organize raft trips down the Bhote Kosi)*
35.2	88 960		Barabise village 🍽 ⵏ ⌫ *(asphalt road all the way to Kathmandu!)*
36.5		945	Barabise bridge
41.5	82/83	875	Dam across Bhote Kosi
45.7	78	835	Khadchaur village 🍽 ⵏ *(undulating road) large suspension bridge on LHS – turn off to Jiri, keep to right*
49.2	75	825	Kothe village 🍽 ⵏ
51.9	72/71	785	Balephi bridge
57	67	765	Sukute village 🍽 ⵏ
62.2	62	745	Start of hill climb for 2.5km
64.6	61/60	870	Top of pass
67.3		735	Dolalghat bridge over Sun Kosi river
67.5	57/56	735	Dolalghat village 🍽 ⵏ ⌫
68.4	56	745	First marker out of Dolalghat – '10km to Lamidanda'
			(start of 26km climb to Dhulikhel – approx 2-3hr cycling!)
78.2	47/46	1010	Lamidanda village 🍽 ⵏ
84.5	40	1100	Tinpiple village 🍽 ⵏ
90		1350	Last 5km to Dhulikhel are the steepest!
94.5	30	1605	Dhulikhel village 🍽 ⵏ ⌫ *(turn right at 'T' intersection)*
98	27/26	1535	Banepa village 🍽 ⵏ
109		1415	Bhaktapur city environs *(road dangerous/busy from here to Kathmandu!)*
112.7	12/11	1410	Turn-off on right to Bhaktapur 'old city'
118.9	6/5	1390	Road junction at entrance to Kathmandu – veer right to Thamel
			(just past airport which is on right)
119.4	no markers	1390	Veer left
	in city		*(may need to ask directions to Thamel district/pronounced Tamel)*
120.1		"	Cross over bridge
120.65		"	Pass large white building (on right side of road)
122.5		"	'Welcome to Kathmandu' monument 🍽 ⵏ ⌫
		"	*(veer around to right – tricky move on one-way system)*
123		"	'T' intersection – continue straight ahead *(various routes to Thamel from here)*
126.3		1395	Thamel district – Kathmandu 🍽 ⵏ ⌫ *(Congratulations)*

Notes: 🍽 = Food, ⵏ = Water, ⌫ = Accommodation available

Route guide
Central Friendship Highway

The 270km Central Friendship Highway is the most direct route from Lhasa to Shigatse. The roads are relatively smooth and flat and the scenery is pleasant but lacks the magnificence of the southern route.

On both the central and the southern route to Kathmandu, the first day out of Lhasa is the same – a long flat cycle from Lhasa to Chaksam Bridge. The road is fast, flat and sealed as it winds alongside the Lhasa River. The cost of the excellent road condition is that the traffic is relatively heavy (or at least heavy for Tibet).

The tarmac continues on the Central Friendship Highway, right up to Shigatse, making the route easier on the bike but also busier in terms of other traffic.

ROUTE GUIDE – LHASA to SHIGATSE (CENTRAL FRIENDSHIP HIGHWAY)

CYCLO-METER (KM)	ROAD MARKER (KM)	ALTIMETER READING (M)	NOTES AND KEY POINTS OF INTEREST
0	None	3600	Barkhor square
			(head west towards Potala and turn left at Lhasa Hotel)
4.5		3595	Lhasa – main bus station
12	4646/47		Road junction
			(veer left for Central Friendship Highway/veer right to Golmud)
63	4696/7	3560	Chüsül (Quxu Xian) ⦿ Ⴎ ↶
70	4703	3565	Dagar village ⦿ Ⴎ ↶
70/71	4703/4	3565	Chaksam Bridge
			(continue straight to 'Rigaze', cross bridge for Gyantse)
79	4712	3565	Views across Tsangpo to Lake Yamdrok 'radar/met centre dome'
			(high on top of hill)
91	4724	3590	Sa-me village with ruined dzong
114	4747	3685	Village
125	4758	3670	Road junction
			(route north leads 8km to Nyemo)
127/8	4760/1	3690	Village with restaurants ⦿ Ⴎ
148	4781	3695	Bridge across Tsangpo (to south side)
168	4801	3760	Turn-off for Rinphuk/Rinpung – possible checkpoint
182	4815	3735	Climb small 35m rise
188	4821	3735	Trakdruka vehicle ferry ⦿ Ⴎ ↶
			(cross for road along North Friendship Highway to Yangpachen)
202/3	4835/6	3770	Drakchik ferry across to Tobgyel valley
220	4853		Shigatse Airport is situated north of village
243	4876	3790	Tama ferry across to Shang valley and Ringon
270/1	4903/5	3825	Shigatse ⦿ Ⴎ ↶

Notes: ⦿ = Food, Ⴎ = Water, ↶ = Accommodation available

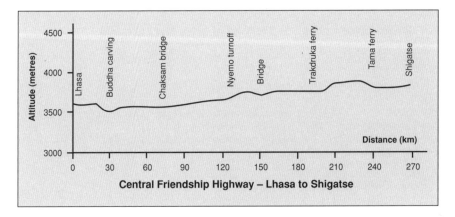

Central Friendship Highway – Lhasa to Shigatse

Route guide
Northern Friendship Highway

The Northern Friendship Highway is 340km from Lhasa to Shigatse and is the least popular route – primarily because it is 70km longer than the Central route and it does not pass by the magnificent Yamdrok Tso, the jewel of the Southern route.

The primary reason why cyclists or overlanders would undertake the northern route (apart from just trying something a little bit different) is because it can be incorporated into a separate trip to Nam Tso. The route turns off towards Shigatse at a side road close to the Yangpachen hot springs (en route from Lhasa to Golmud). Cyclists may wish to make a trip up to Nam Tso and then head directly back to Shigatse without returning to Lhasa.

With this route (as with the Central route) it does not mean that travellers will miss out on Gyantse and Yamdrok. There are regular buses from Shigatse to Gyantse (or it is a one-day each-way side trip by cycle) and it is possible to arrange transport for a trip to Yamdrok from Shigatse.

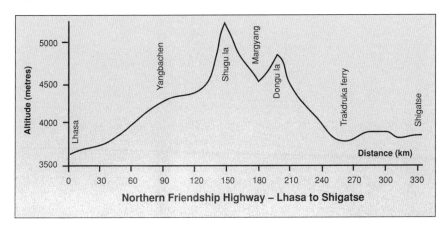

Northern Friendship Highway – Lhasa to Shigatse

ROUTE GUIDE – LHASA to SHIGATSE (NORTHERN FRIENDSHIP HIGHWAY)

CYCLO-METER (KM)	ROAD MARKER (KM)	ALTIMETER READING (M)	NOTES AND KEY POINTS OF INTEREST
0	None	3600	Barkhor square
			(head west towards Potala/turn left at Lhasa Hotel)
4.5		3595	Lhasa – main bus station
12	3879/80		Road junction – 'Goodbye from Lhasa' sign
			(veer right for Yangpachen and North Friendship Highway)
87	3804/5	4260	Yangpachen 🍽 Y ⌂
			(see p74 for route notes between Lhasa and Yangpachen)
89	3803/4		Road junction – turn left/west for Northern Friendship Highway
			(new system of road markers starts from here)
91.5	2/3		Village 🍽 Y
96 7			Yangpachen thermal station and hot spring 🍽 Y ⌂
108	19	4310	Yangpachen monastery
			(situated upon hill on right side of road above village)
109	20		Turn-off for trek to Dorjeling monastery and Tsurphu monastery
116.5	27/28		Bridge at entrance to Lhorong valley
123	34		Valley narrows and road steepens
138.5	49/50		Steep switchbacks for next 6km up to pass
145	56	5260	Shugu la *(excellent views across to Mt Jomo Gangtse 7048m)*
175	86	4500	Margyang village 🍽 Y ⌂ *(low point between passes)*
178	89		Valley on left leads south-east to Nyemo about 50km away
182.5	93/94		Senshang village 🍽 Y
			(start of trekking route leading north as far as Nam Tso)
189.5	100/1		Road climbs for next 5km
193.5	104/5	4845	Dongu la
203	114		Bridge over river
220.5	131/2		Rinchenling village
227.5	138/9		Oyuk Qu – administrative town on right bank of river 🍽 Y
245.5	156/7		Numagang town on left 🍽 Y ⌂
258	168/9		Trakdruka vehicle ferry
			(Yungdrungling monastery lies a few km east behind estuary)
258	4821	3735	Trakdruka village on south bank of Tsangpo 🍽 Y ⌂
			(turn west to Shigatse, east route returns to Lhasa 184km away)
272.5	4835/6	3770	Drakchik ferry – across to Tobgyel valley
290	4853		Shigatse Airport situated north of village
313	4876	3790	Tama ferry – across to Shang valley and Ringon
340	4903/4	3825	Shigatse 🍽 Y ⌂

Notes: 🍽 =Food, Y = Water, ⌂ = Accommodation available

It takes approximately eight to nine hours to cycle the 89km from Lhasa to Yangpachen (see pp170-178). ***Accommodation*** is available at the Yangpachen hot springs. The owner of the guesthouse is also the owner of the pool and poolside ***restaurant***. You will probably find him inside the complex.

It is then another 250km from Yangpachen turn-off to Shigatse, via two major passes and the Trakdruka vehicle ferry.

Everest Base Camp

It's not the summit that's important – it's the journey.
Graeme Dingle

INTRODUCTION

Everest Base Camp is a detour of 85km off the main route from Lhasa to Kathmandu; 85km in normal conditions is an easy day ride. However, even on a good day, the Everest environs do not constitute 'normal' conditions. They are as far from normal as mountain biking conditions can be – but this ride is the ultimate Tibetan mountain-biking experience. It will take a good three days to get up to Base Camp (two if you really push it but this would be hard work carrying full panniers). However, it is easily the most satisfying part of the entire adventure.

If your reason for heading to Tibet is to find genuine off-road mountain biking at altitude, the 85km/three-day ride from the Friendship Highway to Base Camp will surpass your expectations! Seven kilometres short of Base Camp is Rongphu monastery (the highest monastery in the world) and a genuine outpost for Tibetan Buddhism.

If you do not feel up to the 85km ride (and 1000m altitude gain), do consider hitching a ride with a truck or an organized jeep tour. The best place to do this is at the village of Shekar, just before you reach the turn-off to Everest. However you do it, do not miss the opportunity to visit the north face of Everest.

In the spring of 2002, the Chinese embarked on a major development of the road into Everest Base Camp. Starting from Chay the plan is to dramatically improve driving conditions along the entire route. Obviously this should encourage more cyclists to reach Base Camp.

Altitude and climate

As you turn off the Friendship Highway, it is 4175m above sea level. You are already very high. You will almost certainly spend the first night on the Friendship Highway side of the Pang la pass – the pass that stands between you and the beginning of your climb up to Base Camp.

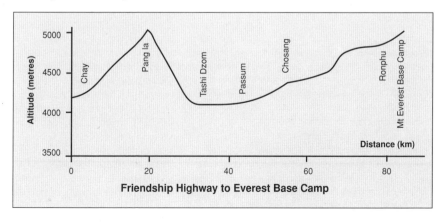

Friendship Highway to Everest Base Camp

Although Pang la reaches a height of 5050m, it is reasonably warm up there and it just gets warmer as you sink into the valley below (at 4090m), which is sunny and sheltered from the winds. The reasonably pleasant climate stays with you up until you start to climb again, just 10km out from Base Camp. Up at Rongphu monastery and Base Camp it is extremely cold so make sure you are well prepared.

Everest Region Maps

The most detailed and accurate map of Mt Everest ever produced is *Mt Everest* (National Geographic Society & Boston Museum of Science, 1984, scale 1:50,000). This survey was created from 160 aerial photographs (scale 1:10,000) shot from a Swiss Lear Jet flying at 12,000m. Copies of the map can still be obtained from bookstores in Kathmandu.

Another map, more easily obtainable and nearly as detailed, is *Mount Qomolangma (Sagarmatha)* (Lanzhou Institute of Glaciology and Geocryology & Chinese Academy of Sciences, 1991, scale 1:100,000).

These maps only cover the area between North Base Camp and Mt Everest and do not include the trekking routes in from Dingri (Tingri). The best map including the main trekking/cycling routes from Dingri into the Mt Everest national park is *Tingri* (Russian World Series 08-45-33, 1976, scale 1:200,000).

To obtain these maps, see the list of specialist map dealers on p33.

CHAY TO MT EVEREST BASE CAMP   [SEE MAPS 8 & 9]

The route across Pang la, into the valley below and up to Rongphu monastery and Base Camp is spectacular. It is completely worth the effort – even at this late stage in the ride when you really just want to push on to Kathmandu for a hot shower and decent meal.

Turn-off to Everest

The Everest turn-off is on the left-hand side of the Friendship Highway soon after Baipa village and the road to Shekar. There is an asphalt road just after Baipa and a turn-off to the left heading to Tingche Xian. Just after that (but still on the sealed part of the road) is a major checkpoint. We were just waved through here on our bikes, although we expected we would need to show our passports and permits. Have them ready in any event.

The asphalt ends soon after the checkpoint and there is a small concrete bridge. Just 300m after the bridge is the turn-off to the left (south) with a sign that says 'Qomolangma National Level Nature Reserve'. It is just less than 12km from Baipa to the turn-off.

Chay

As you cycle up the metal road towards Everest Base Camp, you will come to the little village of Chay. You must check in with the local Chinese officer and your Qomolangma Nature Preserve permit will be inspected.

In Chay you have a couple of very basic accommodation options. You can cycle on a little bit further and set up tent or, alternatively, find a local *Bed & Breakfast*. Don't expect bacon and eggs when you get out of bed – in fact don't expect a bed.

CYCLING TIMES – CHAY to EVEREST BASE CAMP
Turn-off to Chay – 35min
Chay to Pang la – 2hr 30min-3hr
Pang la to Tashi Dzom – 90min
Tashi Dzom to Passum – 1hr-1hr 30min
Passum to Chosang – 1hr-1hr 30min
Chosang to Rongphu monastery – 2hr 30min-3hr 30 min
Rongphu monastery to Mt Everest Base Camp – 1hr
ESTIMATED CYCLING TIMES – NOT INCLUDING STOPS

ROUTE GUIDE – CHAY to MT EVEREST BASE CAMP

CYCLO-METER (KM)	ROAD MARKER (KM)	ALTIMETER READING (M)	NOTES AND KEY POINTS OF INTEREST
0	5145/46	4175	Turn-off south to Rongphu monastery and Mt Everest *(from sign ' Qomolangma National Level Nature Preserve')*
4.0	no markers	4260	Chay (Tse) village ⏍ ⌔ ⌁ – checkpoint, permit required!
4.5		4285	Start steep climb to Pang la – at least 40 'switchbacks'! *(road surface rocky, slippery and difficult with full panniers)*
10			Halfway – first 6km in around one-hour's cycling time
		5050	Pang la *(awesome views across to Himalayas including Mt Everest)*
26.9			Village on left *(fast bumpy descent – 'brake burner')*
29.8			Unusual rock structures – Tibetan 'Stonehenge'
30/31			Possible campsite in next 3km *(road surface improves and flattens out)*
31.2		4150	Nyomda village – right trail leads to Gara valley and Dingri
34.9		4090	Tashi Dzom (Peruche) village ⏍ ⌔ ⌁ *(turn right to Rongphu monastery, left road goes to Kharta)*
36.4			Road forks – turn left towards Dzaka Chu, follow west bank *(variable road surface with some minor creek crossings)*
44.6		4140	Passum village ⏍ ⌔ ⌁ *(Zaphu monastery on ridge to right of road)*
46			Small concrete bridge – Ding valley on right leads to Ding la *(road can be very muddy for next 3km, find route amongst rocks beside road, aim for right/east side of valley ahead)*
48.5			Road forks – leave river, veer to east entrance of valley ahead *(trail left/west heads to Kharta via Doya la)*
50.7			Zaphu village – first half of Zaphu – only a few houses
51.3			Second half of Zaphu village – again only a few houses
52			Large concrete bridge over Dzakar Chu *(road continues to hug west/east side of valley away from river)*
56.9		4360	Chosang (Chö Dzong) village ⏍ ⌔ ⌁
61			Road forks – veer left for shortest route *(right trail down to river, Zamphuk valley on right leads to Dingri)*
63.1			Prayer flags *(Kyelung hermitage cave ruins high on right valley cliff)*
64/65			Possible campsite *(reasonable fine metal surface road)*
67.1			Short descent then road turns south into Rongphu valley
67.4			Partial view of Mt Everest *(large tributary on right from Gyachung glacier, wooden bridge)*
67.9			Couple of large stone mounds *(road surface deteriorates and is undulating for next 9km)*
70.4			Gyelung Dezeng Chöling retreat visible high in north-west valley
72.2			Peyul stone chorten
75.9			Concrete bridge – final steep 1km climb
76.8			Top of rocky moraine – can see Rongphu monastery
77.7		4825	Rongphu (Rongbuk) monastery ⏍ ⌔ ⌁
81.5			Stone chorten
81.8			Small stone temple – Padmasambhavas monastery *(Tundrupling Caves and ruins of nunnery to the left up the ridge)*
85.1		5020	Mt Everest base camp (sign 'Mt Qomolangma Base Camp')

Notes: ⏍ = Food, ⌔ = Water, ⌁ = Accommodation available

The road heads south from Chay and winds back towards the east before heading up the pass in a series of switchbacks. The road meanders backwards and forwards across the face of the mountain and seems needlessly long. If you are pushing you may like to shortcut a few of the switchbacks but it really is steep enough (even just pushing) on the road.

It is possible to hire someone in Chay who will take your panniers up the pass by donkey or horse, making Pang la much more bearable.

Pang la
There are a lot of magnificent sights for cyclists in Tibet but the view from Pang la is truly extraordinary. Spend a little bit of time on the pass if you have a clear day and just revel in the wonder of your world. It really is something else up there. There is another monument to Mt Everest (erected by the Chinese) and a sign that helps you to identify all the major peaks along the range.

From the top of the pass there is a brilliant downhill, for less than 20km, to the little village of **Tashi Dzom**, where you will get wonderful accommodation and food. The downhill is good fun but quite technical territory for mountain-bikers. The gravel is very fine and, in places, very deep. There is very little friction and the sharp switchbacks are built for skidding. Be a little sensible coming down here because there is a rather nasty drop to the right (once you get down the first bit) into a gorge and river. Also, trucks tend to come down pretty quickly too (although they chug up at a safer speed) so keep your wits about you.

Tashi Dzom
This place is fun. It is a little village spread across both sides of the road at a junction where the valley leads to Rongphu in one direction, and to a separate valley and the village of Kharta in the other. Its position makes this a busy little town with a surprising number of bars and restaurants – well two or three.

The best *accommodation* is the first guesthouse that you come to as you enter the town. There is a *restaurant* down below and the bedrooms upstairs. The toilet is a pretty spectacular hole in the back balcony from where you can look up to the magnificent Himalayas. Well worth the trip and extremely refreshing!

The cook from Rongphu monastery makes his way back down here in the winter season (from around mid-November), as his brother owns the restaurant in Tashi Dzom. If he is around, ask him to make you some pancakes – these are the most delicious thin crêpes: with a sprinkle of sugar and a squeeze of lemon they are absolutely divine. If he is not around, don't worry – the pancakes will be waiting for you at Rongphu!

Passum village
The next village towards Everest Base Camp is Passum. *Accommodation* is available here too and the town provides pretty spectacular views of Everest. This is the nice part of the trip: the long flat valley is warm, sunny and sheltered from the wind.

To get to Passum, head through the main street of Tashi Dzom and turn off to the right across the little bridge. Keep following that road; it will meander to and fro across a number of stream crossings and it is sometimes difficult to know where the best road is. This does get muddy when it rains. Stay on the right side of the river as far as Passum.

Even though there is food and accommodation in Passum, if you plan to head up to Rongphu the next day you are advised to keep going and spend the night near or in the next large village called Chosang.

The road between Passum and Chosang is not great and if it is warm it is likely to be flooded from melting snow. This is difficult cycling and if it were any further than

12km it would get frustrating. But it is worth persevering and if it is not wet, it is actually a very easy ride through here.

Chosang

Chosang is on the left of the river so you need to cross the huge concrete bridge (built for a Chinese expedition making an assault on Everest in the early 1990s) and from there it is plain-sailing. Head along the little road that runs across the right side of the village (effectively along the front) until you reach the school. The local teachers (a young woman and an even younger man) will let you stay in one of the unused classrooms. You will have an opportunity to eat with them and meet some of the students. These teachers are doing a great job with extremely limited resources.

The road from Chosang to Rongphu is uphill for 20km. It may not seem far but you are at an extremely high altitude here and the road conditions make it fairly hard going. It is possible to cycle right up, however, and this part of the ride is certainly easier than Pang la. The road follows a gorge where the mighty Rongphu glacier feeds the river – hence its unique green-blue colour that reflects the glacial minerals running through the gorge.

Rongphu monastery

The highest monastery in the world is a wild place. There are a lot of expeditions that pass through Rongphu monastery and the residents' perception of Westerners is shaped by the presence of these expedition groups. Frequently, the expedition groups will leave their sponsored equipment behind with the local residents (in the same way that climbers in Nepal give their used gear to their sherpas as a thank-you gift). If you come into Rongphu on a nice bike with trendy-looking equipment, don't be surprised if people ask for your boots, gloves, jacket, cooker and bike.

The monks here will help you out. Be a little patient and eventually you will find someone that will lead you to the *Monastery Guesthouse* which also contains a small restaurant.

The other delightful thing about the effect of Mt Everest expeditions is that there is a very well-stocked **shop** at Rongphu. There is delicious chocolate and cans of Kola for sale as well as pots of dried noodles (though it is wise to carry some supplies up as well).

Rongphu was once the largest monastic complex in the region and remains the site through which all pilgrims to the highest point on earth must pass. It is the sacred threshold to Mt Everest and has some of the most dramatic views in the world. An early British explorer described the view of Everest from here as follows:

Some colossal architect, who built with peaks and valleys, seemed here to have wrought a dramatic prodigy — a hall of grandeur that led to the mountain.

Mallory described the peak as 'a preposterous triangular lump' from this vantage point as it towers over the Rongphu glacier, which is shining white at the foot of the mountain.

Rongphu monastery is situated halfway up the 1.5km-wide and 30km long valley at 4825m. In earlier times, it took Mallory and Irvine some five weeks of trekking, starting from Darjeeling in India, to reach this site. Now it is accessible by jeep in a day or two.

Rongphu monastery was founded in 1902. For 400 years before that, nuns and hermits occupied meditation huts in the area. The remains of the hermitage meditation caves are dotted around the cliff walls that encompass the monastery, as well as right up the valley to Base Camp. There is an array of mani walls and stones, all of which are inscribed with sacred syllables and prayers.

At Rongphu, there is a beautiful, large, round chorten, with prayer flags fluttering in the breeze, framing the magnificent vista that is Mt Everest. The chorten has a ter-

❏ Who conquered Everest first?

It is an historic fact that New Zealander Sir Edmund Hillary and Nepalese sherpa Tenzin Norgay were the first men to ever reach the summit of Mt Everest, on 29 May 1953. Yet a dispute rages on that the British climber Mallory, who lost his life at the north face, beat Hillary to the summit almost 30 years earlier.

In 1924 a British expedition made an attempt on Mt Everest. Thirty-eight year-old George Leigh Mallory had been on two previous British expeditions to Everest in the 1920s. He was celebrated as one of Britain's most able rock climbers, and he had proven himself as a strong high-altitude climber on the Everest expeditions of 1921 and 1922. Andrew 'Sandy' Irvine, only 22 at the time, had no Himalayan or high-altitude climbing experience. But he was adept at repairing the controversial oxygen apparatus used by the British climbers at high elevations. The local Tibetans and Sherpas laughed at the strange bottles containing what they referred to as 'English Air'.

On 6 June 1924, Mallory and Irvine set off from the top of the North Col in the hope that they would reach the summit three days later. They passed Howard Somervell, who loaned his camera to Mallory. The last person to see the two was geologist Noel Odell, who was following the climbers to provide back-up, on 8 June. Odell was reported to have seen the two approach and climb a rock step, called the 'Second Step', on the mountain's skyline, 'nearing the base of the summit pyramid'. Odell reported that they seemed to be going strong and, although they were lower than he expected by that time, he felt sure they should make it to the summit.

Later, a storm blew over the mountain and Mallory and Irvine's tent was found with the gear hastily left as they departed for their summit bid. Neither man was seen alive again. An American expedition in May 1999 uncovered the body of Mallory but could not find the sought-after camera to prove that he had reached the summit in 1924. However, important artefacts were found – Mallory's wristwatch and altimeter and Irvine's ice axe.

In June 2001, historian Tom Holzel published a theory that the location of the axe and rust stains on Mallory's watch indicate the climbers only reached the 'First Step' before turning around and fatally falling on their descent. Further conjecture, based on rust marks also found on the altimeter, leads further support to this hypothesis. The general consensus of opinion is that Noel Odell must have seen the two climbers on the lower 'First Step'. Something Odell himself later admitted, albeit reluctantly.

In his autobiography, Sir Edmund Hillary recalled his thoughts from 1953 as he stood on the summit of Everest:

'The view to the north was a complete contrast – hundreds of miles of the arid Tibetan plateau. One scene was of particular interest. Almost under our feet it seemed, was the famous North Col and the East Rongbuk Glacier, where so many epic feats of courage and endurance were performed by the earlier British expeditions....It was a sobering thought to remember how often these men had reached 28,000 feet without the benefits of our modern equipment and reasonably efficient oxygen sets. Inevitably, my thoughts turned to Mallory and Irvine who had lost their lives on the mountain 30 years before. With little hope I looked around for some signs that they had reached the summit, but I could see nothing'.

From *View from the Summit*, Sir Edmund Hillary (1999).

raced structure and crown of emblems of the sun and moon, symbolizing the light of Buddha's teaching. Historically, Rongphu monastery was an active site for religious teachings and a place of special pilgrimage during annual mask-dancing ceremonies. Pilgrims came from neighbouring valleys for the annual event although it is now celebrated at the nearby Tengboche monastery. Rongphu's vast treasury of books and costumes had been taken for safekeeping to Tengboche but were tragically lost in a fire at the monastery in 1989.

Everest North Base Camp

It is a short 7km ride from Rongphu to Everest Base Camp. It is not the easiest ride in the world because it is very cold and very high but it is certainly worth the effort. If you get an early start, you will be able to leave your bike locked up at Base Camp and walk up to the base of Rongphu glacier. Just head across the shingle towards Everest and follow the narrow walking tracks on the left side of the terminus. These tracks eventually lead to the beginning of Rongphu glacier – a spectacular sight in itself – and even closer views of breathtaking Mt Everest.

Back to the Friendship Highway

It is a two-day ride back to the Friendship Highway, including the extremely challenging ascent back over Pang la. There is always the option that you hitch on a truck or with a tour group in a jeep back to the main road.

Alternatively, cyclists have tried to exit through the Ding valley, directly to Dingri. Be warned, this is a trekking route and you will end up carrying your bike a good deal of the way. You won't save any time with this shortcut.

Depending whether you get a ride out or not, you can either spend another night back in Tashi Dzom or Chay or head directly to Dingri. It is approximately four to five hours from the turn-off at Chay to Dingri by cycle.

Qinghai-Tibet Highway
(Xining to Golmud to Lhasa)

With assistance from Coen Koomen

Make voyages. Attempt them. That's all there is.
Elaine Dundy

INTRODUCTION

The only official overland route open for independent travellers between China and Tibet is the Qinghai-Tibet Highway, which stretches for around 1969km from Xining to Lhasa via Golmud (Kermo in Tibetan).

The road is monotonous and mainly uninhabited throughout Qinghai province especially the Tsaidam desert and Yangtse basin areas. Most overlanders take the train from Xining to Golmud then catch an overnight bus to Lhasa as quickly as possible.

Golmud has been described (fairly accurately) as a very boring town and the bus ride from Golmud to Lhasa, reaching an altitude over 5100m, has been described (also fairly accurately) as one of the worst bus rides in the world.

In Qinghai province there is minimal annual precipitation but the winter is bitterly cold. The optimum period for overland travel is between June and September.

Although the Qinghai-Tibet Highway sounds rather bleak and uninspiring, given the continuing visa/permit regulation changes that occur on the other Tibetan overland routes, travelling into Lhasa from Golmud is still the only 'guaranteed' overland route into Tibet for independent travellers, albeit from the most isolated starting point.

Qinghai-Tibet Highway

HIGHLIGHTS
Lake Kokonor: largest salt water lake in China, rare bird sanctuary
Tsaidam desert: vast arid, salt plains in Qinghai province
Kumbum/Ta'er Si monastery: birthplace of Je Tsongkhapa, near Xining
East Changtang region: high-altitude nomadic terrain, experience 'old Tibet' lifestyle
Nam Tso Lake: 'Sky Lake', stunning, high-altitude vistas

ROUTE INFORMATION

	DISTANCE	DRIVING TIME*	CYCLING TIME*	NO OF MAIN PASSES	HIGHEST PASS
Xining to Golmud	780km	1-2 days	8-10 days	2	3600m
Golmud to Amdo	710km	1-2 days	8-10 days	5	5160m
Amdo to Damshung	308km	½ day	3-4days	2	4880m
Damshung to Lhasa	171km	½ day	2 days	1	4590m
Xining to Lhasa	1969km	3-5 days	21-25 days	10	5160m

* ESTIMATES ONLY – DO NOT INCLUDE STOPS FOR RESTS/SIGHTSEEING OR SEVERE WEATHER

CHECKPOINTS
30km south of Golmud
Amdo – occasional checkpoint (driver licence checks) on edge of town
Nakchu – north side of town
Yangpachen – south edge of town (frequently not in operation)

Golmud is a large city in the Qinghai Province situated directly north of Lhasa. It is a lengthy journey to get to Golmud from any direction. If you commenced your journey in Hong Kong or Beijing, you may travel by air or rail to the nearest gateway cites of Lanzhou and Xining then on to Golmud. If you do approach Golmud from Hong Kong or Beijing, chances are that you will spend at least one night in Lanzhou and/or Xining.

For travellers who enter China from Pakistan or Uzbekistan, the most reliable overland option to reach Lhasa is to travel by bus to Kashgar then by train to Urumqi and Golmud (as opposed to trying to enter Tibet from Kashgar, via Ali and Kailash). The Urumqi option has an established transport infrastructure which will get you there, albeit slowly.

Cyclists

Very few cyclists attempt the 13- to 16-day cycle ride from Golmud to Lhasa (and even fewer try the 21-to 25-day cycle from Xining to Lhasa). Water and food is scarce as there are very few towns scattered along the main route and most cyclists tie their bicycles onto the roof of the overnight buses and commence their Tibetan cycling adventure when they finally reach Lhasa. However, the East Changtang region between Amdo and Nakchu is a spectacular, high-altitude terrain where you can glimpse the 'old Tibet' lifestyles and camp amongst the nomads.

Hitching

I have met hitchhikers who have successfully avoided the CITS in Golmud and made it to Lhasa on the back of trucks and others who have tried similar feats only to have paid horrendous backhanders en route either to their drivers or PSB officers. As the terrain is so barren and the evenings are freezing, simply refusing to pay more and getting off the truck is not a recommended strategy for hitchhikers.

LANZHOU

Lanzhou is the capital of Gansu province and is located on the old Silk Road. There isn't much reason to hang about in Lanzhou if you are trying to get to Tibet except for a visit to Labrang monastery in Xiahe.

Getting to Lanzhou

There are daily **trains** from many main cities including Beijing, Shanghai, Xian, Chengdu, Guangzhou, and Urumqi.

There are **flights** from Beijing (two daily, 2hr); Guangzhou (one daily, 2hr 10min) and Shenzhen (three a week, Wed/Fri/Sat, 2hr 30min). Lanzhou Airport is 78km from Lanzhou and the bus ride into town will take approximately 90 minutes. Unfortunately, the bus is not big enough to take bikes so you will need to negotiate a taxi instead.

Note: all foreigners are required to purchase 'travel insurance' for all bus journeys in Gansu province.

Accommodation

Accommodation at Lanzhou is varied but a clean, reasonably secure and inexpensive option is *Lanzhou Fandian Hotel* (located on a large roundabout directly north of the railway station).

Excursion to Xiahe – Labrang monastery

Labrang, a major Gelug monastery, is in Xiahe near Lanzhou. You will be able to make a day-trip by minibus (7hr each way) from Lanzhou or spend a few nights there (buses for Xiahe depart daily from Lanzhou 'West' Bus Station).

From Lanzhou (to Xining)

From Lanzhou you can catch a train or bus to Xining and then on to Golmud. The train is best and tickets can be bought at the station. The **train** from Lanzhou to Xining takes four hours; it is possible to connect on the same day in Xining with the onward evening train to Golmud.

Transporting bikes on Chinese trains Bikes will usually be transported in a different carriage to you and, often, on a different train altogether. It may take a while for your bike to catch up with you in Xining if it is on a different train, depending on the length of journey and route. We met a French guy who checked his bike in at Beijing to go through to Golmud and it finally arrived one week after he did!

With a bit of determination, you should be able to carry your bike onto the train with you from Lanzhou to at least as far as Xining. Then it is reasonably certain that your bike will be put on the same train you board to Golmud (being the terminal destination), meaning you can collect it from Golmud Station baggage area when you arrive.

XINING

Xining (in Tibetan Sulang) is the capital of Qinghai Province and is considered by most overlanders to be the entry point for the Tibetan Plateau.

If you decide to stay in Xining, you will have the opportunity to visit the beautiful Ta'er Si monastery (in Tibetan Kumbum) or the village of Taktser, the birthplace of the current 14th Dalai Lama (located about 50km south-west of Xining).

The final leg of the trip to Golmud is the bus or train trip from Xining to Golmud. The train is overnight and reasonably comfortable. You will ascend approximately 1000m but will probably not notice a lot of difference.

Getting to Xining

Trains There are a number of daily trains from the main cities including Beijing, Shanghai, Xian and Lanzhou.

Flights Xining is connected to most main cities (but not Shenzhen) via various airlines: **Beijing** (daily flights, 2hr); **Guangzhou** (Xijiang Airways Tue/Sat, 3hr); **Chengdu** (China Southwest Airlines Tue/Fri/Sun, 2hr 30min); **Shanghai** (Shanghai Airlines Tue/Sat, 3hr 30min). Xining Airport is about 25km south-east of the city.

Accommodation

Clean accommodation is a short bus/taxi trip from the train station at *Xining Binguan (Hotel)*. The reception is in building No. 2.

You Zheng Gong Yu is an inexpensive hotel much nearer to the train station a few minutes' walking distance (even with luggage). It is located immediately opposite the China Travel Service – turn left as you come out of the station.

Excursion to Ta'er Si (in Tibetan Kumbum)

Huangzhong village is about 27km south-east of Xining and is renowned as the birthplace of Je Tsongkhapa (founder of the Gelug order) and site of the Ta'er Si (Kumbum) monastery built in 1577. Kumbum is one of the 'six greatest Gelug monasteries' (along with Labrang, Ganden, Sera, Drepung and Tashilhunpo monasteries).

Ta'er Si monastery is a short bus trip out of Xining. The one-hour ride departs next to the Xining Sports Arena (Xining Tiyuguan). Most tourists visit the monastery on a day trip but there are a number of **dormitory hotels** available in the monastery itself for overnight visitors.

Leaving Xining

There are daily overnight buses/trains leaving Xining for Golmud.

By bus Buses leave from Xining Station or the long-distance bus terminal (located opposite the train station on the other side of the river).

No 781 – departs daily at 16:00, arrives 12:00 the next morning.

You are also likely to be offered a 'discount' ride on a sleeper bus direct to Lhasa; it will take at least 48 hours. Unfortunately you will not have a permit and may encounter problems during the ride from either the PSB or the bus driver!

By train No 603 – departs alternate days at 18:30, arrives 12:00 the next day; No 759 – departs alternate days at 08:18, arrives 07:56 the next day.

If you travel by train, which is certainly the most comfortable option, you will need to check in at the baggage transport section at the station with your onward ticket and bicycle. As there is only one route from Xining to Golmud, your bike should travel that leg with you and arrive at the same time as you. It will, however, be in a different part of the train.

We had no difficulty in getting our bikes to Golmud – it was trying to get them off the station manager at the other end that created some stress. He tried to insist that we pay him some money before he would return our bikes and did the same with other tourists who had checked in large items of luggage.

Xining/Lhasa by air In 2000 a twice-weekly direct flight opened from Xining to Lhasa, costing approximately US$250 – similar to the bus fare from Golmud to Lhasa, and the flight is a lot more comfortable. You still have to purchase tickets/permits via CITS and form a 'tour' of five or more people. Check current timetable and restriction details when you arrive in Xining.

XINING TO GOLMUD

Golmud is situated approximately 780km due west of Xining. Leaving Xining the journey commences with a long climb up to Nyima la pass (3400m), the entrance to the Tibetan plateau, where there are two small shrines.

The area from here until Golmud remains one of China's poorest. The landscape is a great plain consisting mainly of arid desert littered with salt marshes and saline lakes.

Lying approximately 150km west of Xining is the largest salt lake in China – Kokonor (in Chinese Qinghai Hu, in Tibetan Nying Tso – meaning 'Blue Lake'). The western edge of the lake is renowned for its bird sanctuary, which is a breeding ground for thousands of wild birds including the rare black-necked cranes (breeding season is March-June).

Once past Kokonor the somewhat monotonous route towards Golmud is basically uninhabited and water and food stops are few and far between. The plateau basin is dominated by strong easterly winds on flat stony terrain. The final section of the route includes huge salt flats and the last 300km of road is in a very poor state (with large parts under construction).

ROUTE GUIDE – XINING to GOLMUD

DISTANCE (KM)	ALTIMETER READING (M)	NOTES AND KEY POINTS OF INTEREST
0	2200	Xining (*Tibetan* Siling) ▮ ⟙ ↵
		(Ta'er Si 'Kumbum' monastery nearby)
53	2400	Tongkor/Huangyuan
		(turn south, then commence climb to pass)
103	3400	Nyima Dawa la (in Chinese Riyue Shan)
106	3100	Small town ▮ ⟙ *(turn west to reach Lake Kokonor)*
150	3050	Edge of Lake Kokonor (in Chinese Qinghai Hu) ▮ ⟙ ↵
		(excellent flat road along southern edge of lake for next 75km)
223	3000	Tanakma (in Chinese Heimahe) ▮ ⟙ ↵
		(road leaves lake and after 10km starts climb up pass)
245	3600	Pass
300	2950	Tsaka (in Chinese Chaka) ▮ ⟙
		(start of 135km of desolate terrain – stock up on supplies!)
335	2500	Low point
375	3460	Minor pass
432	3050	Dulan ▮ ⟙ ↵
		(minor pass 25km out of Dulan, then on to the desert basin)
495	2850	Redezhen ▮ ⟙
534	2750	Balang
585	3000	Town is located 5km off to the right
630	2750	Nomahung (Neolithic ruins) ▮ ⟙
780	2700	Golmud (in Tibetan Kermo) ▮ ⟙ ↵

Notes: ▮ = Food, ⟙ = Water, ↵ = Accommodation available

GOLMUD

Golmud (pronounced *Ger-moo*), which lies on the southern edge of the Tsaidam desert, gets a bad rap from most visitors as being depressing and forlorn. It is certainly an isolated place for anyone to visit but it is still the only 'guaranteed' entry town for independent travellers trying to journey overland into Tibet.

There isn't really anything to see in Golmud and most travellers won't spend any more time than they require to get a permit and bus ticket on to Lhasa.

Accommodation

Accommodation for foreigners is limited to ***Golmud Hotel***. Fortunately, it is relatively clean and inexpensive – but the price comes with a catch. The CITS is situated in Golmud Hotel and will police your every move from the moment you check in with them. In the event that you wish to cycle from Golmud to Lhasa, do not register with the CITS in the hotel – despite the signs demanding that you do so.

From Golmud (to Lhasa)

By bus The 'official' overland mode of travel from Golmud to Lhasa is by overnight bus. The options are sleeper or non-sleeper and the bus journey is at least 36 hours – but often much longer depending on the number of breakdowns.

The bus station staff (found in the room marked Xizhang, Lhasa Yunshu Gongci) will require that you first register with the CITS at the Golmud Hotel. CITS will require that you pay them a large amount of money, which covers the cost of: a return sleeper bus ticket, insurance, a permit, and a three-day Lhasa tour. The CITS staff will arrange for your permit and you will be collected from Golmud Hotel and taken to the bus station.

It is difficult, although not impossible, to avoid this red tape. Some travellers, usually those who speak some Chinese or at least look Asian, have been able to purchase bus tickets directly from the bus station staff at a discount rate. The bus station staff, unlike CITS employees, are cordial and willing to assist you in your journey. However, bureaucracy does hamper their desire to help.

The overnight sleeper bus from Golmud to Lhasa will cost around US$200 per person. There are also a number of private bus operators who will offer you '30-50%' tickets (which includes a bribe for PSB officers en route). Travellers have had mixed success with private operators.

It is a long and difficult journey from Golmud to Lhasa by bus. Take plenty of water and food. The bus will stop for food and toilet stops (frequent stops for the latter as the diuretic effect of acclimatization is compelling) but the journey is generally uncomfortable. Leaving Golmud, at 2700m, the road crosses several passes over 5000m and you will definitely experience the effects of altitude. Take it easy: sleep passes the time (try to keep your head higher than your feet!) and drink plenty of water. Make sure you carry your sleeping bag with you on the bus as it is extremely cold at night – whenever the bus stops at night the drivers continuously run the engine to stop the fuel freezing.

● **Checkpoints** There are two main checkpoints between Golmud and Lhasa. The first is 30km south of Golmud (road marker 2772km). The second is on the north side of Nakchu. There are also occasional checkpoints at Amdo and Yangpachen.

By train The TAR is the only provincial-level region which does not have a railway link to the 'rest of China'. There are regular announcements by the Chinese State Railway Ministry about proposed plans to build a 1110km Qinghai-Tibet Railway from Golmud to Lhasa, which would include 31km of tunnels. The more recent plans claim the final section of tracks will be completed by 2005.

Given the harsh climate and the constant state of disrepair on the roads, it is difficult to imagine such a railway ever operating successfully – although no doubt the project will continue to proceed.

Cycling to Lhasa from the Qinghai area It is a 13-to 16-day cycle from Golmud to Lhasa – with several high passes over 5000m. The scenery is desolate on the Qinghai section but spectacular once you reach the TAR. Only a few cyclists have ever ridden all the way from Xining to Lhasa (via Golmud) taking approximately 21-25 days.

GOLMUD TO LHASA

Golmud to Tanggu la

The Qinghai-Tibet Highway leads south-west out of Golmud. After 30km the road passes through a particularly vigilant checkpoint near road marker 2772km. After the checkpoint the road starts to ascend a large gorge reaching the truckstop town of Dronglung (meaning 'Wild Yak' valley) at around 3580m. The road continues to climb a further 70km to the East Kunlun Shankou la at 4772m, where the snow-capped mountain Yuxu (5933m) is visible to the west. It is only a slight descent into the

Yangtse basin, an endless, undulating plateau surrounded by the East Kunlun mountain range. The desolate region, containing a number of small isolated lakes, is characterized by strong dry winds and low temperatures. Occasionally gazelle have been spotted beside the road.

Tuotuohe, known for the first bridge over the Yangtse, is the first main town along the route located 425km south of Golmud. It is then a further barren 120km to Wenquan, purportedly the 'highest town in the world' at 5100m. The town is actually lower than this and barely qualifies as a town with just a few concrete barracks and houses.

The Qinghai-Tibet Highway finally crosses the TAR/Qinghai border at Tanggu la pass (5136m) around 622km south of Golmud and 567km north of Lhasa.

Tanggu la to Lhasa

After crossing the Tanggu la pass it is around 88km to the crossroads town of Amdo at an altitude of 4625m. At Amdo there is a westerly route across the inhospitable Changtang Plateau towards Ali, over 1330km away. Only the occasional adventurous tour group and a few trucks traverse this lonely route famed for its wildlife and isolated lakes.

ROUTE GUIDE – GOLMUD to TANGGU LA

DISTANCE (KM)	ALTIMETER READING (M)	NOTES AND KEY POINTS OF INTEREST
0	2700	Golmud (in Tibetan Kermo) 🍴 Y ⌁ *(780km ex Xining)*
30	3130	Checkpoint – guarded 24hr, all vehicles/permits checked! (road marker 2772km)
60	3360	Shunitan 🍴 Y ⌁
87	3580	Dronglung/Nachitai 🍴 Y
127	4080	Xidatan 🍴 Y ⌁
160	4772	East Kunlun Shankou la *(Mt Yuxu 5933m can be seen to the west)*
181	4540	Budongquan 🍴 Y
215	4450	'Green River Environment Centre' 🍴 Y
245	4540	Wudao bridge
273	4560	Wudao Liang 🍴 Y ⌁ *(very cosy restaurant near town entrance)*
286	4685	Minor pass
310	4600	Low point
330	4650	Beilutte 🍴 Y
345	4910	Fenghuo la
360	4700	Erdao Gu 🍴 Y ⌁
368	4565	Low point
400	4600	Minor pass
425	4525	Tuotuohe (in Tibetan Mar-chu Dram) 🍴 Y ⌁
		(first bridge over the Yangtse River just to the north of town)
445	4710	Minor pass
470	4540	Tongtianhe
520	4675	Yanshiping 🍴 Y ⌁
545	4735	Wenquan (in Tibetan Toma) 🍴 Y ⌁
		(purportedly the 'highest town in the world' at 5100m)
603	4955	Town *(undulating road up to pass)*
622	5160	Tanggu la/Dang la
		Notes: 🍴 = Food, Y = Water, ⌁ = Accommodation available

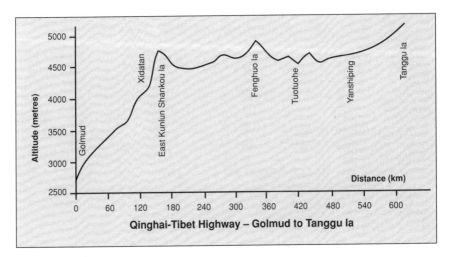

Qinghai-Tibet Highway – Golmud to Tanggu la

The main highway continues south through nomadic countryside for another 140km to another important junction town at Nakchu. This large town has grown dramatically in the last five years due to its strategic location on the Qinghai-Tibet Highway for both Tibetans (as a trading centre) and Chinese (as a military provisions station).

Many trucks travelling to Chamdo from Lhasa will travel via Nakchu. The condition of the 700km easterly road between Nakchu and Chamdo is more reliable for heavier vehicles than the more known southern route via Bayi.

The sealed Qinghai-Tibet Highway continues south out of Nakchu for another 168km to Damshung where there is the opportunity to turn-off the main road for explorations in the Nam Tso region. From Damshung it is another 77km to the hot springs near Yangpachen and a final 87km descent into Lhasa (see pp70-80 for more detailed route guides and other information relating to the roads from Damshung to Lhasa or Damshung to Nam Tso).

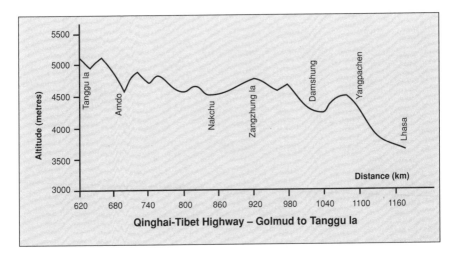

Qinghai-Tibet Highway – Golmud to Tanggu la

ROUTE GUIDE – TANGGU LA to LHASA

DISTANCE (KM)	ALTIMETER READING (M)	NOTES AND KEY POINTS OF INTEREST
622km ex Golmud	5130	Tanggu la/Dang la
645	4915	Low point
663	5110	Touerjiushan la
705	4680	Checkpoint before Amdo – driver licence checks
710	4625	Amdo ⦿ Y ↩
725	4880	Minor pass
753	4630	Low point
772	4815	Minor pass
810	4525	Ziri/Tsaring
850	4475	Nakchu, junction – south to Lhasa, east to Chamdo ⦿ Y ↩ *(severe checkpoint north side of town)*
877	4525	Lomar *(nice colourful town but no food available!)*
930	4750	Zangzhung la
945	4680	Koluk ⦿ Y ↩
960	4545	Low point
976	4660	Kyogche la
987	4490	Horru ⦿ Y ↩
1008	4290	Natung Kamu
1018	4260	Damshung, turn-off for Nam Tso ⦿ Y ↩ *(see pp78-80 for route)*
1069	4590	Gyama la
1096	4260	Yangpachen ⦿ Y ↩
1144	3700	Tsurphu monastery turn-off – 28km up valley over river
1177	3650	'Welcome to Lhasa' sign – entrance to Lhasa City
1189	3600	Lhasa – Barkhor Square ⦿ Y ↩ *(see p70 for Damshung to Lhasa route)*

Notes: ⦿ = Food, Y = Water, ↩ = Accommodation available

Sichuan-/Yunnan-Tibet Highways

Travel has a way of stretching the mind. The stretch comes not from travel's immediate rewards, the inevitable myriad new sights, smells and sounds, but with experiencing firsthand how others do differently what we believed to be the right and only way.
Ralph Crawshaw

INTRODUCTION

All the routes along the Yunnan-Tibet and Sichuan-Tibet highways are closed to individual travellers but a handful of cyclists and hitchhikers manage to reach Lhasa each year.

Chengdu and Kunming are the principal staging towns for overland travel into eastern Tibet. Both are accessible by air/train from other main Chinese cities including Beijing, Xian, Shenzhen, Guangzhou and Hong Kong. International flights exist into Kunming from Bangkok, Singapore, Osaka and Kuala Lumpur and into Chengdu from Bangkok and Singapore.

From both Chengdu and Kunming it is possible to reach the present-day China/TAR border utilizing public transport. Thereafter keen overlanders tend to pass the main checkpoints during the darkness of night but face the possibility of fines and being turned back at any village or hotel they stay in. There have even been reports of PSB officers on motorcycles stopping cyclists!

There is very little public transport west of Batang and truck drivers face heavy fines for carrying foreigners. However, food and accommodation is more widely available along the way than in most other parts of Tibet.

Sichuan-Tibet Highway

The Sichuan-Tibet Highway links Chengdu to Lhasa. The road is officially open as far west as Batang or Derge and public buses are available from Chengdu to Kangding. Past Kangding the road splits – the longer 250km north branch goes via Derge to Chamdo and the south branch goes through Litang and Markham. Both branches merge again near Pomda and then continue west to Lhasa past the mountain Namche Barwa (7756m) and Bayi township.

From Chamdo there is a rarely travelled 1057km overland route to Lhasa heading due west via Nakchu. This route is used by heavy vehicles and can be more reliable than the main Sichuan-Tibet Highway in the rainy season. The first 700km section out of Chamdo crosses five major passes (all over 4700m) before joining the Qinghai-Tibet Highway at Nakchu.

Yunnan-Tibet Highway

The Yunnan-Tibet Highway joins Kunming to Lhasa. The last open town along the Yunnan-Tibet Highway is Zhongdian although some overlanders have reported getting permits as far as Dechen. Both Dali and Zhongdian can be easily reached by public bus from Kunming.

The overland route from Dali is spectacular and passes the scenic towns of Lijiang and Zhongdian. The route joins the main Sichuan-Tibet Highway near Markham.

Sichuan-/Yunnan-Tibet Highways

HIGHLIGHTS

Chengdu or Dali to Lhasa: exciting transition from China to Tibet, challenging and sometimes thrilling road conditions
Chengdu: home of Sichuan cuisine and giant pandas
Lijiang/Zhongdian road: scenic route in Yunnan province, close to Tiger Leaping Gorge
Mt Namche Barwa: views of the spectacular 'world's highest unclimbed mountain'
Tongme; low-lying rainforest settlement
Ganden monastery: founded by Tsongkhapa, first of the great Gelug monasteries

ROUTE INFORMATION – SICHUAN-TIBET HIGHWAY

SOUTHERN ROUTE	DISTANCE	DRIVING TIME*	CYCLING TIME*
Chengdu-Litang-Pomda-Bayi-Lhasa	2160km	7-10 days	35-45 days
NORTHERN ROUTE			
Chengdu-Karze-Chamdo-Pomda-Bayi-Lhasa	2427km	8-12 days	45-55 days
CHAMDO-NAKCHU ROUTE			
Chengdu-Karze-Chamdo-Nakchu-Lhasa	2350km	8-12 days	42-50 days

*ESTIMATES ONLY – DO NOT INCLUDE STOPS FOR RESTS/SIGHTSEEING OR SEVERE WEATHER

ROUTE INFORMATION – YUNNAN-TIBET HIGHWAY

YUNNAN-TIBET ROUTE	DISTANCE	DRIVING TIME*	CYCLING TIME*
Kunming-Dali-Markham-Pomda-Bayi-Lhasa	2401km	8-12 days	35-40 days (ex Dali)

*ESTIMATES ONLY – DO NOT INCLUDE STOPS FOR RESTS/SIGHTSEEING OR SEVERE WEATHER

CHECKPOINTS

Checkpoints/PSB along Sichuan-Tibet Highway south route (Chengdu to Lhasa)

Kangding – checkpoint west edge of town
Nyangchu – guarded bridge before town
PSB present at Litang
PSB present at Batang
TAR/Sichuan border – possible checkpoint on Druparong bridge, 32km past Batang
Markham – checkpoint on east side of town, heavy PSB presence
Pome – checkpoint
Bayi – checkpoint and notorious PSB presence
Minor checkpoint – 5km before Lhasa

Additional checkpoints along Yunnan-Tibet Highway (Dali to Markham)

Dechen – possible checkpoint on south side of town
Yanjiang – checkpoint south of town, 12km after TAR/Yunnan border

SUGGESTED ITINERARY – SICHUAN-TIBET HIGHWAY

SOUTHERN ROUTE	DISTANCE	DRIVING TIME*	CYCLING TIME*	NO OF MAIN PASSES	HIGHEST PASS
Chengdu to Kangding	362km	1-2 days	6-8 days	1	2900m
Kangding to Litang	276km	1 day	4-6 days	3	4320m
Litang to Markham	299km	1 day	5-7 days	2	4675m
Markham to Pomda junction	277km	1-2 days	4-6 days	3	5020m
Pomda junction to Pome	311km	1-2 days	5-7 days	2	4618m
Pome to Bayi	233km	1 day	4-5 days	1	4515m
Bayi to Lhasa	408km	1-2 days	6-8 days	1	5000m
Chengdu to Lhasa	**2166km**	**7-10 days**	**35-45 days**	**13**	**5020m**

*ESTIMATES ONLY – DO NOT INCLUDE STOPS FOR RESTS/SIGHTSEEING OR SEVERE WEATHER

CYCLING/BY BUS/HITCHING

There are plenty of buses available to independent travellers throughout the Sichuan and Yunnan provinces and also some inside the TAR. The main routes pass through the most prosperous, and therefore populated, sections of Tibet with plenty of food and water available.

Chengdu to Lhasa is 2166km via Markham (south route) and 2416km via Chamdo (north route). The more direct south route crosses seven passes over 4200m and will take seven to ten days hitching/busing or 35-45 days cycling. There are numerous checkpoints including the particularly notorious ones at Markham and Bayi.

Dali to Markham is around 785km and it is a further 1229km from Markham to Lhasa. If you are lucky you could hitch to Lhasa in under a week but it will take 35-40 days to cycle from Dali to Lhasa.

ROUTE OPTIONS

To reach Lhasa from Sichuan or Yunnan provinces there are four principal overland routes: three from Chengdu (two via Chamdo, one via Markham), and one from Kunming (via Dali and Markham).

Most independent travellers that do attempt to reach Lhasa overland chose the more direct Sichuan-Tibet Highway 'southern' route and a few, more recently, the Yunnan-Tibet Highway. The longer routes via Chamdo are primarily only traversed during the wet season (June-September) when the roads are more reliable than the southern routes.

This section describes in detail the Sichuan-Tibet Highway 'southern route' from Chengdu to Lhasa and briefly describes the 'northern route' as well as the section of the Yunnan-Tibet Highway from Dali to Markham.

CHENGDU

A former capital of China and famous for its spicy Sichuan cuisine, Chengdu is the capital of Sichuan Province. Chengdu is also a popular starting point for entry into Tibet, usually by air but occasionally overland by the odd ambitious traveller.

Getting to Chengdu

With a population of around ten million, Chengdu is well connected to other Chinese cities by air and train.

By air There are daily flights from Beijing, Kunming, Lanzhou, Chongqing, Xian, Shanghai, Guangzhou, Lhasa, and Hong Kong. There are also a couple of international flights each week from Bangkok (Thailand) and Singapore. Shuangliu airport is 18km west of Chengdu.

By train Daily trains run to Chengdu from Beijing, Shanghai, Chongqing, Xian, Guanzhou, Kunming and other main centres.

Accommodation

The most popular accommodation and general hangout for backpackers is still the *Traffic Hotel* (77 Linjiang Road), which is clean and comfortable. To get to the Traffic Hotel, take bus No 16 from the North Train Station.

Giant Panda Breeding Research Centre (Daxiongmao Fanzhi Yanjiu Zhongxin)

While waiting for tickets and permits to be finalized a worthwhile excursion is a visit (taxi or cycle) to the Giant Panda Research Centre located about 12km north-west of Chengdu (past the Zoo). There are about a dozen pandas on view and the best time to arrive is during feeding time (08:00-10:00).

Heading to Tibet

Many travellers arrive in Chengdu for the sole purpose of booking a flight on to Lhasa. If you are patient, obtaining a ticket is not too difficult.

By air to Lhasa Flights to Lhasa depart twice daily (at 06:55 and 11:20) and take 1hr 50min. The fare (around US$250 one-way/US$450 return) includes permit (approximately US$85), airport transfer and 'three-day tour'. Peak months are July and August.

● **Booking a flight** You must book your flight from one of the travel agents in the lobby of the Traffic Hotel (the China Southwest Airlines office will not sell air tickets for Lhasa to individuals). The agent will arrange your ticket and permit by including you in a temporary five-person 'tour party'. It will take a day or two to arrange all the paperwork.

● **Flying with a bicycle** There are mixed reports about the difficulties of flying bicycles into Tibet. Most people (exercising a little patience) have no problem. Officially there are no regulations against carrying bikes and no extra baggage fees (although some agents will try to charge extra). It appears optional whether your bike needs to be boxed, but it would be wise to protect your bike during transit as on any longhaul flight.

By bus For those intending to travel overland into Tibet, the first step is to catch a long-distance bus, which depart daily from the South Bus Station (outside the Traffic Hotel) for Kangding (Dartsedo). The price is about Y100 for the 8- to 9-hour journey (you will be required to purchase travel insurance). Once in Kangding you should be able to purchase onward tickets further west to Batang or northward to Derge (en route to Chamdo).

There are actually long-distance sleeper buses that go as far as Chamdo and even Lhasa but foreigners have traditionally been prohibited from purchasing tickets on these routes.

SICHUAN-TIBET HIGHWAY (SOUTHERN ROUTE) – CHENGDU TO LHASA

Chengdu to Batang and Pomda Junction

To Tibet border The most direct route into Tibet from Chengdu is via Ya'an and over Mt Erlang Shan crossing to the traditional border between China and Tibet at the Luding Bridge.

The recently opened tunnel under Mt Erlang Shan (turn-off to the tunnel between road markers 2752km and 2753km) makes the journey easier and more manageable. The cycle ride up to the summit of Erlang Shan is as tough as any climb in Tibet. The road is subject to landslides and provides a true introduction into what mountain biking across Tibet entails. On a clear day from Khakha Buddha la pass there is an excellent view of Mt Minyak Gangkar (7556m), the highest mountain in Asia east of the Himalayas.

Once past the old wooden suspension bridge at Luding it is a further 50km to Kangding (in Tibetan Dartsedo) an old tea trading centre and the gateway to the

ROUTE GUIDE – CHENGDU to POMDA (SOUTHERN ROUTE)

DISTANCE (KM)	ALTIMETER READING (M)	NOTES AND KEY POINTS OF INTEREST
0	500	Chengdu 📷 ⛨ ⌇
149		Ya'an 📷 ⛨ ⌇
		(road markers – old 2632km/new 146)
252		Turn-off for new tunnel under Mt Erlang Shan at road marker 2735km
269	2900	Khakha Buddha la (in Chinese Erlang Shan, in Tibetan Yarla Namtse)
		(tunnel recently opened avoids pass)
313	1330	Luding (traditional Tibet/China border) 📷 ⛨ ⌇
		(suspension bridge built in 1706)
362	2580	Kangding (in Tibetan Dartsedo) 📷 ⛨ ⌇
		(checkpoint on west edge of town, buses possible from Chengdu)
395	4290	Gye la/Sheduo la *(Yalong/Gyarang watershed)*
429		Minyak Chakdra chorten *(turn-off to the Mt Minyak Gangkar 7556m)*
437	3500	Dzongzhab/Ranaka (in Chinese Xinduqao) 📷 ⛨
441		Major turn-off – road markers missing 2924km/446km
		(head north to Chamdo 852km away, west to Litang)
457	4100	Kabzhi la
513	2700	Nyangchu/Yajiang 📷 ⛨ ⌇ *(guarded bridge over Yalong – before town)*
4320		Lama la *(pass before Li/Yalong watershed)*
579		Nub Golok
638	4000	Litang 📷 ⛨ ⌇ *(PSB present)*
718		Ronko
748	4675	Haizishan la *(Batang/Li watershed)*
791		Taksho
833	2670	Batang 📷 ⛨ ⌇ *(PSB present)*
865		Druparong Zampa – bridge over Yangtse
		(TAR/Sichuan border – checkpoint at bridge, checking trucks)
937	3900	Markham (in Tibetan Gartok) – checkpoint on east side of town 📷 ⛨ ⌇
		(main intersection – continue west to Lhasa, 760km south to Dali)
952	4360	Lao-shan la
		Rongme 📷 ⛨
1002	2700	Druka Zampa *(bridge over Mekong)*
1022	3900	Joba la *(there is a low point at 3600m – 10km after the pass)*
1067	5020	Dungda la
1107	3780	Tsawa Dzogang (in Chinese Zogong) 📷 ⛨ ⌇
1150		Temtho
1214	4050	Pomda (in Chinese Bangda) junction – major intersection 📷 ⛨
		(continue west to Lhasa, north to Chamdo 184km away)

Notes: 📷 = Food, ⛨ = Water, ⌇ = Accommodation available

Minyak Gangkar region. Public buses run daily from Kanding to Karze and Litang/Batang. A further 33km west of Kangding is Gye la, the first time you rise above 4000m.

The next village to stock up in is Dzongzhab (in Chinese Xinduqao) which is 4km before the main intersection on the Sichuan-Tibet Highway, where the direct southern route continues west to Lhasa via Litang and the longer route heads north towards Chamdo.

Litang to Batang Litang is 200km west of Dzongzhab and lies at an altitude of 4000m. It is a good place to stock up on warm clothing.

From Litang there is a daily bus to Batang which takes about 6 hours and crosses the Haizishan la (4675m) before descending into the low-lying Batang valley.

Batang is 195km from Litang and is situated 32km before the TAR/Sichuan border (a bridge over the Yangtse). The PSB in Batang (and at a checkpoint on the border bridge) have been known to fine and return travellers to Chengdu.

Batang to Markham After leaving the one-street town of Batang you cross the TAR/Sichuan border and climb steeply to over 4100m before descending quickly into Markham.

Markham is where the Yunnan-Tibet Highway joins the Sichuan-Tibet Highway; the PSB have a particularly strict reputation here. If caught you will likely face a hefty fine and expulsion (by bus) back to Chengdu. The checkpoint is located on the east side of town.

From Markham the Yunnan-Tibet Highway leads south to Dali approximately 785km away.

Markham to Pomda junction From the prosperous Markham valley ascend to Laoshan la (4360m) and then gradually descend to Druka bridge over the Mekong. From the bridge there is a long series of switchbacks up a sandstone gorge to Joba la (3900m) and then over the first 5000m pass at Dungda la (5020m).

From Dungda la, where you have excellent views of the mountain Dungri Karpo (6090m), descend to Tsawa Dzogong (in Chinese Zogong) overlooking the river Ya chu.

After Tsawa Dzogong continue down a forested gorge until the Ya chu valley widens and you reach the small collection of buildings at the Pomda intersection (which is actually 6km south of Pomda).

The northern branch of the Sichuan-Tibet Highway joins the southern branch at Pomda junction which is around 1214km west of Chengdu, and still a further 952km east to Lhasa.

Pomda junction to Pome

From Pomda junction ascend gradually from the Ya chu valley to the Gama la (4618m) and then descend steeply on over 70 switchbacks to the Po bridge situated at the confluence of Salween and Ling chu.

Continue uphill from Po to Pema (in Chinese Baxoi) and then ascend out of the barren Ling chu valley for 67km to Ngajuk la (4468m) – the watershed between the Parlung Tsangpo and Salween river.

Descend for 23km to Rawok located on the north shore of Ngan Tso. From Rawok the Sichuan-Tibet Highway swings around to the north-west and enters a heavily forested landscape. Follow the Tsangpo downstream for 86km to Sumdzom and then a further 41km to the county capital at Pome (where there is a checkpoint and heavy PSB presence). This stretch of road can be particularly treacherous in the wet season.

Pome to Bayi

Continue along the east bank in a north-west direction for 89km to reach Tongme (2100m), a low-lying rainforest settlement. The section of road before Tongme is prone to landslides and is often closed during the rainy season. Past Tongme you reach Tongjuk and, after passing some logging depots, start a long climb up multiple switchbacks to Serkhyim la (4515m).

ROUTE GUIDE – POMDA to LHASA (SOUTHERN ROUTE)

DISTANCE (KM)	ALTIMETER READING (M)	NOTES AND KEY POINTS OF INTEREST
1214	4050	Pomda (in Chinese Bangda) junction – major intersection 🍴 ⊤
ex Chengdu		*(continue west to Lhasa, north to Chamdo 184km away)*
1227	4618	Gama la *(multiple switchbacks on descent)*
1272	2700	Po bridge
1285		Turn-off to Lingka
1308	3200	Pema (in Chinese Baxoi) 🍴 ⊤ ⌁
1333		Chidar
1375	4468	Ngajuk la *(23km descent, Tsangpo/Salween watershed)*
1398	3850	Rawu *(on northern side of Lake Ngan Tso)*
1450		Yupuk
1484		Sumdzom
1525	2745	Pome – checkpoint 🍴 ⊤ ⌁
1541		Kanam
1614	2100	Tongme 🍴 ⊤ ⌁
		(the valley low point of 1950m is located about 10km after Tongme)
1661	2300	Tongjuk
1707	4515	Serkhyim la *(awesome views of Mt Namche Barwa 7756m)*
1739	3000	Nyingtri 🍴 ⊤ ⌁
1758	3000	Bayi 🍴 ⊤ ⌁ *(heavy PSB presence)*
824		Baipa
1843		Namse Zampa bridge over Ba chu 🍴 ⊤ ⌁
		(a road branches north-east to Draksum Lhatso 38km away)
1891	3400	Kongpo Giamda 🍴 ⊤ ⌁
1954		Gyashing 🍴 ⊤
1987	4200	Shungdor 🍴 ⊤ ⌁
2016	5000	Mila la
2036		Hot springs 🍴 ⊤ ⌁
2042		Rutok monastery
2078		Balo 🍴 ⊤ *(turn-off to Sephu valley)*
2098	3800	Medrogongka Xian 🍴 ⊤ ⌁
2125		Turn-off for Ganden monastery
		(trail on right leads to Ganden 9.5km away, 550m ascent)
2146	3670	Taktse (Dechen Dzong) 🍴 ⊤
		(Dzong ruins on north spur overlooking village)
2161		Minor checkpoint *(say you are returning from Ganden monastery if questioned)*
2166	3600	Lhasa bridge 🍴 ⊤ ⌁ *(a further 3km to Barkhor square)*

Notes: 🍴 = Food, ⊤ = Water, ⌁ = Accommodation available

From the Sichuan-Tibet Highway you get awesome views of the mountains Gyala Pelri (7150m) and Namche Barwa (7756m) further south – the latter being the world's highest unclimbed mountain. The mighty Tsangpo flows east between these giant peaks and then miraculously swings back west, south of Mt Namche Barwa, and cascades down into north-eastern India, descending 3000m within a mere 80km!

From the Serkhyim la it is a 32km descent into Nyingtri, which lies near the base of the mountain Bonri (a sacred Bon mountain), and a mere 19km further north to Bayi. Bayi was once just a Chinese military base but it is now a county capital and a principal settlement along the Sichuan-Tibet Highway. The PSB are particularly vigilant in Bayi and it is not a wise place to hang around without the proper permits. Most overlanders who get 'past' Bayi make it all the way to Lhasa.

Bayi to Lhasa

Bayi to Medrogongka Large sections of the 408km road from Bayi to Lhasa are sealed.

Theoretically, it is also possible to reach Lhasa (via Tsetang) from Bayi taking a road south out of town over the Bayi bridge crossing the Nyang chu. From Bayi it is a tough first 53km to a heavily guarded checkpoint just before a bridge over the Tsangpo. If you make it though that checkpoint it is a relatively unchartered 387km to Tsetang (then a smooth 194km of sealed road onto Lhasa).

The main Sichuan-Tibet Highway heading upstream out of Bayi along the east bank of the Nyang chu is very scenic with alpine conifer forests on both river banks. About 60km past Bayi is Bepa and a further 21km is the Namse Zampa bridge where there is 38km dirt track on the north bank of the Ba chu leading right (east) to Draksum Tso (a popular Chinese tourist attraction).

The small county capital of Kongpo Giamda is 48km past the Namse Zampa bridge from where it is a final 124km push over the Mila la (5000m) – the last pass before Lhasa. At the base of the Mila la are some hot springs near Rutok (an excellent spot to relax for a day) and just over another 60km to the dull township of Medrogongka.

Medrogongka to Lhasa Medrogongka to Lhasa is 68km of fast flat road (mainly sealed). Look out for the turn-off to Ganden monastery 27km out of Medrogongka (near road marker 4591km) and also the minor checkpoint 5km before Lhasa. For those hitching it is straightforward to jump on the daily public bus (three hours) out of Medrogongka to Lhasa.

For a more detailed route description from Lhasa to Medrogongka see pp63-69.

SICHUAN-TIBET HIGHWAY (NORTHERN ROUTE) – CHENGDU TO LHASA

Chengdu to Chamdo

The northern branch of the Sichuan-Tibet Highway turns north towards Chamdo at a barren junction, 440km after leaving Chengdu. Past the junction the road crosses nine passes over 4000m (highest of 4900m) before reaching Chamdo a further 852km away.

Most trucks will travel on this route between Chengdu and Lhasa especially in the rainy season (June-September) when the road is relatively more stable than the shorter southern branch.

The turn-off on the Sichuan-Tibet Highway lies 4km past Dzongzhab (in Chinese Xinduqao). You can now travel freely throughout the Kandze Tibetan Autonomous Prefecture which is now open to foreign tourists. Therefore it is possible to get a bus from Kangding (without a permit) as far as Derge.

The main towns along the way are Dawu and Karze (the provincial capital) that have numerous shops, restaurants and a few guesthouses catering to foreigners. The bus from Kangding takes around 12 hours to reach Karze and a further eight hours to Derge. About 110km before Derge you will pass the junction town of Manigango where roads to the Amdo and Kham regions meet.

ROUTE GUIDE – CHENGDU to CHAMDO (NORTHERN ROUTE)

DISTANCE (KM)	ALTIMETER READING (M)	NOTES AND KEY POINTS OF INTEREST
0 (441km ex Chengdu)		Turn-off north to Chamdo 852km, marker missing 2924km/446km *(west for Sichuan-Tibet Highway Southern Route)*
37	3700	Lhagang *(cluster of chortens)*
43	4420	Drepa la
63	3420	Garthar/Barme (in Chinese Qianning) 🍴 ⍾ ⌂
106	4115	Nedreheka la
139	3125	Tawu (in Chinese Daofu) 🍴 ⍾ ⌂
209	3475	Drango (in Chinese Luhuo) 🍴 ⍾ ⌂
275	4000	Latseka la *(Yarlong/Zhe watershed)*
306	3580	Karze (in Chinese Garze) 🍴 ⍾ ⌂
342	3500	Rongpatsa
401	3960	Manigango 🍴 ⍾ ⌂ *(major turn-off north to Xiling)*
442	4900	Tro la
511	3300	Derge (in Chinese Dege) 🍴 ⍾ ⌂ *(possible checkpoint)*
539	3200	Kamtok Drukha – TAR/Sichuan border, checkpoint *(bridge over Yangtse, 980km road marker from Chengdu)*
572	4245	Nge la
602	3400	Tangpu
624		Gyamda/Jomda 🍴 ⍾ ⌂
636		Khargang
665	4352	Gele la
680		Chunyido
720	4481	Lazhi la
743		Toba
4680		Jape la
4511		Tama la
852	3240	Chamdo 🍴 ⍾ ⌂ *(a rarely travelled route heads due west 700km to Nakchu)*
863		Jagka
917		Kyitang
950	4572	Lona la *(Mekong/Salween watershed)*
964		Yiqing/Shayag
998	4330	Chamdo airport – reopened in 1995 *(inbound flights from Chengdu – only for 'group tours')*
1030	4080	Pomda (in Chinese Bangda) 🍴 ⍾ ⌂
1036	4000	Major intersection – 6km past Pomda *(turn west to Lhasa 952km away, south-east to Sichuan/Yunnan)*

Notes: 🍴 = Food, ⍾ = Water, ⌂ = Accommodation available

Derge is famed for wood-block printing of Tibetan religious and academic texts. The printing factory was established in 1729 and still produces many of the Tibetan sutras.

The Tibet/Sichuan border lies 28km past Derge at a bridge over the Yangtse. There is usually a checkpoint by the bridge.

Chamdo is one of Tibet's largest cities but is not officially open to foreigners. There is a daily bus departing to Lhasa (via Nakchu) over the rarely travelled 1028km-long overland route heading due west from Chamdo. The first 700km stretch of road from Chamdo to Nakchu crosses five major passes (all over 4700m) before joining the Qinghai-Tibet Highway. Chamdo is also serviced by direct flights from Chengdu. Unfortunately foreigners are barred from purchasing tickets for either of these journeys.

The north branch of the Sichuan-Tibet Highway rejoins the south branch at Pomda approximately 184km south-west of Chamdo.

Alternatively, it is a one- to two-day bus ride from Kangding to Batang and a one-day bus ride from Chengdu to Kangding.

YUNNAN-TIBET HIGHWAY – DALI TO MARKHAM/LHASA

The 1989km Yunnan-Tibet Highway connects Dali with Lhasa. The overland route from Dali is spectacular and passes many scenic towns. The route joins the main Sichuan-Tibet Highway near Markham. If you are lucky you could hitch to Lhasa in under a week, but it will take 35-40 days to cycle from Dali to Lhasa.

The Yunnan-Tibet Highway commences from Dali, which is easily reached from Kunming (412km away). There are international flights to Kunming from Hong Kong, Bangkok, Yangon, Vientiane and Singapore with daily domestic air and rail services from Beijing, Shanghai, Guangzhou, Chengdu, Shengzhen and others.

China Southwest Airlines has introduced a weekly flight from Kunming to Lhasa (via Zhongdian). Tickets can be purchased only as part of a 'tour group' from a travel agent for about US$300 (one-way including permits).

Dali to Markham

Dali Dali lies on the western edge of Erhai Hu (meaning 'Ear-Shaped Lake') and is a nice place to relax for a few days and prepare your route into Tibet. Dali can be reached from Kunming via a daily 8-to 10-hour bus ride or a 45-minute flight. Note many of the buses from Kunming terminate at Xiaguan, the prefectural capital, 14km south of Dali.

For accommodation in Dali try the *'Pop MCA' Guesthouse* (700 Wenxiang Lu) or the newer *'Siji Kezhan' Inn* (Boai Lu). Before leaving Dali stock up on warmer clothes for Tibet, sort out your money requirements and send friends and family an email with your intended plans.

Lijiang Lijiang, a scenic town about 200km north of Dali, is another possible town to plan an overland trip into Tibet. Lijiang can be reached on a 3- to 5-hour bus ride from Dali or by a daily 45-minute flight from Kunming on Yunnan Airlines. Lijiang lies 13km east of the main Sichuan-Tibet turn off at Baihanchang.

Zhongdian Zhongdian (3250m) was formerly the last open town on the Yunnan-Tibet Highway and traditionally where most overlanders commence their hitching or cycling campaigns into Tibet.

However, since 1998, Dechen (in Chinese Deqin), which lies 190km north of Zhongdian, has been officially open and can be reached by public bus from Zhongdian (10hr) although there are conflicting reports if this is still the case – check out the current policy while in Zhongdian.

Zhongdian is at the end of the sealed road and can be reached from Lijiang in five hours by bus or by sleeper bus or plane from Kunming three or four times a week. Alternatively, it is a four- to five-day cycle ride from Dali to Zhongdian. The last day approaching Zhongdian involves a 1400m climb to 3200m and the first signs of Tibetan Buddhism become visible.

A good place to stay in Zhongdian is the *'Tibet Hotel'* near the bus station with 24hr hot water and a money change facility.

From Zhongdian there is an alternative 400km route into Sichuan province via Litang. The route goes through Xiangcheng (which 'closes' intermittently) and crosses nine passes – including one around 4300m.

Zhongdian to Lhasa is an arduous 1687km route that will take approximately five to seven days to hitch (with lots of luck) or 30-35 days to cycle.

Zhongdian to Markham Past Zhongdian the road quickly drops to a small village at 2100m then it is the start of a long triple pass (the highest at 4350m) before Dechen with descents of up to 150m after each pass.

After Dechen there is a long descent into the Mekong valley. The Yunnan-TAR border is about 100km north of Dechen and 12km before the checkpoint at Yanjing.

It is about another 115km to Markham, where there is a strict PSB presence, via the Hung la (4220m). The Yunnan-Tibet Highway joins the Sichuan-Tibet Highway on the north side of Markham.

		ROUTE GUIDE – DALI to MARKHAM (YUNNAN-TIBET HIGHWAY)
DISTANCE (KM)	ALTIMETER READING (M)	NOTES AND KEY POINTS OF INTEREST
0	1950	Dali 🍴 ⓣ ↩ (*regular bus/train from Kunming, about 400km away*)
80	2635	Minor pass
100	2300	Low point
160	2940	Pass
188	2400	Baihanchang – turn-off to Lijiang 13km away 🍴 ⓣ ↩
		(*flights into Lijiang from Hong Kong/Kunming*)
230	2630	Minor pass
270	1850	Low point
368	3250	Zhongdian (in Tibetan Gyelthang) 🍴 ⓣ ↩
		(*bus from Dali, fly from Kunming, 4hr drive from Litang airport*)
400	3560	Pass
435	2000	Low point
450	2100	Benzilan (in Tibetan Pontselang) 🍴 ⓣ
500	4275	Pass (*start of triple pass, Mekong/Yangtse watershed*)
502	4100	Low point
506	4350	Yak la
508	4120	Low point
511	4313	Pass
560	3300	Dechen/Deqin (in Tibetan Jol) 🍴 ⓣ ↩
		(*possible checkpoint – south side of town*)
565	3500	Minor pass
585	2050	Bridge over Mekong
630	2250	Hongshan 🍴 ⓣ ↩ (*cross Mekong twice before township*)
670	3160	Yanjing (in Tibetan Tsakalho) – checkpoint south of town 🍴 ⓣ ↩
		(*awesome views of Mekong river 900m below*)
730	4270	Hung la
745	3600	Low point
785	3900	Markham – checkpoint on east side of town 🍴 ⓣ ↩
		(*west to Lhasa 1229km, east to Chengdu 937km*)

Xinjiang-Tibet Highway
(Lhasa to Mt Kailash & Kashgar)

Jamie McGuinness

Throughout the East there runs a legend of a great mountain at the centre of the world...Kailas, worshipped by Hindus and Buddhists alike as the home of their gods and the navel of the world. Close by are the sources of four mighty rivers: the sacred Ganges, the Indus, the Sutlej and Tasango-Brahamaputra.

From *A Mountain in Tibet* by Charles Allen

INTRODUCTION

Kailash, or Kang Rinpoche to Tibetans, is considered the centre of the universe and the most holy place in the world for both Hindus and Buddhists and, like Islam's Mecca, everyone hopes to pay homage by circling the mountain at least once in their lifetime. This ritual kora supposedly wipes the sins of a lifetime, enticement enough one would think, but it is also undoubtedly one of the most stunning three- to four-day walks in the world.

But whilst the world has become seemingly smaller in other parts, it is only recently that Kailash has become accessible to the Western traveller. Nomads still spend years herding their yaks and sheep from far away corners of Tibet towards Kailash, whilst other, less self-sufficient pilgrims spend months walking and hitching on trucks. For India's Hindus and Buddhists bureaucracy is the challenge, with only 150 people a year permitted direct access, the rest having to take tours through Kathmandu.

For Westerners during the magical years of 1987-88 there were few travel restrictions, but a Tibetan uprising, encouraged by Western freedom of expression, and the sudden surge in tourist numbers, forced the Chinese to rethink their tourism policy. Since then, officially only tour groups who have an Alien Travel Permit are allowed to visit. Even on a (usually expensive) tour by four-wheel drive, it is still an arduous trip with many days spent bouncing along rough roads and camping in often difficult conditions or braving the filth of Chinese truck stops. Despite the difficulties, for the atheist, ascetic and devout alike, it is the journey of a lifetime, and always will be.

No matter what your motivation, route or method, the experience is pure Tibet, from the arrestingly coloured plains and soft hills, so endlessly captivating, to meeting true Tibetan nomads and pilgrims and exploring places holy since time immemorial. Wildlife is in abundance too: we saw several wolves close up, herds of kiang (Tibet's curious, flighty wild ass the size of a long legged horse), foxes, gazelles, marmots and the bone-breaking vultures and lammergeiers. It is this beauty and diversity that sets a trip to Kailash apart from other overland routes.

The best time of year to visit Mt Kailash is between late-May and mid-October. July and August are the warmest months but this is also the monsoon season.

Cyclists

For all the rewards, it is an exceptionally tough trip. For the cyclist the challenges are the rough road, dust from passing vehicles, the testing winds and, not least, the bureaucracy. Road conditions include awkward rocky sections and tough patches of sand, and

Xinjiang-Tibet Highway

HIGHLIGHTS

Mt Kailash: 'centre of the universe' for Hindus and Buddhists,
the circuit (*kora*) is the holiest pilgrimage of all
Lake Manasarovar: one of Tibet's four holiest lakes, near to Mt Kailash
Tirthapuri: healing waters in remote hot springs, a pilgrimage to Mt Kailash
is considered unfinished without visiting Tirthapuri
Aksai Chin plateau: contains the highest roads in the world (two passes over 5200m)
Kashgar: bustling 'ethnic melting pot' along the ancient Silk Road

ROUTE INFORMATION (OVERLAND ROUTES TO MT KAILASH)

	DISTANCE	DRIVING TIME*
Southern Kailash route (Lhasa-Lhatse-Saga-Darchen)	1219km	5-7 days
Northern Kailash route (Lhasa-Lhatse-Tsochen-Gertse-Ali-Darchen)	1942km	6-8 days
Changtang route (Lhasa-Damshung-Amdo-Ali-Darchen)	2113km	6-8 days
Paiko Tso route (Zhangmu-Nyalam-Paiko Tso-Saga-Darchen)	788km	4-5 days
Xinjiang-Tibet Highway (Kashgar-Karghilik-Mazar-Ali-Darchen)	1665km	5-8 days

* ESTIMATES ONLY – DO NOT INCLUDE STOPS FOR RESTS/SIGHTSEEING OR SEVERE WEATHER

ROUTE INFORMATION

	DISTANCE	DRIVING TIME*	CYCLING TIME*	NO OF MAIN PASSES	HIGHEST PASS
Lhasa to Lhatse (via Central Friendship Highway)	421km	1-2 days	5-6 days	1	4450m
Lhatse to Saga	299km	1-2 days	5-7 days	3	5080m
Saga to Darchen (Mt Kailash)	499km	2 days	7-10 days	3	5180m
Darchen to Ali	310km	1 day	5-7 days	1	4850m
Ali to Tibet Border (Satsum la)	379km	2 days	8-10 days	4	5250m
Satsum la to Mazar	463km	1-2 days	12-15 days	3	5100m
Mazar to Kashgar	513km	2 days	7-10 days	2	4900m
Lhasa to Kashgar	**2884km**	**10-13 days**	**45-55 days**	**17**	**5250m**

* ESTIMATES ONLY – DO NOT INCLUDE STOPS FOR RESTS/SIGHTSEEING OR SEVERE WEATHER

CHECKPOINTS/PSB ON XINJIANG-TIBET HIGHWAY (LHASA TO KASHGAR):

Rinphuk turn-off – 98km past Chaksam bridge on Central Friendship Highway
Mt Kailash turn-off – 6km west of Lhatse
Raga – occasional checkpoint
Saga – east side of town
Bridge – 14km past (north-west) Old Dongbar
Bridge – 19km past Paryang
Hor Qu – western edge of village
Barga – before turn-off to Darchen, 4km past Barga
Darchen – PSB present
Mensa – 66km from Darchen
Ali – PSB present, checkpoint 6km north of Ali
Rutok Xian – 10km out of Rutok towards Kashgar
Karghilik/Aba – PSB present

on the good stretches, the corrugations will drive you to distraction. If it has rained or snowed heavily the ruts turn to treacherous mud and normally placid streams become dangerous torrents. Just as annoying are the constant afternoon winds, especially the long dust plumes thrown up by passing traffic. Except during the summer monsoon, the wind picks up late morning and gusts with savage force, enough to flatten light tents, only dying down as darkness descends. There is virtually no shelter from this wind, and true to Murphy's Law, it is always a headwind. During the monsoon the wind decreases and is replaced by an irregular drizzle.

The police do their utmost to prevent cyclists reaching Kailash from the Lhatse direction; they would prefer that you pay the money for a tour instead. However, once you have reached Kailash they don't stop you from leaving provided you don't antagonise them. From Kashgar bureaucracy comes to your rescue; initially you aren't in Tibet and therefore can travel semi-legally, and where you cross into Tibet it is rugged and inhospitable and therefore not the place to base a check post. Once at Ali you are fined and sent on your way, with a permit to get you out of the region.

Hitching

For the individual on foot, the main challenge is getting rides. It is not always fun to wait days, so have the right gear to walk, which can be a pleasant interlude. When a vehicle does stop, the next hurdle is to negotiate a reasonable price (as you usually have to pay the driver; there are no 'free' rides in west Tibet). Trucks are the buses of remote Tibet, but without fixed fares. And you are a foreigner, wealthy by worker standards, probably tired of waiting or walking so you'll be expected to pay considerably more than what the bus fare should be. Also, once a week a bus runs from Lhasa to Ali via the northern route. As a hitch-hiker you're in a weak negotiating position.

Group tours

Vehicles for organized 'group tours' can be rented in Lhasa. You will never be permitted to hire a land cruiser of your own and invariably you will need to hire a driver and a guide through a travel agent (for tips on negotiating contracts with agents see p58).

A typical 'long' trip could last 24 days – taking 13 days to reach Mt Kailash via the north road (via Ali) and five days to return to Lhasa on the south road including four days at Mt Kailash and one day visiting Lake Manasarovar. Expect to pay around US$2500 to US$3000 for a four-wheel drive vehicle or US$1200 to US$2000 for a large truck, generally split between 15 passengers.

GETTING TO MT KAILASH

To reach Mt Kailash there are five main overland routes: from Kashgar (Xinjiang Province), from Zhangmu/Dram (Nepal border) via Paiko Tso, and three routes from Lhasa (two via Lhatse, one via Amdo). There are also a few travel agents in Kathmandu organizing trips to Mt Kailash via Simikot (Nepal) and Purang.

From Kashgar

From Kashgar (in Chinese Kashi) to Mt Kailash (1665km) the route is extremely trying and it is hard to imagine a more challenging route anywhere in the world. The journey skirts the Taklamakan desert, crosses the Kun Lun mountains and bisects the controversial Aksai Chin plateau that contains the highest motorable roads in the world.

The total journey along the Xinjiang-Tibet Highway (Kashgar to Lhasa) is a long and arduous 2884km and should be only undertaken by those with plenty of time and suitable equipment.

From Amdo

Traversing the width of the huge Chang Tang Plateau, this route is famed for its wildlife and lakes; there is little else. Only the occasional adventurous tour group and a few trucks traverse this long road to Mt Kailash from Lhasa (2113km).

From Lhatse

In years gone by the debate raged about the merits of the so-called 'Northern Route' and the 'Southern Route'; the circuitous and long northern road without serious river crossings, and the short southern route with its dangerous rivers that are definitely not crossable during the monsoon. Trucks travel at approximately 35-40km/hr along this route.

The Northern Route (1942km) is from Lhatse to the turn-off just before Saga, then north to Tsochen and around Gertse to Ali, before it heads back to Mt Kailash. The Southern Route (1219km) is also from Lhatse but via Saga and Paryang to Mt Kailash. This route is considerably more direct and 723km shorter.

With tourism as the driving force, during the late 90s the Chinese built several bridges and the beginnings of a road along the Southern Route, which effectively ended any debate; the direct Southern Route now may be travelled during any season, provided it is snow-free.

Paiko Tso (lake) shortcut (also spelt Pelku, Paiku and Peiko)

If you are starting or ending in Nepal there is a much shorter way to Mt Kailash that avoids Lhatse (this 'short-cut' will save you about 325km). The views are spectacular and the route is little travelled but it is also rough and should be avoided during the monsoon, particularly if it has been raining heavily.

Mt Kailash circuit (kora)

Reaching Mt Kailash (6714m) is the journey, but the goal is to circumambulate the mountain. For Buddhists and Bons, the more koras the greater the merit gained, with three and 13 having particular significance, whilst 108 is the fast-track to enlightenment. Prostrating oneself around the first circuit is most meritorious.

Travelling light and walking the hard way, the 52km kora takes only 12 hours. With three or four days you can really experience it. The pastel colours, the multitude of pilgrims and the presence of the mountain itself is almost surreal, and the extreme altitude doesn't lessen this; Darchen, the starting point, is at 4650m and the Dolma la, the pass at the halfway point, is 5630m.

Side trips If the Kailash road hasn't sapped your strength there are plenty of worthwhile detours. A visit to Tirthapuri and Lake Manasarovar completes the Kailash pilgrimage and features some hot pools to bathe in. Relatively close by is the stunningly set Guru Gem Bonpo monastery, now rebuilt and functioning once again.

SOUTHERN ROUTE TO MT KAILASH (KANG RINPOCHE)

Introduction

This section describes in detail the 'southern route' to Mt Kailash from Lhatse to Darchen via Saga, the shortcut from Saga to the Nepalese border and also briefly covers the route from Kashgar to Ali.

Originating from Kailash, the Tsangpo flows past Saga, Lhatse and Shigatse, however the road does not follow the river all the way: instead it climbs side valleys and explores parallel routes. During the 1990s at least three long sections were substantially re-routed as more efficient or more easily passable routes were found.

Facilities Alongside the road improvements the facilities improved too and, being China, the change is rapid. Restaurants have sprung up where there were none and locals are more welcoming to foreigners, although still almost nobody speaks English. The rate of change in the larger villages is likely to further increase. West Tibet (in Tibetan Ngari) is nomad country so camping is common.

Water The route traverses many long valleys that are often flat and very wide. Usually a stream flows down the centre so most sections of the road are not too far from water. That is the theory, anyway. In practice however, this stream can be distant and elusive, hard to reach though the long tussock.

Refill when you can. Going over most passes there is no water, at least during the dry seasons; however, the distances between water are generally manageable.

Lhatse to Saga
The turn-off to Mt Kailash is a few kilometres south of Lhatse, at a checkpoint where your Aliens' Travel Permit (ATP) and usually your visa are scrutinized.

The first section to Saga (293km) traverses pleasant country with occasional scattered settlements, and frequent camping spots where water is plentiful.

Saga With more than one street, Saga is a developing town by Ngari (West Tibet) standards. The handful of shops sell all the basics and although you may be able to restock at New Dongba, it may be wiser to have enough supplies to reach Darchen. Naturally there are a collection of restaurants, a large army base and international telephone calls can be made from the post office.

Entering from Lhatse, first you see a petrol depot then, abruptly, around a 90° bend, there is the town. Heading straight at this intersection leads to the ferry across the Yarlung Tsangpo and the Paiko Tso route to Nyalam and Nepal.

If entering from Darchen the descent is long and pleasant with a scattering of houses to warn you of the town. Saga's dogs mostly relax during the day but riding in at night requires more care. There is a vigilant checkpoint on the east side of town.

Saga to Paryang
This 142km stretch to old Dongba has plenty of roadworkers' *accommodation* (called 'compounds') and although two are separated by 34km intervals, most are much closer together. Water, too is frequent and the only dry stretches are over the two minor passes.

The climb to the first pass (Torkyo la) begins soon after leaving Saga but just as the climb steepens there is a good, obvious and watered **camping spot** off the road.

Old Dongba/Zhongba A glance at the ruins along this one-street town suggests that it has been ravaged by the Cultural Revolution or some later repression. The truth is more mundane: when a new town was established nearby (imaginatively named New Dongba), half the population moved there, abandoning their houses. Incidentally, dong is the name for Marco Polo sheep.

Blocking the road is a police **checkpost** barrier. Here, when you can find the boy soldiers, often without uniform, they note down your visa and passport details. For travellers heading towards Kailash, the police will usually wish to see an ATP. If you are coming from Kailash, they are usually less bothered.

Around a sandy corner and on a small rise is a traditional entrance kani and to the south a small gompa. Here, the roadworkers have stopped because the road has been rerouted.

New Dongba/Zhongba Situated on the edge of the vast Thang Kiang Naga (or 'plain of the wild donkey and grass'), New Dongba is a typical truckstop that you might simply want to pass by.

ROUTE GUIDE – LHATSE TO SAGA (SOUTHERN KAILASH ROUTE)

DISTANCE (KM)	ALTIMETER READING (M)	NOTES AND KEY POINTS OF INTEREST
0	3990	Lhatse 🍴 Y
6	4050	Turn-off, checkpoint (permit/passport inspected), **reset** odometer (*veer left to Shekar, turn right to Mt Kailash 793km away*)
2		Cross concrete bridge over Tsangpo (road marker 2136km)
20		Grassy plains – can view Lang Tso (*possible campsites for next 10 km*)
24		Lulung village (*houses are painted with the distinctive Sakya tricolour*)
28		Travel around Lang Tso (saltwater)
46		Start of uphill section for 1.5km
47		Small lake, no grass
47.5	4575	Choctse la (table mountain pass) (*steep descent for 3km*)
53	4390	Kaga (Kaika) 🍴 Y (*Ngamring village and lake 6km away from main road*)
64		Village 🍴 Y
73		Road maintenance compound
80		Road maintenance compound
84	4725	Ka la
93		Road maintenance compound
99		Start of steep ascent for 4km
103	4800	Tok-yo la
113	4550	Sangsang 🍴 Y
120		Lake
126		Road maintenance compound
131		Water – available all year round
143		Turns up a watered side valley start ascent
144		Road maintenance compound
149	4900	Sangsang la (Gye la)
156		Cross stream and meet river
167		Route opens out
168		Road maintenance compound
179		Road maintenance compound 🍴 Y
185		Road maintenance compound 🍴 Y
190	5040	Thongsa la
199		Road maintenance compound
208		Road maintenance compound
218		Road maintenance compound
228	4930	Raga (Raka) village 🍴 Y (*occasional checkpoint*)
235	4950	Turn-off for northern route to Ali – no English signage road markers 1905/6km
250	5080	Pass
255		Steep descent for 7km
262	4650	Road maintenance compound 🍴 Y
272		Road maintenance compound
280		Road maintenance compound
293	4600	Saga 🍴 Y (*last major village before Mt Kailash, checkpoint*)

Notes: 🍴 = Food, Y = Water, = Accommodation available

ROUTE GUIDE – SAGA to PARYANG (SOUTHERN KAILASH ROUTE)

DISTANCE (KM)	ALTIMETER READING (M)	NOTES AND KEY POINTS OF INTEREST
293	4600	Saga 🍽 Y ⌁
ex Lhatse turn-off		*(last major village before Mt Kailash, checkpoint)*
298		Start of ascent for next 4km
300		Possible camping – water accessible *(route steepens for next 2km)*
302	4880	Torkyo la
304		Road maintenance compound
305.5		Bridge across small river
315		Road maintenance compound
319	4600	Village – some medical services 🍽 Y *(road marker 1820km)*
324		Possible campsite
327		Road maintenance compound
334		Monastery – above and away from the road
338		Bridge across river
349		Road maintenance compound
357		Road maintenance compound
357/8		Minor pass
363		Small lake
365		Road maintenance compound
379		Store 🍽 Y
383		Road maintenance compound
290		Enter Yalung valley (for next 5km)
393		Road maintenance compound
403	4530	Start ascent
408		Spring Possible campsite next to water *(steep ascent for next 2km)*
412	4900	Sing la
418		Road maintenance compound
425		Road maintenance compound – enter valley *(last compound on this route)*
429		Holy spot with prayer flags and red-painted rock
435	4600	Old Dongba (Zhongba) 🍽 Y ⌁ *(road marker 1704km)*
436		Kani monastery Y *(road markers end)*
		(expect bad corrugations in road and patches of sand for13km)
449		Bridge across clean water (with fish)
		(occasional police post checking driver licences, far side of bridge)
450		Junction – go straight on to avoid New Dongba *(veer right/north for ND)*
452		Junction – go straight on to avoid New Dongba *(turn left/north for ND)*
459		Junction – go straight on to avoid New Dongba *(turn left/north for ND)*
465		Junction – go straight on to avoid New Dongba
		(turn left/north for New Dongba; possible camp/supplies 3-4km away)
471		Bridge – patches of sand
477		Bridge – road turns up a wide side valley
479		Turn up another side valley
488		STOCK UP! – last water for 27km 🍽 Y *(dunes and sandy desert begin)*
503	4750	Soge la – double pass
515		Water available
525	4600	Paryang (Paiyang) 🍽 Y ⌁

Notes: 🍽 = Food, Y = Water, ⌁ = Accommodation available

ROUTE GUIDE – PARYANG TO DARCHEN (SOUTHERN KAILASH ROUTE)

DISTANCE (KM)	ALTIMETER READING (M)	NOTES AND KEY POINTS OF INTEREST
525	4600	Paryang (Paiyang) 🍴 ⟁ ⌂
ex Lhatse turn-off		
528		Water available – occasional sand patches
540		Water available
544		New bridge – **stock up on water** (*no more water for next 35km, possible checkpoint*)
578		Bridge
579		Bridge – water available
582		Bridge
587		Cross deep stream (no bridge) – small restaurant in nomad tent (*possible camping for next few km*)
614		Minor pass
630		Bridge across the Mayum Tsangpo – water available (*a series of camping spots popular with trucks*)
651		Junction – continue straight rather than left (*start of ascent for next 6km, no more water for next 20km*)
657	5180	Mayum la
667		Stony section
671		Bridge – water available
682		Two bridges – but not reliable water
694		Sandy patches (*no water for next 12km*)
706		Water available
717	4700	Mt Gurla Mandhata (in Tibetan Memo Nani) 7728m becomes visible
730		Bridge – water available
735		Often a tea shop here
742		Manasarovar Tso visible for the first time
745		Bridge – in gully
746		Turn off to Manas to camp (*chorten with prayer flags*)
750		Return route turn off to Manas to camp
751	4530	Hor-te (Hor Qu) 🍴 ⟁ ⌂ (*bridge or shortcut over stream, army checkpoint far side of town*)
754		Bridge; Beautiful lake – not Manasarovar
769		Bridge
774		Hor-re Village
777		Barga 🍴 ⟁ ⌂ (*turn-off for Purang & Nepal border 90km away*)
783		Start of multiple stream crossings and turn-offs to Darchen (*watch for possible checkpoint just before turn-off to Darchen*)
792/3	4650	Darchen 🍴 ⟁ ⌂ (*starting point for Mt Kailash trek*)

Notes: 🍴 = Food, ⟁ = Water, ⌂ = Accommodation available

Paryang to Darchen

Paryang/Paiyang This dusty village is centred around a gompa. It is a windy place, hence the high walls protecting each modest compound. Among the many houses are a few shops and a couple of family homes that can pass for restaurants. The best water is from a small well 50m south of the village. There is an occasional checkpoint at a new bridge 19km out of town.

A further 55km past Pariyang are three small but distinctive hillocks call the Pomo Pe Sum, or Ngari Pe Sum (also called the 'Three Sisters'). This place can now also be called three bridges, for these follow in quick succession. There is another checkpoint at Hor Qu on the far side of town.

Barga Approaching Barga, a key junction town near Lake Manasarovar (4580m), are the worst dogs on the route. They delight in chasing cyclists and vehicles. With a bike it is safer to walk it, preferably with one person wheeling two bikes while the other can keep up a steady fusillade of stones. Locals will often come to your assistance.

The 100km kora around Lake Manasarovar (in Tibetan Mapham Yum Tso) takes four to five days. The trail can be very marshy with many river crossing.

Approximately 5km past Barga is the start of various turn-offs towards Darchen and Mt Kailash.

To Purang and the Nepal border From Barga a road heads south between lakes Manasarovar and Raksas Tal. Purang (in Nepalese Taklakot), the largest town in the Mt Kailash region, is 90km from Barga via Gurla la (4650m).

From Purang (3880m) the Tibet/Nepal border is a further 28km south-east at Sher (3750m) where visas and permits are checked. This border is closed to independent travellers but a few tour groups are receiving permits to enter Tibet from Nepal via Purang on their way to Mt Kailash.

From Sher a five-day trek follows the Karnali river over Nara la (4550m) to Simikot (2890m) in Nepal. The official Nepal Immigration Office is en route near Muchu. From Simikot there is a weekly flight or overnight buses to Kathmandu. The Sher-Simikot trek is definitely not suitable for cycling!

Darchen

A few years ago to call this place even a settlement was an exaggeration, however it perhaps now deserves the title. It is a ramshackle collection of houses and **simple restaurants** swollen during the season by a huge collection of pilgrims' tents and traders setting up shop. There are two large compounds: one is the **tourist hotel**, complete with **tent platforms**, and the other is a Tibetan medical college.

Also roaming around in plain clothes is the local PSB officer. It pays to keep a low profile and to be pleasant to this person should you run into him/her. An ATP from Ali will usually allow you to stay in Darchen, but you will still need to purchase a trekking permit. To avoid unnecessary complications begin the kora immediately and don't stay the night in Darchen.

Kora of Kang Rinpoche (52 km circuit) Although yaks do trek the kora (and thus have acquired enough merit to escape slaughter), they destroy their loads in the process. Expect nothing less for your panniers if you wheel your bike over the Dolma la (5630m). Leave the bike in Darchen, even if it means slinging a couple of panniers over your shoulder.

Around the entire kora are good camping spots, alternatively, it is possible to stay in simple lodges at Drira Phuk and Zutrul Phuk, although the half a dozen or so cold rooms are often full during the season. It is not necessary to stick to the itinerary described in most guidebooks.

Mt Kailash to Ali
Darchen to Tirthapuri For the devout, the Kailash and Manasarovar pilgrimage is completed with a visit to Tirthapuri (4320m). Known for its hot springs, Tirthapuri is

ROUTE GUIDE – MT KAILASH/DARCHEN TO ALI

DISTANCE (KM)	ALTIMETER READING (M)	NOTES AND KEY POINTS OF INTEREST
0	4650	Darchen ●| Y ↵ (*starting point for Mt Kailash trek*)
6		Turn-off for Ali (*veer north to Ali, south to Lhatse 814km away*)
21	4800	Flat pass
66	4500	Mensa (Moincer) ●| Y ↵ (*turn-off south for Tirthapuri 9km away, checkpoint*)
92	4850	Jerko la
106	4750	Lower pass
120		Songsha (Sungsha) army base ●| Y (*turn-off to Zanda 122km away*)
159	4480	Army base
169	4650	Minor pass
178	4300	Namru (Baer) – new Namru 3km earlier ●| Y (*turn-off to Zanda 130km away via Ayi la 5610m*)
189		Bridge (*turn-off for short-cut to Ali about 80m away*)
217		Gar
270		Langnar bridge
278		Turn-off to Rudong (*confluence of Indus and Gar rivers*)
310	4150	Ali (in Tibetan Senge Khabab, in Chinese Shiquanhe) ●| Y ↵ (*Ali is 1108km ex Lhatse*)

Notes: ●\| = Food, Y = Water, ↵ = Accommodation available

approximately 75km north-west from Darchen towards Ali. To reach the hot springs, turn-off at Mensa (Moincer) and head south for a further 9km. There is a checkpoint at Mensa.

Mensa to Ali The 112km section of road from Mensa to Namru can be difficult in the rainy season, with numerous river crossings along the undulating terrain.

There are turn-offs for Zanda (Tholing) and Tsaparang from Namru and at the army camp in Songsha 56km north of Mensa.

Around 10km north of old Namru there is a possible short cut to Ali (weather permitting) – via a bridge across the Gar River and up a valley for 52km to a pass (approximately 4600m), then north-east for about 25km into Ali. If you are unable to cross the Gar River the traditional route continues 80km up the west side of the river, crossing a bridge (near the confluence of the Gar and Indus rivers) then veering directly east for a further 40km into Ali. This is the road marked on many maps that loops west initially out of Ali (and actually heads towards the Indian border and Leh).

Ali/Shiquanhe On the banks of the Indus (in Chinese Shiquanhe) river, Ali is the administrative headquarters and the largest town in Ngari. Once it was only a military base. The *hotels* and truck stops are dismal but the **shops** are surprisingly well stocked (dried fruit and nuts and other Uighur specialities from Xinjiang). The kebabs make a change and even the *Chinese restaurants* are passable. The place is a comparative paradise for the Ngari traveller, except that you are not supposed to be here. The PSB police will hunt for you so it is better to go and see them directly. We made the excuse of needing a visa extension, which was granted, and were fined. The staff were pleasant (to us) but clearly had a job to do: the translator read out the riot act and then gave us a permit. You may also be able to get a visa extension from the PSB (up to 30 days).

ROUTE GUIDE – SAGA to FRIENDSHIP HIGHWAY (via Paiko Tso shortcut)

DISTANCE (KM)	ALTIMETER READING (M)	NOTES AND KEY POINTS OF INTEREST
0	4450	Saga Village ⦿ ⊤ ↵
		(road marker 1846/7km)
3	4390	Ferry across Tsangpo
7		Road heads up small watered valley
14		Village
20		Very steep climb for next 2km
22	4680	Pang la
27		Villages to the left side
29	4500	Steep climb for next 5km – stony and very rough
34	4800	Pass
36		Drolung Tso visible (salt lake)
41		Some water available ⊤
48		Water available ⊤
51		Beautiful open country
60	4650	Pass lake (with bad water) – Himalayas visible
64		Water available ⊤
67	4650	Road maintenance post *(east for Friendship Highway, west for Kyirong 103km away via Ma la 5150m)*
73		Start of uphill for next 2-3km
78		Steep section – two streams
82	4850	Follow the river down through gorge
		(sometimes too much water, sometimes none)
90		Climb out of gorge
91		Descend down stream bed
		(route skirts around south edge of Paiko Tso)
93	4760	Turn-offs left to nomad camps
94		Turn-offs left to nomad camps
96		Stream and sand patches
98	4500	Bridge ⊤
102		Good views of the mountain Kambachen
		(stony ground for 2km)
104		Bridge *(sand patches over next 7km)*
111		Cross large plain (Digur Tang) for next 32km
119		See all of Mt Shishapangma (in Nepalese Gosainthan) 8012m
129	4650	Village ⦿ ⊤ ↵
		(grass tax is collected in this village)
136	4700	Village to the north ⊤
145	4600	Selung (turn-off south to Mt Shishapangma base camp)
149	4600	Cross bridge then veer left ⊤
150		Undulating trail until Friendship Highway
175	4495	Join Friendship Highway *(road marker 5265/6km; some vehicles join the main road further along towards Lalung la)*

Notes: ⦿ = Food, ⊤ = Water, ↵ = Accommodation available

Unfortunately, getting out is more difficult that you might think. Once a week a bus runs to Lhasa via the northern route. There is some traffic for the road to Kailash but Tibetan drivers are wary of picking up foreigners; waving your ATP sometimes reassures them. Heading to Kashgar you are better dealing with Chinese or Uighurs since they have less problems at checkposts.

THE PAIKO TSO SHORTCUT

The shortcut from Saga to the Friendship Highway via Paiko Tso is generally used only by tour groups travelling directly between Kathmandu and Mt Kailash. The road surface is rough and is difficult during heavy rain. However, by avoiding having to travel via Lhatse this route saves overlanders 325km.

The route commences with a ferry across the Tsangpo just east of Saga and climbs over a couple of steep passes before descending a narrow gorge to the grassy plains a few kilometres from the southern edge of Paiko Tso.

Along the way there are turn-offs to Kyirong (including the 'Valley of Happiness') and the northern base camp of Mt Shishapangma (8012m) – the only 8000m peak situated wholly inside Tibet.

KASHGAR TO ALI

The journey from Kashgar to Ali is a tortuous 1355km along the highest roads in the world and should be only undertaken by those with plenty of time and suitable equipment.

Kashgar

Kashgar (1290m) has been a main trading post along the Silk Road for over 2000 years and conjures up romantic images of knife-wielding nomadic Muslims amongst colourful markets. Unfortunately, the Chinese influence is overbearing but Kashgar still remains an intriguing ethnic melting pot of Uighurs (still the majority), Tajiks, Kyrgyz, Uzbeks and Han Chinese.

Kashgar can be reached from Pakistan via the Khunjerab la (4730m) or from Kyrgyzstan via the Torugart la. There is also a train link from Urumqi. However, the most popular overland route into Kashgar is from Pakistan over the Karakoram Highway (which is also an excellent cycle ride!). The highway is open between May and November and Islamabad is a relatively painless place to obtain a three-month Chinese visa.

For convenient and clean accommodation in Kashgar stay at the *Chini Bagh Hotel* (93 Seman Lu).

Kashgar to Karghalik (in Chinese Yecheng)

It is now possible to get a daily bus from Kashgar as far as Karghilik 250km away (5-6hr). From Karghilik you need to head 3-5km further out of town to Aba where the road diverges south and where you may be able to hitch a ride on any truck heading to Ali.

Cycling to Karghalik is about 3-5 days of town hopping along mainly flat hot dusty roads toward the Taklamakan desert and the foot of Kun Lun Shan mountains.

Beware of PSB officers who are consistently turning overlanders back from Karghilik. With a lot of luck and some expensive lifts it is possible to hitch from Kashgar to Ali in about 4-6 days.

Karghalik to Mazar

After more desert, the road passes through Pusha (2050m) then climbs to the first pass, a mere 3350m, still high enough to get the head pounding before you descend back to about 2500m.

ROUTE GUIDE – KASHGAR to ALI (via Xinjiang/Tibet Highway)

DISTANCE (KM)	ALTIMETER READING (M)	NOTES AND KEY POINTS OF INTEREST
0	1290	Kashgar (in Chinese Kashi) 🍽 Υ ↪
198	1300	Yarkand/Shache 🍽 Υ ↪
260	1370	Karghilik/Yecheng 🍽 Υ ↪
265	1410	Aba – main turn-off at truckstop 🍽 Υ
		(head south for Ali/Tibet, main road continues east to Hotan)
330	2050	Pusha 🍽 Υ ↪
369	2650	Akmeqit 🍽 Υ
380	3350	Kudi la
395	2600	Village, low point
430	2980	Kuda
489	4900	Chiragsaldi la
		(descend 1100m in next 24km)
513	3800	Mazar 🍽 Υ ↪
583	4850	Kekeate la *(ascend 550m over previous 13km, then descend 500m over next 14km)*
641	3650	Xiadulla
705	4270	Kangxiwar la
716	4000	Kangxiwar
768	4230	Dahongliutan 🍽 Υ
		(start long climb over next 50km)
818	5100	Qitai la – entrance to Aksai Chin region
		(descend 200m in 3km, then remain on high plateau for next 200km)
863	4810	Tianshuihai 🍽 Υ ↪
960	5050	Tielong 🍽 Υ
976	5250	Satsum la – steep climb!
989	5070	Second lower pass
1003	5090	Xinjiang/TAR border marker
1013	5080	Sumzhi 🍽 Υ ↪
1020	5250	Qieshan la
1033	5050	Small shelter
1047	4650	Small shelter – water nearby
1115	4300	Domar 🍽 Υ ↪
1131	4550	Pass
	4200	Lake Palgon – road runs around eastern end of lake
		(look for Muslim fishermen from whom you can buy fresh fish)
1222	4150	Derup/Rutok Xian 🍽 Υ
		(checkpoint about 10km before town)
1226	4150	Turn-off to 'old' Rutok *(old town is 10km from main road)*
1260	4180	Prehistoric rock carvings – petroglyphs
1315	4650	Lame la
1350		Checkpoint
1355	4150	Ali (in Tibetan Senge Khabab, in Chinese Shiquanhe) 🍽 Υ ↪

Notes: 🍽 = Food, Υ = Water, ↪ = Accommodation available

The second pass, the 4900m Chiragsaldi la across the Kun Lun Shan range, has killed several unacclimatized travellers and soldiers, and there is only partial relief down at Mazar (3800m), approximately 250km from Karghilik. At this important junction there is merely a collection of tents and restaurants.

From Mazar it is possible to cycle to a point where you can see K2 – continue 35km past Mazar to a side road then continue along this for a further 55km. From here it is a mere 25km to the summit of K2 (8611m) the world's second-highest mountain.

Once on the Tibetan plateau there is no road, merely many parallel tracks and, if you are lucky, telephone poles, heading across the velvet plains. Route finding is not always easy.

Aksai Chin region
To reach Tibet proper turn east from Mazar and continue along the southern side of the Kun Lun Shan range. There are seven more passes before Ali (including two at 5250m) making this the highest road in the world.

After ascending the Qitai la pass (5100m) you enter the Aksai Chin, a disputed territory between India and China which was the main cause of a border war in 1962.

Cycling from Karghalik to the Tibet border at Satsum la will take approximately 15-20 days.

Tibet Border (Satsum la) to Ali
The first Tibetan settlement inside the TAR is at Sumzhi. It is then a barren 102km to the military outpost at Domar where you can stock up on supplies. After another pass and a further 75km the road skirts the eastern shoreline of the 113km-long Lake Palgon (4200m), which straddles the Indo-Tibetan border. Near the lake it is possible to buy fresh fish from Muslim fisherman.

The new Chinese town of Rutok Xian lies just south of Lake Palgon. There is a checkpoint about 10km before town. The 'old' Rutok village is about 10km west of the main road, at a turn-off 5km south of Rutok Xian.

It is a further 89km to Lame la and then a 40km descent into the Indus basin and a final checkpoint before reaching Ali. Cyclists will take between 8-10 days to ride from Satsum la to Ali.

4 MOUNTAIN BIKING IN NEPAL

Peter Stewart

*Trips start when the last familiar face recedes from view
and end the instant one reappears.*
from The Art of Tripping by Lance Free

INTRODUCTION

This part provides a brief outline of some 'classic' cycle rides in Nepal –
that you may wish to consider if you are still feeling energetic after your
tour in Tibet.

Unlike the trekking seasons for which there are two main periods,
mountain biking can be done at almost any time of the year, mostly with
perfect to near-perfect riding conditions.

WHEN TO GO

Prime time

The best time is October to December. The days are sunny and fine with little chance of rain. It gets dark by 16:00 to 16:30 later in December, but visibility is as good as it gets. The first months are the busiest on the trails, so
it's no surprise that this is also prime trekking time, whereas December and
the colder conditions make for perfect day-time biking without the tourists.

Close behind

January to March is a great time to bike as few people are about, trails are
empty, hotels mostly quiet and the views brilliant. But it is cold, although
Pokhara is on average about 5°C warmer than the rest of Nepal and the
area provides stunning mountain trails and vistas.

Sizzle time

April to June sees the warm weather emerge and increase in intensity in
the latter weeks before the summer rains are welcomed in. It gets dusty
and the air and views are hazy but there are long daylight hours and with
a full Camelbak the riding is still great.

Monsoon time

July to September is generally not the best season for cycling. However, it
can still offer superb riding time as the rains are limited to an hour or two
per day and mud trails dry fast. The land is lush and green and offers sights
to behold and unavailable in any other season. The mountains are generally covered in fluffy clouds as the Himalayas go on holiday along with
many of the locals. This is prime riding time for Tibet and Ladakh and
those regions, which fall in the shadow of the monsoon.

With the growing number of mountain-biking tour groups in Nepal,
there are now a large number of established mountain-bike trails off the

main roads. In addition, a few adventurous mountain bikers have taken bikes into trekking areas hoping to find great riding but these areas are generally not suitable for mountain biking (70-80% of the time bikes need to be carried) as trails are subject to avalanches and have frequent obstacles. Also there are always trekkers, porters and local people in the way. Some of these trail users see bikers as an intrusion and just add one more problem to these heavy-traffic areas in peak season.

An organized mountain-bike tour is often the best option. The longest-serving operator in Nepal is **Himalayan Mountain Bikes** (HMB; ⌨ www.bikeasia.info), which is foreign operated and was established in 1988. This is the company that introduced mountain-bike tours to Nepal and has pioneered most of the trails and bike activities there. They operate tours through Asia but specialize in Tibet. Its Thamel office at the entrance to North Field Café. HMB offers a full range of tours from one day to ten days or more (all-inclusive) up to a 21-day fully catered-for trip. Other options are barebone tours and customized group tours. It has a complete workshop service centre in Lazimpat-Radisson Lane, Kathmandu (☎ 01-442345), with a full-time mechanic offering bike servicing, bike clothing, spare parts, plus tour and rental bikes (hire cost is between US$10 and $15 per day for a modern bike). Bikes are also bought and sold.

Nepal offers a number of options for hiring bikes. First, a rented bicycle (*saikal*) can be found on almost any of the main downtown tourist precincts, especially Thamel. Little attention is given to maintenance and reliable repairs, however, and they care little if it breaks down once you're out of sight. These are usually Indian or cheap Taiwan brand bikes that can loosely be termed 'mountain bikes', only because they resemble the look of a mountain bike and the sticker says so! Their components are cheap and will not withstand the rigours of off-road riding. Don't plan to take these far unless you are prepared to walk them home. They are fine for city riding and getting around the local sights at a very reasonable rate (around Rs20/hr or Rs150/day).

Nepal also hosts Asia's most popular mountain-bike race series around November each year. This is an adventure-styled race over three days and incorporates village stays; all competitors are entertained each night by host villages. For those who enjoy racing or just participating, this event is not to be missed.

VISAS AND PERMITS

All nationalities need a passport valid for at least six months after the completion of travel. Nearly all nationalities need a visa for Nepal. Visas may be obtained in your country of origin in advance or obtained from customs control at the Nepalese border.

Tourist visas
The 15- and 30-day visas have been abolished: all visiting tourists must now apply for a 60-day visa (US$30). It is still possible to apply for a single, double or multiple entry visa at an additional cost of US$25, US$40 and US$60 respectively. This visa can be obtained from a Nepalese embassy abroad or upon arrival at the international airport.

This 60-day visa can be extended for 30 days at a cost of US$50. The rule is still in place that a tourist can only stay in Nepal for up to 150 days in each year. If a visitor has previously entered Nepal within the last 150 days they can obtain a 30-day visa at a cost of US$50. Again this visa can be obtained from a Nepalese embassy abroad or upon arrival at the international airport.

Note: It is very important that all visitors travelling to Tibet via Nepal obtain a **single re-entry** visa at the extra cost of US$25 to avoid having to pay a further US$50 upon their return to Nepal.

Trek permits

These have now been abolished for the main trekking areas of Everest, Annapurna and Langtang. The National Park and Conservation fees (through ACAP) have not been abolished so are still applicable. Trekking permits for all remote regions are still in effect.

All foreigners wishing to trek in Nepal need a Conservation Fee Permit. An application form can be obtained on your arrival in Kathmandu; make sure you bring four passport photographs with you if you intend to do any trekking before or after your bike trip. At present this permit fee is Rs2000 or approximately US$16.

There are additional minor permit fees to cover local areas such as Bhaktapur City, Rani Ban Forest, Shivapuri Reserve and some monasteries such as Swayambhunath and Changu Narayan. Permit fees vary from Rs10 to Rs800.

OTHER USEFUL INFORMATION

Language

Nepali, which is not a difficult language to pick up, is spoken throughout the country. There are many local dialects and most Nepalis speak at least two languages, often three or four. English is widely understood in Kathmandu, but not so much in the hills.

Currency

The Nepalese unit of currency is the rupee (Rs), divided into various rupee notes plus minor 100 naya paise coins. At the time of writing (June 2002) £1 = Rs105 and US$1 = Rs78. It is illegal to import or export rupees, but foreign currency is not limited, provided it is declared on arrival.

Take your personal spending money in travellers' cheques; any well-known currency is accepted in Nepal and India. Travellers' cheques can be changed easily at hotels in Kathmandu, but may be harder outside the main population centres. Credit cards are also accepted in many of the better shops and restaurants in Kathmandu.

Business hours

Saturday is the weekly holiday and all government offices and some shops will be shut. Sunday is a normal working day for the general public; however, a five-day working week has been introduced for all government offices and banking institutions. Normal shopping hours are 09:00/10:00 until 17:00/18:00 depending on the time of year; in the Thamel areas they can be as late as 21:00.

Nepalese time is GMT + 5 hours 45 minutes.

Tipping

There is a tradition of tipping in Nepal and in relation to biking tours we recommend that you allow about US$1.50-2 per day of the tour to be shared between your guides and staff. This is only a guideline and also depends on group size. Also, excess clothing and other small items etc are often much appreciated.

Food

The food in Kathmandu is generally good and varied; Nepali, Indian, Chinese, Tibetan, Japanese and European food are all available. A meal in a reasonable restaurant will cost about US$5-6, while in the more sophisticated eating spots you can pay up to US$10-14 or so plus drinks.

The native food in Nepal is very simple: *dal bhat tarkari* – rice, lentils and curried vegetables is often all that is available outside of the few large towns.

Four classic mountain-biking routes in Nepal

CLASSIC ROUTE 1: NAGARKOT VISTA TOUR
(KATHMANDU– NAGARKOT–SANKU–BODHNATH)

Summary
This is a short ride of two to three days. It includes places of cultural interest, a sustained uphill climb and a classic off-road downhill, making it an ideal warm up for greater things.

Route guide
First, head south-east out of Kathmandu via the ring road. Take the first left off the Bhaktapur road to get on to the backroad to Thimi. Some 5km further on you reach the heart of Bhaktapur, the best-preserved example of Newari architecture in the valley and certainly a beautiful place to walk or ride around (entrance fee of Rs750 which goes towards city restorations).

The asphalt road to Nagarkot heads north-east out of the city, climbing gently through the rural landscape of fields sown with millet and rice, and passing the occasional stand of feathery bamboo, until it reaches the top of the ridge at Nagarkotphedi. From here the gradient increases and the switchbacks follow the ridge up to Nagarkot, situated just below 2000m (a 650m gain from Kathmandu). This route will take the average rider 90 minutes.

There is an optional but more demanding ride which involves a detour north out of Bhaktapur on the sealed road, which is generally so pot-holed you could almost class it as unsealed. This 5km route takes you (with a gain of 221m) to the rarely-visited ancient temple of Changu Narayan. There is basically nowhere to stay overnight here and sustenance is limited, however, there is a small **café** in the car park at the entrance to the city and a reasonable meal can be bought here. You may want to push on to Nagarkot for the night, so it's best to pace yourself and check that you have enough daylight to complete your day.

Retrace your steps east out of Changu Narayan for a short distance and then head in an easterly direction along the ridge, rather than taking the road back down to Bhaktapur (if you are uncertain of the direction, ask for 'Paudeldanda'). From here it's off-road and a gradual climb for at least two to three hours. Follow the tracks along the forested ridge-top and eventually you will join the smooth blacktop road to Nagarkot after a thrilling downhill out of the forest.

There are a couple of small **teahouses** along this ridge ride that could accommodate you overnight depending on the season. Nagarkot's **lodges** and teahouses **stretch** north from the main intersection. Those with the best views of the mountains are at the northern end but those to the south are closer to the observation tower – great for seeing the sunrise. If you have time make the extra climb, stay on the sealed road to the tower.

The return route is a rewarding downhill, and it's one screamer of a ride through beautiful country with the most amazing backdrops and little if any traffic (but do watch out for buffalo and locals).

Again, there are options, both of which take you to Sanku. The more technically advanced route heads north-west straight down from the bus stop along the south side of the forest. It's very steep and may involve some bicycle carrying. This will deliver you to the Vishnu Temple just out of Sanku. The more usual route is to follow the jeep track past the northern lodges along the ridgeline (via 'The Farmhouse'), with Narayan Ban Forest to your left, before barrelling down 500m to the Sali Nadi Valley and river. It's a wide, double jeep track (well rutted after the rains) and an all-out epic downhill that ends too quickly.

Explore the small township of Sanku, which hardly seems to have progressed since the 16th century. Do a little reading in advance as there are some historic landmarks in the area and a bike is the ideal way to explore them.

To return to Kathmandu, one option is to stay on the sealed road from Sanku, which will lead you to Bodhnath Stupa. Alternatively, just after departing the village of Sankhu, head south (on the sealed road) down to the river via 'Salambutar' back towards Changu Narayan. You'll need to cross the river at a small footbridge and make a 2km climb or portage (depending on trail conditions) from Bramhakel or Chhap back up to the temple.

If you continue to Bodhnath, after about 5km you can branch off the sealed road to the south and follow the village trails in a westerly direction eventually leading you into Pashupatinath along the Bagmati River. At the northern entrance to the Pashupatinath temple complex cross the metal foot bridge and head north: this will bring you out within 10 metres of the Bodhnath Stupa's main entrance.

Allow a bit of time to relax around the stupa and by late afternoon you'll experience the twice-daily *kora* prayer of the local Tibetans around the stupa. It's also a great place to grab a coffee and lunch.

CLASSIC ROUTE 2: NORTHERN VALLEY RIM

Summary

This is a gutsy ride traversing the northern watershed of the valley, from Kakani in the west to Shivapuri in the east. The entire ridge is more than 40km of gnarly off-road terrain (mostly jeep track).

There are numerous dramatic 'escape' routes from the ridge down to the valley. The route can be extended by exploration of the tracks passing through Manicur Dara and eventually linking to Nagarkot. It is best to ride with at least one another person and advise a friend of your plans.

Route guide

Leave Kathmandu heading towards Balaju on the Ring Road for 2km to the north of Thamel and from there onto the Trisuli road. At this point you start to climb 23km on the sealed road out of the valley to Kakani (altitude 2073m). The road twists and turns on an even gradient past the Nagarjun Forest Reserve (or Rani Ban) that provides the road with a leafy canopy.

Once in Kakani take the turn to the right, leaving the Trisuli road. The intersection is signposted with a 'Taragoan Resort' board; almost immediately you pass under some high-voltage power lines.

From the intersection the route starts with a 4km uphill on a paved road and passes a police checkpoint and training centre. The road comes to an abrupt end at a short, wide descent that's a popular Saturday picnic area, and offers a relaxing place to stop for the view and grab a Nepali chai (tea) and some cooked noodles (chow chow).

Continuing on, the track becomes a single trail that is mostly all rideable. After some 10 to 15 minutes you will enter an abandoned gateway. From there you will need t carry your bike for 10 minutes to an army checkpoint where you will be relieved of

Rs300 to enter the reserve (Rs10 for Nepalese). Hang onto your pass as you'll need it later. A short ride/carry leads into the camp.

The army-built road actually loops in a 'figure 8', taking in both sides of the ridge, however for this ride you need to keep to the south. There is not much water available once you leave Kakani, so be prepared. After some 20km the track widens at the spur above Budhanilkantha for a steep 7km downhill all the way into the township. The road has a heavy gravel surface.

Option A: To Bodhnath If you have got through this by afternoon (say four to six hours' riding), it's a pleasant late-afternoon ride back to the city of Bodhnath.

Take the dirt road turning left, just after the right turn at the Budhanilkantha 'T' intersection, or the one 1.5km north of Basbari. This is the first escape route back into Kathmandu and it leads you past a small Kali Temple above the river.

Option B: To Gokarneswar The next option is to make the trip to Gokarneswar (add another two to three hours). The way to Gokarneswar is to continue on from the last army checkpoint above Budhanilkantha (before the gravel road down). If you wish to continue on further, don't take the right gravel road.

The alternative is to continue along the ridgetop to Shivapuri by keeping left and contouring up through the Tare Bhir. There's a radically steep descent trail 3km from the fork – a drop of 700m in just 2.5km.

Just 2km beyond this the ridge peaks at 2732m in the Tare (Shivapuri) forest. You head due south for 4km to Nagi Gompa (a Buddhist nuns' retreat centre and former seat of the great Buddhist Master Tulku Urgyen) located 2251m above sea level, overlooking the valley.

It's 6km from here to Gokarneswar, or 10km to Bodhnath, making it the longest consistent downhill of the northern rim and a total buzz.

Option C: From Nagi Gompa Mulkharka Continue from Nagi Gompa Mulkharka (add another one to two hours). It's an additional hard 7km to the next good descent, from Mulkharka and Sundarijal. This is a good wide track, less gnarled than from Nagi Gompa, but beware of the pits and occasional rocky sections. Also watch out for the uphill trekkers from Sundarijal (although this is a less popular trekking route these days). The stone steps down into Sundarijal will be obvious as they cross the dirt track. This is the trekking path from below starting on the Helambu trail.

There is overnight *accommodation* in Mulkharka at the 'Karma Lodge'.

From Sundarijal follow the main road in the only direction available (south-west) that brings you to the main junction on the Bodhnath road. Turn right, pass the main gateway into the Stupa (on your right) and continue straight ahead towards Kathmandu.

From the base of the steps back to Kathmandu (Thamel) it is approximately one hour's ride.

CLASSIC ROUTE 3: TOURING ROUTES

The Rajpath to Daman – summary

This route has all the makings of an epic four-day plus ride from the Kathmandu valley all the way through to the Royal Chitwan Wildlife Park.

You start from Kathmandu and head west on the Tribhuvan Highway (or Rajpath) that was the first highway to connect Kathmandu with the rest of the world.

Route guide – Kathmandu to Daman

Your first destination is Naubise, on the highway, which is the junction and turn-off point for Daman and is well signposted. The road switchbacks 150 spectacular kilometres from Naubise to Hetauda, crossing a 2488m pass just above Daman. Most traffic from the Terai and India uses the Tribhuvan Highway between Narayanghat and Mugling, which, although longer, is a lot quicker. In monsoon times this may not be the case as the highway can often collapse.

The Rajpath is a different adventure and has a great mixture of light traffic and magnificent scenery, culminating at Daman, with exceptional Himalayan views: it's a classic ride on the first day. From the lookout at Daman you can see eight of the ten highest peaks and all the way through to Cho Oyo in Tibet.

The ride begins on the Kathmandu–Pokhara Highway, which gives the only access to the valley by road, although construction is underway for a new access route out of Dhulikel to the eastern rim of the valley. After leaving the valley, the highway descends to Naubise, at the bottom of the Mahesh Khola Valley, 27km from Kathmandu, where the Rajpath intersects with the Kathmandu–Pokhara Highway. Take the Rajpath, which forks to the left.

The mammoth descent from the pass at Thankot is one to take precautions with given a blacktop surface, slick with oil spills, and Tata trucks and buses that have no hesitation travelling two-abreast around blind corners into unsuspecting traffic or novice bikers! The other option is to take a bus to Naubise. Take care!

From Naubise, your last chance for some time to purchase water and supplies, you start with a 35km climb to Tistung at a height of 2030m. You climb through terraced fields carved into steep hillsides. On reaching the pass you descend for 7km into the beautiful Palung Valley before the final steep 9km climb to Daman, at a height of 2322m.

(**Option**: From Palung Valley you can take the left turn down into the Khulikani Dam area which also offers some nice biking around the dam fringe. Accommodation is limited.)

This is a long day's ride, almost all of it climbing. It will take between six and nine hours in the saddle so the recommendation is to start early and maybe take a local bus, with your bike, to Naubise to avoid the area of the tour with the heaviest traffic. Thus, with an early start it is possible to make it to Daman.

If you have time break the ride into smaller sections because for most cyclists Daman would be an ambitious target for one day. Once in **Daman**, the reward is to wake up to one of the broadest Himalayan panoramas Nepal has to offer. On a clear morning you can see from Dhaulagiri to Everest.

There is a fair selection of *lodges* in Daman offering anything from a few beds to tented camps and deluxe accommodation a few kilometres up the road at Everest Panorama Resort (EPR).

Our recommendation is that you stay overnight in Daman and make a day hike around the hilltops. There is a delightful Bhutanese monastery just above Daman: head into the forest to the right, and after a 20-minute walk you should arrive at the gompa. The Lama is most accommodating, although little English is spoken. A donation to the gompa will be put to good use and well appreciated.

Daman to Hetauda The next day the road climbs a further 3km to the top of the pass, at 2488m. At this point, you can savour the prospect of an exhilarating 2300m descent in 60km! In one short plunge you'll be transported from the chill of the mountain into the warm and steamy heat of the Terai all in just a few hours. Don't rush the ride as there is abundant wildlife, including huge white headed monkey's that look big enough to take your bike and ride it themselves.

From the almost alpine climate of Daman cast your eyes to the south, all the way across the vast Indian plains and notice a contrast, on your descent with the side you've just climbed – the south side is lush and semitropical. With innumerable switchbacks and an endless downhill run you should watch out for the occasional bus and truck looming around a blind corner. Make a note to check your brake pads so that you've got a bit of 'meat' on them. They'll be looking thinner by Hetauda.

The road eventually flattens out when you make a right turn to cross a newly constructed bridge and the first main river crossing. A further 10km brings you to **Hetauda**. Here is your best opportunity to take a **lodge** for the night rather than trying to make Chitwan before evening.

After a night's rest you can continue along the Rajpath towards India or turn right at the statue of the King in the centre of town and head towards Royal Chitwan National Park, another half-day's ride.

Welcome to the Terai.

Hetauda to Narayanghat and Mugling

The Bazaar of Hetauda (with its strong Indian influence) is just to the east of Royal Chitwan National Park, and once in Sauraha there is a wide selection of *accommodation*, both in the park and in the town.

Chitwan offers a lot to do and many flat bullock/village trails to explore by bike. Maps are available that can provide a guide to the selection of runabout trails, mostly to the south of the main road, that can eventually lead into Sauraha.

Following the main road, it is approximately 67km from Hetauda to Tadi Bazaar and the turn-off for Sauraha, reached by a 6km jeep track, which maybe partly sealed.

This is vastly different riding to that of Kathmandu and in the summer months (May to September) it can be very hot and you may find the asphalt road becoming rather sticky under your tyres.

Narayanghat, 20km from Sauraha on the banks of the Narayani River, gives a choice of further routes. From here you can return to Kathmandu or Pokhara via Mugling. Although some would say this section from Narayanghat to Mugling is probably best avoided on bike due to bus and truck traffic, it is nonetheless a very beautiful section of road to ride and traffic during many times of the day can be light. The alternative is to catch a bus.

Option: Bike through to Pokhara from Narayanghat or Mugling

If you're heading to Pokhara (96km) it's up to you to assess whether to bike further or to miss the highway between Mugling and Pokhara and catch a bus in Mugling. Here, the road is now much improved and vehicles travel a lot faster in what is still quite dusty conditions. However, this is a great route and traffic is limited mostly to those travelling to and from Pokhara. A little care and you'll have great rolling landscapes with river and valley views to more than entertain you for the five to seven hours of biking. The approach to Pokhara with the Annapurna range and Machapuchare in the near distance is memorable.

CLASSIC ROUTE 4: POKHARA LAKESIDE TO SARANGKOT AND BEYOND (1 TO 2 DAYS+)

Summary
This ride offers a nice mixture of off- and on-road riding and even if you're not fond of riding roads the scenery is worth the few kilometres of asphalt for the off-road and exceptional views awaiting you. This is a good trail to wear a helmet on.

Route guide
Simply put, the ride is directly north from Pokhara Lakeside, providing an excellent and challenging day of biking. This is in fact the biking leg of the now defunct 'Annapurna Triathlon' which was last run in 1996.

Leave early and ride along the lakeside (towards the mountains) to the last main intersection and sealed road, known as the 'camping chowk'. Make a right turn at the 'chowk' which now heads into central Pokhara. After 2km and at Road marker '0' you turn left and continue north. After a further 2km there is a smaller sealed road to the left, sign-posted as the road to Sarangkot. A well sealed and smooth road winds its way along a ridge into Sarangkot, providing outstanding views of the Himalayas and one of the best of 'The Fishtail' that seems close enough to reach out and touch.

After 6km a few **teashops** mark a welcome refreshment stop just where the stone steps commence the walking trail to the summit lookout. Take the unsealed jeep track, which closely hugs the edge of the mountain overlooking Phewa Tal (the lake fronting Lakeside). Continue until you join a 'Y' intersection which doubles back sharply to the right and makes the final climb to Sarangkot Point.

Option: Take the right turn up to the point for 360° views. Also consider staying here and continuing the ride tomorrow.

From the 'Y' junction you can also continue straight ahead (keep left) riding the narrower motorbike trails leading to Naudanda. What was in past years only a single track, is now a road that a car can drive on. However, it still makes for a great day out on the bike mixing challenging climbs, fast rocky downhills with some gravel and muddy village sections, but always with a stunning panorama. The trick is to keep your eye on the trail. Once over the top of the hill at Kaski you follow the trail through to Naudanda. You are now at an approximate altitude of 1590m, having gained approximately 840m altitude from Pokhara. The trail is rocky in parts and will test your equipment to the extreme, so don't consider riding this trail on a cheap hire bike.

The view from the ridge at Naudanda is spectacularly beautiful. Dhaulagiri, Manaslu, the Annapurnas and Machapuchare create a classic Himalayan panorama, especially on a cool, clear morning. Although the trail keeps mostly to the south of the ridge, which shields you from the mountain panorama, it does offer you the best perspective of the Pokhara township and Phewa Tal lake.

From Naudanda.... onwards

Now that you have reached Naudanda you have the choice of continuing left or right. Heading left or west, the sealed road continues along the spine of the ridge, the Pokhara–Baglung Highway, which connects Pokhara with Lumle (a popular starting point for trekking in the Annapurnas). If you choose to head towards Lumle and on to Beni you have a mostly downhill run on sealed roads except for the last 10km into Beni. Riding on to Birathanti maybe a good mid-point if Beni is too far. This is initially a 5km mild uphill, followed by a 20km switchback downhill. There are nice **lodges** in Birathanti (walk in from Birat) for an overnight stop before returning to Pokhara.

Your return from Naudanda to Pokhara is 32km long. You can either return via the Sarangkot trail (described above) or follow the highway back. The latter starts with a twisting 6km descent into the Madi Khola Valley. The highway has an excellent asphalt surface and descends gently as it follows the river, allowing an enjoyable coaster of a ride almost all the way back to Pokhara.

Take a map and study the surrounding areas as there are a few side routes worth exploring.

APPENDICES 5

A brief history of Tibet

This centre of heaven
This core of the earth
This heart of the world
Fenced around by snow
The headland of all rivers
Where the mountains are high and
The land is pure.
The *Dunhuang Documents* (8th & 9th centuries)

OVERVIEW

Ancient Tibetan history is a complex fabric woven from threads of myth and mystique. Recorded Tibetan history reveals two main periods beginning in approximately the first century AD. The first is the period of rule of the Tibetan monarchy until AD1000, and the second is the period of Tibetan Buddhism, from AD1000 to the present. Whether the monarchy or religion provided the leaders of the state, wars within Tibet and with the neighbouring countries have been a fact of life throughout its lengthy history.

The one element that consistently flows through myth and recorded facts is that the history of Tibet is unique and individual. It is not the history of China or any other neighbouring state. Tibet was influenced by its neighbours (Buddhism itself originated in India) but the main element that shaped Tibetan history is the land itself.

Historically, Tibet covered a total of approximately 2.5 million sq km. It was divided into the three provinces of Amdo (now split by China into the provinces of Qinghai and Gansu), Kham (largely incorporated into the Chinese provinces of Sichuan and Yunnan), and Ü-Tsang (which, together with western Kham, is today referred to by China as the Tibet Autonomous Region).

The area that the Chinese government has designated the Tibet Autonomous Region (TAR) comprises less than half of historic Tibet. The TAR was created in 1965 for political and administrative reasons. It is important to note that when Chinese officials and most publications in the West refer to 'Tibet' they are referring only to the area within the TAR.

CHRONOLOGY OF TIBETAN HISTORY (AD2–2002)

Prehistory Neolithic culture exists in Tibet.

2nd century King Nyatri Tsenpo becomes ruler of separate tribes in Yarlung and founds Yarlung Dynasty.

7th century King Songsten Gampo introduces Buddhism into Tibet, moves the capital to Lhasa. King Songsten Gampo takes Chinese and Nepalese princesses as his wives and builds Jokhang Temple in Lhasa.

8th century King Trisong Detsen brings Buddhist masters from India to Tibet and founds the scholastic Buddhist monastery at Samye.

9th century King Lang Darma rejects Buddhism in favour of the ancient Bon religion, leading to his assassination. The dynasty collapses and the kings' descendants flee to western Tibet to set up smaller kingdoms.

10th century Second phase of Tibetan Buddhism begins to spread, led by teachers such as Atisha, Milarepa, Marpa and Rinchen Zangpo.

11th century Three principal Buddhist sects rise: Kagyu, Kadampa and Sakya.

12th century Mongolian and Tibetan relationships develop and, in the aftermath of Genghis Khan's invasions throughout the region, Kublai Khan grants the Phagpa Lama authority over Tibet.

13th century Sakya sect rules Tibet and establishes the first form of Tibetan monastic government.

14th century Yuan Dynasty falls in China and Tibet regains its independence. The Sakya sect rule over Tibet. Tsongkhapa, the reformer of Tibetan Buddhism, is born in 1357 and founds the Gelug sect of Tibetan Buddhism.

15th century Three great monasteries of the Gelug sect are established: Ganden, Drepung and Sera. Gedun Truppa (later named the 1st Dalai Lama) founds Tashilhunpo monastery.

16th century 3rd Dalai Lama, Sonam Gyatso, is given his title by Altan Khan, descendant of Genghis Khan.
4th Dalai Lama, Yonten Gyatso is born in 1589.

17th century The rise of the Tsangto clan in Tsang led to the rescue of the Gelug by Gushri Khan. Supreme authority is conferred on the 5th Dalai Lama, Ngawang Lozang Gyatso ('the Great Fifth'). Modern style of Tibetan government (as maintained in exile) is established.
6th Dalai Lama is born in 1683.

18th century 6th Dalai Lama dies in 1706. Tibet is invaded by Mongols prior to 1720 and the Chinese in 1728, after which China is granted suzerainty of Tibet.
Tibetans create the Kashag Council and a succession of Dalai Lamas with very short reigns follows.

19th century 13th Dalai Lama is born in 1876. In 1887, Britain and the Qing (Manchu) Dynasty conclude a treaty relating to Burma and Tibet.

20th century
● **1902** Rumours that Russia has signed a secret treaty with Tibet spread. Preparations begin for a military invasion.
● **1904** Younghusband marches with 3000 troops to Gyantse and the 13th Dalai Lama flees and shelters in Mongolia and in China.
British withdraw after signing the Anglo-Tibetan Convention, allowing them to have Trade Agents at Gyantse and at Gartok in Western Tibet.
● **1909** 13th Dalai Lama returns from exile and Chinese troops occupy parts of Kham (eastern Tibet). Dalai Lama appeals to Britain for assistance.

- **1910** Chinese Army invades Tibet and enters Lhasa and 13th Dalai Lama flees to India.
- **1911** In Beijing the Qing (Manchu) Dynasty is overthrown and the Republic of China is established under Yuan Shih-Kai, who declared Tibet, 'Xinjiang' (East Turkestan) and Mongolia to be provinces of China.
- **1912** Tibetans uprise against the Chinese and on 12 August 1912, China signs a Surrender Agreement with the Tibetans. Chinese return to China via India.
- **1913** 13th Dalai Lama returns to Lhasa and issues a formal Proclamation of Independence.
- **1914** Tibet, Britain and China attend the Simla Convention as equal powers and initial an agreement to settle the Sino-Tibetan border dispute.
- **1920** Sir Charles Bell sent to Lhasa to reassure the Tibetans of British support for its self-rule and self-defence.
- **1923** 9th Panchen Lama disputed tax liability to the Tibetan Government and flees to China.
- **1933** Chokyi Gyaltsen, the 13th Dalai Lama, dies in Lhasa aged 58.
- **1937** The 9th Panchen Lama dies in Jyekundo on the Chinese border.
- **1940** Tenzin Gyatso, 14th Dalai Lama, is enthroned in Lhasa.
- **1941-44** Tibet remains neutral during WWII, refusing permission for America or China to transport military supplies through its territory.
- **1947** Tibet sends delegations to India, China, Britain and America to discuss trade and open formal relations abroad.

  Former Regent Rating, supported by the monks of Sera, attempt coup.
- **1949** China's People's Liberation Army overcomes Nationalists (KMT) and on 1 October proclaimed the People's Republic of China. 10th Panchen Lama sends telegram to Mao Tse-tung asking him to 'unify the motherland' (when he is 11 years old). PLA sent to 'liberate Tibet from foreign imperialists'.
- **1950** 14th Dalai Lama, at 15 years old, takes over Tibetan government. On 7 October, China invades Tibet and destroys the small garrison force at Chamdo in Kham. The Tibetan Government and the Dalai Lama move to Yarlung and send appeals for help to the United Nations (UN). The British and Indian delegates persuade the Assembly not to discuss the matter.
- **1951** Tibet signs (under duress) a 17-Point Agreement, which promised cultural and political autonomy but relinquishes independence.
- **1957** Eastern Tibetans revolt when Chinese begin destroying monasteries. Tibetan resistance movement established and drives Chinese out of southern Tibet.
- **1959** National uprising against the Chinese on 10 March. Thousands of Tibetans march in Lhasa and fight the Chinese troops. Dalai Lama flees to exile in India, followed by 100,000 other Tibetans.

  China imposes military rule under the façade leadership of the 10th Panchen Lama. 'Democratic reforms' introduced and hundreds of thousands of Tibetans are executed, imprisoned, or sent to labour camps. Destruction of monasteries begins.
- **1965** Beginning of the Cultural Revolution and systematic destruction of 98% of the monasteries in an effort to eradicate Tibetan culture.
- **1976** Cultural Revolution ends with the death of Mao Tse-tung and China acknowledges 'past mistakes in Tibet'. China attributes mistakes to Cultural Revolution and extreme policies of the Gang of Four.
- **1979** China, facing economic collapse, initiates a policy of opening up to the rest of the world. Invites 14th Dalai Lama to return to Tibet, on the condition he remains in Beijing. 14th Dalai Lama sent fact-finding mission to Tibet and delegates greeted by

huge demonstrations calling for independence and the return of the Dalai Lama. Many demonstrators imprisoned.

• **1980** Party Secretary Hu Yaobang visits Tibet and initiates some liberalization in relation to trade and religious activities, and recalls several thousand Chinese cadres.

• **1983** Tibetan economy, depleted by Chinese development policies, re-centred on tourism. Signs of a renewed attempt by Beijing to encourage the resettlement of large numbers of Chinese people in Central Tibet emerge.

• **1987** Dalai Lama proposes a Five Point Peace Plan during a visit to the US Congress in Washington.

On 1 October, Chinese police open fire on unarmed demonstrators calling for independence in Lhasa: 21 more demonstrations reported in the following 18 months – up to 100 feared dead and over 2000 arrested.

• **1988** Dalai Lama puts forward the Strasbourg Proposal, offering China control of Tibetan foreign policy and defence in return for full internal autonomy. The Chinese promise to negotiate.

• **1989** On 5 March, police open fire and kill further group of demonstrators in Lhasa. Demonstrations spread and martial law declared. PLA take over city and all foreign tourists, journalists and diplomats expelled. Hundreds killed by security forces and thousands arrested. Tibet cut off from the outside world.

In October 1989, the 14th Dalai Lama is awarded the Nobel Peace Prize.

• **1990** Martial law is lifted but restrictions remained in force. Small demonstrations continued but most quickly quelled by police.

Dalai Lama is officially received by Swedish, Dutch, and French governments.

• **1991** Chinese authorities organize 'celebrations of the 40th anniversary of the peaceful liberation' throughout Tibet. Tibet is declared open to foreign investment.

• **1992** Deng Xiaoping's 'spring tide' introduces the 'socialist market economy' to Tibet and the migration of Chinese entrepreneurs and petty traders increases. Chen Kiuyuan takes over as TAR party secretary.

• **1993** Human rights activist Gendun Rinchen is arrested for trying to contact European ambassadors on a fact-finding mission to Tibet. The 24 May demonstration over price rises becomes a pro-independence protest.

China gives permission for an exiled-Tibetan official, accompanied by the Dalai Lama's brother, to discuss negotiations in Beijing (the first such mission since 1984) but by September relations had ended abruptly.

• **1994** Gendun Rinchen freed after international campaign. On 26 May President Clinton withdraws human rights concessions from renewal of China's most favoured nation trading status.

'Third National Work Forum on Work in Tibet' held in Beijing, rubber-stamping faster economic development in Tibet and imposing restrictions on religion.

Potala re-opens after five years of renovation. Yulu Dawa Tsering, former abbot of Ganden monastery and long-term political prisoner, released on parole and meets the UN special rapporteur on religious intolerance during the first UN human rights visit to China and issued a critical report calling for the release of all monks and nuns in prison. On the same day, official statements order a ban on the unauthorized construction of monasteries and the induction of new monks and nuns.

• **1995** January to March demonstrations in Lhasa calling for independence, result in over 100 arrests. Anti-Dalai Lama campaign launched.

Six-year old Gedhun Choekyi Nyima recognized by the Dalai Lama as the 11th Panchen Lama in May 1995. The boy and his family were removed to Beijing and

Chadrel Rinpoche, abbot of Tashilhunpo monastery in Shigatse and head of the search team for the new Panchen Lama, is arrested. Five thousand troops move to Shigatse and on 13 July, up to 30 monks from Tashilhunpo are arrested. Two bombs are reported in July and another later in the year. In November the Chinese press condemned Gedhun Choekyi Nyima for having once 'drowned a dog'. Chadrel Rinpoche is denounced as the 'scum of Buddhism'. China names Gyaltsen Norbu (age 5) as Panchen Lama.

● **1996** Bomb explodes at the home of a supporter of the Chinese-appointed Panchen Lama. Snowstorm kills 56 people and thousands of cattle in north-eastern Tibet.

Patriotic re-education campaign launched with work teams visiting monasteries to 'correct' the historical, legal and religious opinions of monks and nuns. Disturbances in Ganden monastery are reported following the removal by soldiers of photographs of the Dalai Lama.

● **1997** On 19 February Deng Xiaoping dies. Chadrel Rinpoche is sentenced to six years for 'conspiracy to split the nation'.

Britain hands Hong Kong back to China on 1 July and 10,000 Tibetans attend obligatory celebrations in Lhasa. TAR secretary Chen Kuiyuan claims Buddhism is a 'foreign import' and not part of Tibetan culture.

UN human rights delegation visits Drapchi prison and fails to report witnessing a demonstration there. It is announced that the patriotic re-education campaign is to be extended to schools, towns, offices and villages. US appoint a 'Special Coordinator for Tibet'.

● **1998** Zhu Rongji replaces Li Peng as Prime Minister of China. Tibetan Youth Congress organized an 'unto death' hunger strike in India, which results in the self-immolation of Thupten Ngodup.

Three EU Ambassadors visit Drapchi prison, sparking an uprising which results in the deaths of ten prisoners.

In June, US President Bill Clinton visits Beijing and holds a joint live broadcast press conference with Jiang Zemin in which he calls for the Chinese leadership to negotiate with the Dalai Lama.

In September, two monks are arrested for preparing a letter for UN High Commissioner for Human Rights Mary Robinson. Legchog replaces Gyaltsen Norbu as chairman of TAR.

● **1999** Campaign to promote atheism in Tibet launched. China closes all communication with the Tibetan Government-in-Exile.

Two monks protest on 40th anniversary of the Tibetan uprising and are sentenced to several years in jail. It is revealed that the sentence of Ngawang Sangdrol, the longest-serving female political prisoner in Tibet is extended to a total of 21 years. Gyaltsen Norbu, the Chinese-appointed Panchen Lama visits Tashilhunpo monastery in Shigatse.

Karmapa leader of 'Black Hat' monastery in Tsurphu and the third highest Tibetan Buddhist leader escaped into exile.

● **2000** In July, Chinese state media say the government is winning its battle against separatism in Tibet. World Bank officials refuse to back a controversial scheme to resettle almost 60,000 Chinese farmers on traditional Tibetan land.

Dalai Lama not invited to UN worldwide peace conference for religious leaders. In October, British officials claim they were shown photographs of 10th Panchen Lama, Gedhun Choekyi Nyima.

Dalai Lama continues visits to worldwide leaders including a historic visit to Northern Ireland.

• **2001** In May the Dalai Lama meets with US President George Bush in a historic White House meeting. In July, Beijing is awarded the 2008 Olympics Games.

China announce latest plans to build a railway linking Lhasa with Qinghai and other Chinese provinces (to be completed by 2005). Lhasa authorities are currently implementing ambitious plans to more than quadruple the area of urban Lhasa from its current 53 sq km to 272 sq km by 2015 and to increase the urban population by 30% over the next four years.

Dalai Lama attends Noble Peace Prize centennial symposium in Oslo. In November, China granted accession to WTO.

Tibetan Government-in-Exile launch new book *Tibet Under Communist China – 50 Years.*

• **2002** Chinese erect a 37m-high monument in Potala Palace Square to commemorate the 50th anniversary of the 'peaceful liberation' of Tibet.

Tanak Jigme Sangpo, Tibet's longest-serving political prisoner, is released. The 76-year-old was reportedly freed on medical parole, having spent a total of 32 years in prison.

In his annual 10th March Statement (commemorating the 1959 Lhasa Uprising), the Dalai Lama reaffirmed his commitment to dialogue with the Chinese leaders saying that 'as soon as there is a positive signal from Beijing, my designated representatives stand ready to meet with the officials of the Chinese government anywhere, anytime'. Dalai Lama's speech also contains forceful words about the international campaign against terrorism saying it is 'hypocrisy to condemn and combat those who have risen in anger and despair' while ignoring 'those who have consistently espoused restraint and dialogue'.

Tibetan Buddhism

This is my simple religion. There is no need for temples; No need for complicated philosophy. Our own brain, our own heart is our temple. The philosophy is kindness. **His Holiness 14th Dalai Lama**

EARLY TIBETAN MYTHOLOGY

Prior to the beginning of Tibetan Buddhism, Tibetans practised a religion called Bon. The tradition of Bon describes the descent of man from a monkey (the father of man) and an ogress (the mother). The monkey and the ogress were believed to have lived in the valley of Yarlung. The children of the monkey and the ogress played in the valleys and one of the villages in Yarlung, called Tsetang, or 'Playground'. The monkey and the ogress's six sons were believed to have been the original ancestors of six Tibetan clans. The valley itself is now referred to as the 'Cradle of Civilization' of Tibet.

Bon tradition

Bon is really a collection of folk religions that originated in Western Tibet more than 1300 years ago.

It is the integration of many Bon traditions into Indian Buddhism that has made Tibetan Buddhism unique. Tibetan kings were seen as divine objects and the consultation of 'oracle' priests had great importance. Blood sacrifices, generally animal but sometimes human, were offered to the gods of the sky, the earth and the netherworld. Many of the deities were 'man-like', with terrifying aspects. Some of those terrifying images were later incorporated into Tibetan Buddhism as 'protectors of the faith'. These symbols can be seen today in Tibetan art.

Bon traditions still appear in some parts of Tibet, notably the Menri area around the Shang Valley in Western Tibet.

Yarlung Valley: 'Cradle of Civilization'

People settled in the Yarlung valleys and began an agricultural society, which complemented the livelihood of the nomads who continued to live in the higher lands. Local chiefs ruled their own towns (or forts called *dzong*) and different communities were established.

The Yarlung Valley was ruled by a succession of kings and, in 127BC, King Nyatri Tsampo constructed the first fort in Tibet at Yumbu, named Yumbulagang. The same dynasty continued to rule until the eighth king, King Drigum Tsampo, and his sons fell victim of a revolt by the King's Bon followers. Some time later, the younger of King Drigum Tsampo's two sons, Jatri Tsampo, regained power and set about constructing a tomb for his father in the Yarlung Valley. A long line of descendants succeeded King Tsampo and the Yarlung Valley was to remain the seat of power for many years after his death.

ORIGINS OF TIBETAN BUDDHISM

Any study of the origins of Tibetan Buddhism must necessarily start with the origins of Buddhism itself – in India. In approximately 500BC, in the small state of Kapilavastu, south of Nepal, Prince Siddharta, the boy who was to become Buddha, was born. As an adolescent, the boy left his family and joined a group of monks. He tried to find a sense of fulfilment with the monks but was left dissatisfied. Then, one evening the young prince sat under a bodhi tree near Gaya and felt that the revelation he had been seeking was 'illumination'. He discovered that earthly misfortunes created evil in the world and one's moral objective must be to place the conscience on a level where such things are controlled by the spirit. The spirit of conscience must rise to the level of the gods, unburdened by human suffering.

The Buddha's teachings are based on the four noble truths. Those are (1) that misery is an inevitable part of life, (2) that misery originates from desire, (3) that desire can be eliminated, and (4) that the overcoming of desire, and hence suffering, is made possible by following the eightfold path of virtue. The eightfold path of virtue is as follows:

- Right understanding (ie free from superstition and delusion)
- Right thought (ie high and worthy of human intelligence)
- Right speech (ie kind and truthful)
- Right actions (ie peaceful, honest and pure)
- Right livelihood (ie not bringing hurt or danger to any living being)
- Right effort (ie in self-training and self-control)
- Right mindfulness (ie having an active, watchful mind)
- Right concentration (ie in deep meditation on the realities of life)

These teachings spread throughout India and its neighbouring countries. One of those countries was Tibet.

As the scattered tribes of Tibet united under the rule of the Yarlung kings, the country's stability increased and this expansion brought the Tibetan people into closer contact with neighbouring countries and with the teachings of Buddha. Tibetan Buddhism grew into an institution in itself, based on a series of schools.

The Many 'Hats' of Tibetan Buddhism

The four schools of Tibetan Buddhism were established during different periods with different Indian lineages and each has a distinct path to reach enlightenment. The distinguishing feature of Tibetan Buddhism is its assimilation of elements of the indigenous Bon traditions, Sakyamuni Buddhist teachings and the adaptable medium of *Tantra* (a mystic philosophy developed in ancient India that greatly influenced Hinduism and Buddhism).

The Nyingma was the first wave of Tibetan Buddhism, which emerged in the 8th century. The Sakya and Kaygu formed the second wave of Tibetan Buddhism, which emerged in two separate regions in Tibet in the 11th century. The Gelug school is the most recent adaptation of Tibetan Buddhism and it emerged in the 14th century.

Nyingma school (meaning 'Those of the Ancient Tradition')

Nyingma was founded by the Indian mystic Padmasambhava (in Tibetan Guru Rinpoche – 'the precious master') in the 8th century. This is essentially Tantric Buddhism. Tantra schools rely heavily on the recitation of 'secret' mantra and the use of symbols and mandalas (cosmic pictures) as a means of identifying with superhuman powers.

Guru Rinpoche converted Bon priests by displaying how the powers of the ferocious Bon deities could be harnessed for the benefit of all sentient beings.

In the early stages of Nyingma, followers relied solely on the oral teaching of doctrines from master to student. During the 11th century the most important Nyingma lamas were the discoverers (*tertons*) of the treasures (*termas*), which were mostly texts concealed by Guru Rinpoche in mountain caves. During this period, the first Nyingma monasteries were established, including Mindroling, Dorje Drak and Pelyul.

The essential tenet of Nyingma is the belief that the physical world perceived by most human beings is insignificant and that there is an opportunity for those who reach certain stages of higher wisdom to obtain sudden enlightenment.

Sakya school (meaning 'White Earth')

The Sakya school was founded during the 11th century. Originally inspired by the teachings of the Indian master Birwapa (Virupa), the Sakya tradition of Buddhism was introduced into Tibet by Drokmi

MAIN SCHOOLS OF TIBETAN BUDDHISM

Name	Nyingma	Sakya	Kagyu	Gelug
Established	8th century	11th century	11th century	14th century
Tibetan founder	Bon priests	Khonchog Gyelpo	Marpa	Tsongkhapa
Indian lineage	Padmasambhava (Guru Rinpoche)	Birwapa	Tilopa	Atisha
Other prominent figures	Longchen Rabjampa	Sakya Pandita	Milarepa	Dalai Lama Panchen Lama
Original monastery	Katok Sakya	Daklha	Gampo	Ganden
Other main monasteries	Mindroling Dorje Drak	Ngor Gongkar Chöde	Tsurphu Yangpachen Til Drepung	Drigung, Sera Tashilhunpo Labrang Kumbum
Succession	Treasure finders '*tertons*'	Marriage/family inheritance	Transmission of secret doctrines to chosen disciples	Reincarnation

Lotsawa, who had learnt from the master during his travels to India. The first Sakya monastery was founded by Khonchog Gyelpo of the Khon clan. It was located in the Tibetan village of Sakya and, accordingly, the sect was named Sakya. All Sakya school monasteries may be easily identified by their vertical tricolour stripes of red, white and grey. The tricolour stripes represent the three great Bodhisattvas. These are the three celestial beings of Avalokitesvara, the bodhisattva of compassion, Manjusri, the bodhisattva of wisdom, and Maitreya, in whom heaven awaits birth as the next buddha.

Sakya is a mix of old and new Tantra combined with systematic philosophical and logical analysis. That mix, more than any other feature, characterizes the school. The most revered Sakya lamas were the most educated scholars in Tibet, and include Sakya Pandita, who held the position of the fourth Great Lama of Sakya during the period of Sakya's political ascendancy. Succession of the head lamas was limited to the members of the Khon family.

The Sakya school is primarily a monastic school, with an emphasis on intellectual achievement. Sakya members' practice involves the mystical path (called *lamdre*), which is a quintessential Tantric path leading quickly to enlightenment.

Kagyu school (meaning 'Oral Instruction') The Kagyu lineage originates from the Indian masters Tilopa, Naropa and Marpa and emphasizes meditation. Marpa was the first master to enter Tibet in the 11th century, where he had four main disciples including the famous yogi Milarepa (1040-1123).

The biography and songs of the mystic poet Milarepa have been translated into many languages. He is revered in Tibet for his retreat into a cave, robed in a cotton cloth, where he subsisted on nettle soup (and is reputed to have turned green as a consequence) and more importantly, for his rare achievement of attaining enlightenment in one lifetime.

It was Milarepa's principal student, Gampopa, who founded the first school at Daklha Gampo in the early 12th century. Gampopa's own students founded the influential monasteries at Densatil and Tsurphu. The Karmapa Kagyu school at Tsurphu became the most successful in the political arena.

Gelug School (meaning 'Virtuous Ones') The Gelug lineage can be traced back to the Bengali master, Atisha, who arrived in Tibet in the 11th century and formed the Kadampa school (meaning 'Buddha's commandments'). Atisha insisted on a return to Buddha's original doctrines and the observance of monastic disciplines. He looked down upon the coarser forms of Tantric worship that had become popular in Tibet. The Kadampa sect was eventually absorbed within the Gelug school.

The Gelug school emerged in the 14th century, as the strength of the Sakya school was diminishing. It was founded by a gifted man from Amdo, Je Tsongkhapa (1357-1419). Tsongkhapa travelled around Tibet paying homage to the Kagyu, Sakya and Kadampa sects and drawing strength from these established the Gelug school, based on discipline and with equal stress on philosophy and Tantric mysticism.

In 1409, Tsongkhapa established the first Gelug monastery at Ganden. He also organized the first Great Prayer Festival (*Monlam*) in Lhasa. Tsongkhapa also provided the largest and most integrated body of scripture written by a Tibetan – some 24 volumes of text.

Under the doctrines of Gelug, each monk is to undergo 20 years of study, which leads him to his academic degree and title of *geshe*. These are the minimum requirements before yoga and meditation practice in the Tantric tradition is permitted. The study of logic is considered very important and monks take part in regular debates according to formal rules.

After Tsongkhapa's death, the principle of *tulku* ('living Buddha') came into existence. The head abbots of the Gelug school were believed to be successive incarnations of the Bodhisattva Chenresi (the 'Protector of Tibet'). Tsongkhapa's successors were subsequently bestowed the universal title Dalai Lama ('Master Ocean of Wisdom').

The six greatest Gelug monasteries are at Ganden, Drepung, Sera, Tashilhunpo, Labrang in Gansu and Kumbum Jampaling near Xining.

SONGSTEN GAMPO – GREATEST OF TIBETAN KINGS

A key turning point in early Tibetan history came during the period of rule of Songsten Gampo, from AD629 to AD650. Songsten Gampo is known as the greatest of the Tibetan kings. He introduced major welfare and administrative reforms and expanded his territory. He also sent a delegation to India and the sole survivor of that delegation returned and went on to design a script for the Tibetan language.

Songsten Gampo married nine queens of neighbouring countries, including both the daughter of the Nepalese ruler and a Chinese princess. (His marriage to the Chinese princess is now widely publicized in tourist sites in Lhasa, and is touted by the Chinese as a principal source of China's sovereignty over Tibet. Little mention is made of his equally important Nepalese wife, nor his many Tibetan wives.) Songsten Gampo had to defeat a rival suitor for his Chinese Princess, namely the ruler of eastern Tartar. The Chinese Emperor still refused to give his daughter's hand, but Songsten Gampo defeated the Chinese in an armed conflict and the emperor was eventually forced to permit the marriage.

Songsten Gampo asked each of his wives to bring Buddhist artefacts and texts to Tibet and built a series of imperial temples, including the Jokhang and Ramoche, to house them. Around these temples he created his new capital city of Lhasa.

Before his death, Songsten Gampo divided his kingdom into six districts and put a governor in charge of each. Those governors distributed land amongst their subjects and class divisions were created between soldiers, farmers, attendants and landed classes.

For the next two centuries, the descendants of Songsten Gampo continued to rule and carry out his work of cultural transformation and education. The process culminated in the 790s when the then king, Trisong Detsen, together with the Indian mystic Padmasambhava and Indian Buddhist abbot, Shantirakshita, built the first monastic university in Tibet. The monastery was called Samye and is located in the Yarlung valley.

SAKYA AND MONGOLIAN RULE

In 1073, the first chapels of Sakya monastery were founded and the seat of the Sakya sect of Buddhism was established. At the beginning of the 13th century, Genghis Khan invaded much of central Asia and China. In 1239, Genghis Khan's son invaded Tibet. He summoned the leader of the Sakya sect and symbolically vested in him temporal authority over the whole of Tibet. They continued to serve as viceroys of Tibet on behalf of the Mongol emperors until challenged by new sects.

When the Mongolian Empire fell apart in the 14th century, the Tibetan secular dynasty arose and continued until 1959. This became an era of national dedication to the practice of Buddhism and the Great Prayer Festival (*Monlam*) was founded in Lhasa in 1409 (and continues to be practised to this day).

GELUG AND THE DALAI LAMAS

A new leader, Je Tsongkhapa, transformed Tibet spiritually, socially and aesthetically, in the 15th century. Monasteries were built throughout the country and more and more

men and women became members of those monasteries and began to seek enlightenment. This created a peaceful social climate, as there were far fewer available people
for the armies of the remaining warlords.

Tsongkhapa then founded the Gelug sect of Buddhism and established the first
Gelug monastery at Ganden in 1409. Sonam Gyatso became the leader of the sect in
the 16th century. The Mongolian King gave him the title Dalai Lama (meaning
'Master Ocean of Wisdom') and retroactively recognized his two earlier predecessors
also as Dalai Lamas.

The 4th Dalai Lama was the child of a Mongolian tribal chief and he recognized
his teacher as the first Panchen Lama. The 5th Dalai Lama ('Great Fifth') ruled with a
monastic style of government, which was almost completely demilitarized. From the
time of the 5th Dalai Lama, until the entry of the Chinese army in 1959, the Tibetan
government was based on monastic education and literature and philosophy. The ascendancy of power through reincarnation was reinforced when the 5th Dalai Lama recognized the reincarnation of the second Panchen Lama (the second highest leader in the
Gelug school) and installed him in his own seat at Tashilhunpo monastery in Shigatse.

The 5th Dalai Lama built Potala Palace and died in it. His ministers concealed his
death for 13 years until the building of the palace was complete because of their desire
to retain the economic and administrative stability that had endured throughout his reign.

The 6th Dalai Lama was not noted for his respect for the monastic rules nor his
ability to rule the state but is renowned for his extravagant lifestyle (including
romances and drinking) and poetry. The ministers continued to run the country during
his reign. The 7th Dalai Lama was installed in the 18th century but there were differ-
ences between him and his ministers. From his rule until that of the 13th Dalai Lama,
there was a series of quick successions and repeated interference from China.

The 13th Dalai Lama, on the other hand, became a powerful leader of a nation that
was, at the time, politically and economically weakened by a lack of stability in leadership and interference by the Chinese. He devoted himself to improving the standard of
living of Tibetan people and worked on as many development projects as possible, given
the restrictions imposed by the climate, isolation and lack of human resources.

THE 20TH CENTURY IN TIBET

The 20th century has been a period of enormous upheaval for the Tibetan population.
Its years of relative isolation from the rest of the world, especially the West, were to
end and its autonomy was to be lost. Colonel Francis Younghusband of the British
army based in India entered Tibet by force from Sikkim in 1904. The British retained
a small presence in Tibet until the mid 20th century.

By the beginning of the 20th century, China was requesting that Tibet become one
of its provinces. That request was emphatically refused by the 13th Dalai Lama. In
response to the threat from Russia in the north, a tripartite conference was arranged in
Simla (northern India) between China, Tibet and British-India. The resulting Simla
Agreement provided that Tibet was under the suzerainty (caretakership) of China but
that China would not interfere with Tibet's autonomy. China never signed the agreement, although British-India and Tibet did. In 1913, the 13th Dalai Lama asserted the
independence of Tibet and expelled all Chinese troops.

In the 1920s, China's interest in Tibet was increasing and there were repeated invasions. In 1933, the 13th Dalai Lama died and Tibet was once again ruled by ministers.

The 14th Dalai Lama

The 14th and reigning Dalai Lama was installed in 1940. In 1949, China fell to communist rule, headed by Mao Tse-tung. In 1950, the Chinese communist government

marched into Tibet and captured parts of the north-east (particularly the province of Amdo). The Tibetan army was ill-equipped to hold back the massive Chinese army. When India protested against its actions, China declared that Tibet was an integral part of China and that India should not interfere with its internal affairs.

The years from 1950 to 1959 led to a massive transformation of Tibet and years of hardship for the Tibetan people. Despite the young Dalai Lama's visits to India and efforts to secure international support for the sovereignty of his state, he was not able to prevent the Chinese occupation of Tibet.

The Dalai Lama remained in Lhasa until 1959, but by that time Tibet was a country under siege. In 1959 the Dalai Lama was forced to depart Lhasa in fear of his life.

What followed was a period of mass destruction of Tibetan culture and life, all in the name of the 'Cultural Revolution'. Monasteries were systematically destroyed and Tibetan people were forced to carry out labouring work to extend the Chinese road and utility infrastructure through Tibet. Tibet was not treated any differently to China itself under the communist regime. The destructiveness of the 'Cultural Revolution' left no sacred item unturned throughout China. It was a tragic time in China's history – but even more so for Tibet. It marked the beginning of China's assertion that Tibet was an 'inalienable part of the motherland of China', and hence subject to all the destructive forces that were sweeping through China at the time. The effects of the 'Cultural Revolution' have been condemned by subsequent Chinese administrations (although those in Tibet are quick to blame Tibetan recruits of the 'Red Guard' for much of the damage in the region). Over 6000 monasteries and ancient artefacts, books and universities were destroyed across the nation and the damage will never be rectified.

The 14th Dalai Lama currently lives in exile with hundreds of thousands of Tibetan refugees. The message that he continues to preach to the world is one of peace. The systematic destruction and repression of the Tibetan way of life in Tibet goes on.

Tibetan festivals

The Tibetan calendar is based on phases of the moon rather than the sun and as a result lags behind the Western (Gregorian) solar calendar by four to eight weeks. The Tibetan New Year, for example, begins in February. However, as lunar months are not exactly 30 days long, additional days are included in the calendar at auspicious times in order to align the seasons with the months.

The Tibetan calendar commences at the birth of Buddha and runs in 60-year cycles. Each cycle is named after one of 12 animals in combination with one of the mystical elements – fire, earth, iron, water or wood (eg 2000 was the Iron Dragon Year).

The principal religious festivals held throughout the Tibetan calendar are listed below. To check lunar dates against Gregorian calendar dates see the following website: 🖥 www.fpmt.org/resources/dates.asp.

FIRST LUNAR MONTH

Days 1-3 – *Losar* **New Year Festival** Celebrations start by spending time with family and then friends. Prayer flags are replaced and incense offerings are made. All Tibetans don their finest clothing.

Days 4-25 – *Monlam* **Great Prayer Festival** Held in Lhasa and instigated in 1409 by Tsongkhapa, this prayer congregation used to include about 10,000 monks.

Day 15 – Festival of the Great Miracle Celebrating Buddha's defeat of the six non-Buddhist teachers at Sravasti. Huge butter sculptures are displayed all around the Barkhor circuit.

Day 25 – Maitreya Buddha Procession The main statue of Maitreya Buddha (usually housed inside the Jokhang) is carted around the Barkhor circuit symbolizing the coming of Maitreya Buddha upon the fulfilment of Sakyamuni teachings.

SECOND LUNAR MONTH

Days 3-15 – Ganden Tantric Ceremony Sand mandalas are meticulously created during this festival at Ganden monastery.

Day 19 – Great Offering Ceremony Held at Jokhang to commemorate the death of the 5th Dalai Lama (the 'Great Fifth')

Day 29 – Festival of the Demon-Ransom King (Scapegoat Festival) Origins can be traced back to when leading pro-Bon ministers were expelled from Lhasa by pro-Buddhist ministers during King Trisong Detsen's reign.

Day 30 – Golden Procession Traditionally when the tomb of the 5th Dalai Lama in the Potala Place is unveiled for worshippers. Giant, 250ft-long *thangkas* are draped from the Potala's south face.

FOURTH LUNAR MONTH

Day 15 – Buddha's Enlightenment *Saga Dawa* (Full Moon Day) Possibly the most important day for Buddhists. Celebrating Buddha attaining full enlightenment *nirvana* at Bodhgaya under the bodhi tree.

FIFTH LUNAR MONTH

Day 5 – Dalai Lama's Birthday Tenzin Gyatso was born in Takster village, Amdo region near Xining (celebrated on July 6 in the west).

Day 15 – Universal Incense Day Commemorates the completion of Samye monastery (the first Buddhist monastic institution built in Tibet).

SIXTH LUNAR MONTH

Day 4 – Feast of Buddha's First Sermon Commemorating Buddha's first sermon on the Four Noble Truths at Sarnarth Deer Park near Varanasi.

Day 10 – Guru Rinpoche's (Padmasambhava) Birthday The great Indian mystic who was instrumental in establishing Buddhism in Tibet.

Day 29 – *Shoton* Yogurt Festival commences. Dress rehearsals.

**Day 30 – *Shoton* Yogurt Festival at Drepung and Sera. Hanging of large *thangkas*.

SEVENTH LUNAR MONTH

**Days 1-5 – *Shoton* Yogurt Festival in Lhasa. Opera *cham* performances at Norbulingka.

Day 8 – Drepung Lubum Tombs of 3rd and 4th Dalai Lamas, at Drepung monastery, are opened to the public.

Days 1-14 – *Ongkor* Harvest Festival Ceremonies performed by farmers sometime in the first two weeks to ensure healthy crops.

Day 27 – Bathing Festival Commences An auspicious period when all the rivers are said to be purified.

NINTH LUNAR MONTH

Day 22 – Buddha's Divine Descent Celebrating Buddha's descent from heaven where he spent time preaching to his mother.

TENTH LUNAR MONTH

Day 14 – Palden Lhamo Procession Ceremony around the Barkhor to invoke Palden Lhamo, the protective deity of the Jokhang.

Day 25 – Tsongkhapa's Death The celebrated founder of the Gelug sect.

ELEVENTH LUNAR MONTH

Days 6-7 – Nine Evils Day. Extremely inauspicious day to perform any tasks or travel (midday to midday).

Days 7-8 – Ten Auspicious Signs Very auspicious day for socializing and having fun (midday to midday).

TWELFTH LUNAR MONTH

Days 29-30 – Year End Festival Tibetans clean their houses to exorcise the previous years spirits. They eat *guthuk* (dumpling soup) and make *kapste* (fried sweet) as offerings.

Bibliography

Classic travel (many recent editions available)
A Conquest of Tibet, Sven Hedin (1934)
A Journey to Lhasa and Central Tibet, Sarat Chandra Das (1902)
Among the Tibetans, Isabella Bird Bishop (1904)
Bayonets to Lhasa, Peter Fleming (1961)
Captured in Tibet, Robert Ford (1957)
Diary of a Journey Across Tibet, Hamilton Bower (1894)
First Russia then Tibet, Robert Byron (1933)
Forbidden Journey, from Peking to Kashmir, Ella K. Maillart (1937)
Land of the Lamas: Notes of a Journey through China, Mongolia and Tibet, W. W. Rockhill. (1891)
Lhasa and Its Mysteries, L. Austine Waddell (1905)
Lhasa, the Holy City, F. Spencer Chapman (1940)
Lost Horizon, James Hilton (1933)
My Journey to Lhasa, Alexandra David-Neel (1927)
Narratives of the Mission of George Bogle to Tibet and of the journey of Thomas Manning to Lhasa, Clements R. Markham (1876)
Secret Tibet, Fosco Maraini (1952)
Seven Years in Tibet, Heinrich Harrer (1953)
The Opening of Tibet, Perceval Landon (1905)
Three Years in Tibet, Ekai Kawaguchi (1909)

Tintin in Tibet, Hergé (1958)
To Lhasa in Disguise: A secret expedition through mysterious Tibet, William McGovern (1924)

Contemporary travel
A Mountain in Tibet, Charles Allen (1982)
A Stranger in Tibet, Scott Berry (1989)
Among Warriors: A Martial Artist in Tibet, Pamela Logan (1996)
An Explorer's Adventure in Tibet: A Lonely Foreign Traveller Penetrates the Forbidden Land and Attempts to Reach the Province of Lhasa in 1897, A. Henry Savage Landor (2000)
Below Another Sky: A Mountain Adventure in Search of a Lost Father, Rick Ridgeway (2001)
Conjuring Tibet, Charlotte Painter (1996)
Courting the Diamond Sow: A Whitewater Expedition on Tibet's Forbidden River, Wickliffe W. Walker (2000)
Cycling to Xian, Michael Buckley (1988)
From Heaven Lake: Travels Through Sinkiang and Tibet, Vikram Seth (1986)
Himalayan Passage: Seven Months in the High Country of Tibet, Nepal, China, India, & Pakistan, Jeremy Schmidt & Patrick Morrow (1992)
In the Himalayas: Journeys Through Nepal, Tibet, and Bhutan, Jeremy Bernstein (1996)
Journey across Tibet: A woman's lone trek across a mysterious land, Sorrel Wilby (1988)
Mountains of the Middle Kingdom: Exploring the High Peaks of China and Tibet, Galen A. Rowell (1983)
Namma – A Tibetan Love Story, Kate Karko (2001)
On Top of the World: Five Women Explorers in Tibet, Luree Miller (1976)
The Sacred Mountain of Tibet: On pilgrimage to Kailas, Russell Johnson & Kerry Moran (1989)
The Last Barbarians: The Discovery of the Source of the Mekong in Tibet, Michel Peissel (1997)
The Outer Path: Finding My Way in Tibet, Jim Reynolds (1992)
Tibet: A Chronicle of Exploration, John MacGregor (1970)
Tibet's Secret Mountain: The Triumph of Sepu Kangri, Chris Bonington & Charles Clarke (1999)
Trespassers on the Roof of the World: The Secret Exploration of Tibet, Peter Hopkirk (1982)
Yak Butter & Black Tea: A Journey into Tibet, Wade Brackenbury (1997)
Younghusband, the last great imperial adventurer, Patrick French (1994)

Photobooks
A Portrait of Lost Tibet, Rosemary Jones Tung, et al. (1996)
From Manchuria to Tibet, Wong How & Man Wong (photographer), et al. (1998)
Lost Lhasa: Heinrich Harrer's Tibet, Heinrich Harrer (1997)
My Tibet, Dalai Lama & Galen A. Rowell (photographer) (1990)
Spirit of Tibet: Portrait of a Culture in Exile, Chokyi Nyima Rinpoche (1998)
The Face of Tibet, William Chapman (2001)
The Tibetans: A Struggle to Survive, Steve Lehman (photographer), et al. (1998)
The Tibetans: Photographs, Art Perry (1999)
Tibet: Caught in Time, John Clarke, et al. (1998)

Tibet: Journey to the Forbidden City: Retracing the Steps of Alexandra David-Néel, Tiziana & Gianna Baldizzone (1996)

Tibet: Reflections from the Wheel of Life, Thomas L. Kelly (photographer), et al. (1993)

Tibet: The Roof of the World Between Past and Present, Maria Antonia Sironi Diemberger. (2000)

Tibet: The Sacred Realm: Photographs 1880-1950, Lobsang P. Lhalungpa (1997)

Tibetan Portrait: The Power of Compassion, Phil Borges (photographer), et al. (1996)

Tibetan Voices: A Traditional Memoir, Brian Harris (photographer), et al. (1996)

Tibet's Hidden Wilderness: Wildlife and Nomads of the Chang Tang Reserve, George B. Schaller (1997)

Culture

Inside the Treasure House: A Time in Tibet, Catriona Bass (1990)

Nomads of Western Tibet: The Survival of a Way of Life, Melvyn C. Goldstein & Cynthia M. Beall (1990)

Precious Jewels of Tibet: A Journey to the Roof of the World, Jane Bay (1998)

Touching Tibet, Niema Ash (2000)

Warriors of Tibet, Jamyung Norbu (1986)

Political novels

A Poisoned Arrow, the secret report of the 10th Panchen Lama from Tibet Information Network (1997)

Cutting of the Serpent's Head: tightening control in Tibet 1994-95 from Human Rights Watch & Tibet Information Network (1996)

In Exile from the Land of Snows: The Definitive Account of the Dalai Lama and Tibet Since the Chinese Conquest, John F. Avedon (1984)

Red Star over Tibet, Norbu Dawa (1987)

Return to Tibet: Tibet After the Chinese Occupation, Heinrich Harrer (1983)

Sky Burial: An Eyewitness Account of China's Brutal Crackdown in Tibet, Blake Kerr (1997)

Sorrow Mountain: The remarkable story of a Tibetan warrior nun, Ani Panchen & Adelaide Donnelley (2000)

The Dragon in the Land of Snows, Tsering Shakya (1998)

Tibet: Enduring Spirit, Exploited Land, Robert Z. Apte & Andres R. Edwards (1998)

Tibet Since 1950: Silence, Prison, or Exile, Elliot Sperling (2000)

Tibet: The Road Ahead, Dawa Norbu (1998)

Tibetan Buddhism

Inside Tibetan Buddhism, Robert Thurman (1995)

The Iconography of Tibetan Lamaism, Antoinette K. Gordon (1959)

The Religion of Tibet, Charles Bell (1931)

The Sacred Life of Tibet, Keith Dowman (1997)

Tibetan Art: Toward a Definition of Style, Jane Casey Singer & Philip Denwood (1997)

Tibetan Book of Living and Dying, Sogyal Rinpoche, et al. (1992)

Tibet's Great Yogi Milarepa, W. Y. Evans-Wentz (1928)

Dalai Lama

Ethics for the New Millennium, Dalai Lama (1999)

Freedom in Exile: The Autobiography of the Dalai Lama, Dalai Lama (1990)

Kundun: A Biography of the Family of the Dalai Lama, Mary Craig (1997)

My Land and My People, Dalai Lama (1962)
Portrait of the Dalai Lama (The Thirteenth Dalai Lama 1876-1933), Charles Bell (1946)
The Art of Happiness: A Handbook for Living, Dalai Lama & Howard C. Cutler (1998)
The Search for the Panchen Lama, Isabel Hilton (1999)
The Wisdom Teachings of the Dalai Lama, Matthew E. Bunson (1997)
The World of the Dalai Lama, Gill Farrer-Halls (1998)

History

A Cultural History of Tibet, David Snellgrove & Hugh Richardson (1968)
A History of Modern Tibet 1913-1951, Melvyn C. Goldstein (1989)
Tibet and Its History, Hugh Richardson (1962)
Tibet, Its History, Religion and People, Thubten Jigme Norbu & Colin Turnbull (1983)
Tibetan Civilisation, R. A. Stein (1972)
Tibetan Nation: A History of Tibetan Nationalism & Sino-Tibetan Relations, W. W.
  Smith et al. (1996)

Legal status

*The Case Concerning Tibet: Tibet's Sovereignty and the Tibetan People's Right to Self-
Determination* from International Committee of Lawyers for Tibet & Unrepresented
  Nations and People's Organisation (1998)
The Status of Tibet, history, rights and prospects in international law, Michael C. van
  Walt van Praag (1987)
Tibet: Human Rights and the Rule of Law, International Commission of Jurists (1997)
*Tibet: The Position in International Law – Report of the Conference of International
Lawyers in Issues relating to Self-determination and Independence for Tibet,* J.
  McCorquodale & N. Orosz (eds) (1994)
Tibetan People's Right of Self-Determination a Report of the workshop on self-
  determination of the Tibetan People: Legitimacy of Tibet's Case 1994/1996, India
  (1996)

Guidebooks

Mapping the Tibetan World, Yukiyasu Osada et al. (Kotan, 2000)
Nepal, Tibet and Bhutan Edited, Laura M Kidder (Fodor's, 2000)
Odyssey Illustrated Guide to Tibet, Elizabeth Booz (1998)
The Power-Places of Central Tibet – The Pilgrim's Guide, Keith Dowman (1988)
The Tibet Guide: Central and Western Tibet (2nd ed), Stephen Batchelor (Wisdom,
  1998)
Tibet Handbook, Victor Chan (Moon, 1994)
Tibet Handbook: with Bhutan (2nd ed), Gyurme Dorje (Footprint, 1996)
Tibet (5th ed), Bradley Mayhew et al (Lonely Planet, 2002)
Tibet: Lhasa-Kathmandu (Insight Pocket Guides, 1998)
Tibet Travel Adventure Guide, Michael Buckley (ITMB, 1999)
Tibetan Phrasebook – Lonely Planet (3rd ed), Sandup Tsering (2002)
Trekking in Tibet: A Traveller's Guide (2nd ed), Gary McCue (Mountaineers, 1999)

Health

The High Altitude Medicine Handbook (Micro Edition), Andrew J Pollard and David
  R Murdoch (1997)
Medicine for Mountaineering, edited by James Wilkerson (4th edition, 1992)

Useful Tibetan words

Greetings

Hello *tashi deleg* བཀྲ་ཤིས་བདེ་ལེགས་
Goodbye *ga la pheb* ག་ལ་ཕེབས་
Please *cha pe nang* ཕྱག་ཕེབས་གནང་
Thank you *thu je zig* ཐུགས་རྗེ་གཟིགས་
Sorry *thu je chhe* ཐུགས་རྗེ་ཆེ་
Yes *gong dhaa* དགོངས་དག
No (thank you) *re, yin dhoo* རེད། ཨིན། འདུག
Tibet *Bö* བོད་
China *Gya nag* རྒྱ་ནག
Tibetan (person) *Pö pa* བོད་པ
Chinese (person) *Gya mi* རྒྱ་མི་

Time

today *de ring* དེ་རིང་
yesterday *ka sang* ཁ་སང
tomorrow *sang nyi* སང་ཉིན་
now *ta ta* ད་ལྟ
morning *sho gey* ཞོགས་གས
afternoon *gong do* དགོང་དྲོ་
hour *chhu tsö* ཆུ་ཚོད་
day *nyin pa* ཉིན་པ
week *dün trap* བདུན་ཕྲག
month *da wa* ཟླ་བ
year *lo* ལོ་

Family

grandfather *mo mo* རྨོ་མོ་
grandmother *po bo* སྤོ་བོ་
father *pa pa* པ་པ
mother *a ma* ཨ་མ
boy *bu* བུ
girl *bu mo* བུ་མོ་
child *phu gu* ཕྲུ་གུ

Numbers

one *chig* གཅིག
two *nyi* གཉིས་
three *sum* གསུམ
four *shi* བཞི་
five *nga* ལྔ་

Numbers (cont)

six *dug* དྲུག
seven *dhün* བདུན་
eight *gye* བརྒྱད་
nine *gu* དགུ
ten *shu* བཅུ
twenty *nyi shu* ཉི་ཤུ་བཅུ
fifty *na shu* ལྔ་བཅུ
one hundred *gya thampa* བརྒྱ་ཐམ་པ

Transport

bicycle *kan ga ri* རྐང་ག་རིལ
bus *chicho langkor* སྤྱི་སྤྱོད་ལྔ་འཁོར་
truck *mo ta* མོ་ཊ
taxi *leche mota* གླ་བྱེད་མོ་ཊ
aeroplane *nam dru* གནམ་གྲུ
hire *la* གླ
ticket *pa ce* པ་སེ
bus station འབབ་ཚུགས་
airport *namdru babthang* གནམ་འགྲུ་འབབ་ཐང་

Health

hospital *men khang* སྨན་ཁང
sick *ney pa* ནད་པ
doctor *em chi* ཨེམ་རྗེ་
headache *go ney* མགོ་ནད
medicine *men pa* སྨན་པ
dog *kyi* ཁྱི
diarrhoea *shel ney* བཤལ་ནད
fever *tsha wa* ཚ་བ

Money, passport

money *ngül* དངུལ
passport *tang* བང་
visa *tang* བང་
bank *ngül kang* དངུལ་ཁང་

Accommodation

bed *nye tri* ཉལ་ཁྲི
hotel *drön kang* མགྲོན་ཁང་
toilet *san jeu* གསང་སྤྱོད་

hot *tsa bo* ཚ་པོ་

cold *trang mo* གྲང་མོ་

wash *tru* འཁྲུ་

cost *kong* གོང་

Food and drink

food *ka lag* ཁ་ལག

restaurant *sa kang* ས་ཁང་

shop *tson kang* ཚོང་ཁང་

water (bottled) *chu* ཆུ་

hot water *chu tsabo* ཆུ་ཚ་པོ་

tea *sha* ཇ་

Tibetan tea *Bö sha* བོད་ཇ་

sugar *nga mo* མངར་མོ་

beer *pi yu* པི་རུག

Tibetan beer *chang* ཆང་

barley *ney* ནས་

wheat *do* གྲོ་

cheese *chur wa* ཕྱུར་བ་

flour *do ship* གྲོ་ཞིབ་

yogurt *sho* ཞོ་

bread *ta lep* བག་ལེབ་

rice *dey* འབྲས་

milk *o ma* ཨོ་མ་

butter *maa* མར་

meat *sha* ཤ་

egg *ko nga* གོང་

onion *tsong* ཚོང་

potato *sho kho* ཞོ་ཁོག

vegetables *tsay* ཚལ་

noodle soup *tug pa* ཐུག་པ་

dumplings *mo mo* མོག་མོག

salt *tsa* ཚ་

Religious words

monastery *gom pa* དགོན་པ་

nunnery *ani gompa* ཨ་ནི་དགོན་པ་

temple *lha kang* ལྷ་ཁང་

chapel *lha kang* ལྷ་ཁང་

protector chapel *gön kang* དགོན་ཁང་

assembly hall *du kang* འདུ་ཁང་

butter lamp *ma me* མར་མེ་

incense *pö cha* སྤོས་ཆག

circumambulate *kor wa* འཁོར་བ་

monk *dra pa* གྲྭ་པ་

nun *a ni* ཨ་ནི་

deity *lha* ལྷ་

Buddhist *Nang pa* ནང་པ་

stupa *chorten* མཆོད་རྟེན་

religious sect *chö luk* ཆོས་ལུགས་

prayer scarf *ga'u* འདགའ་

prayer wheel *ma ni* མ་ནི་

prayer stones *mani to* མ་ནི་རྡོ་

photograph *par* པར་

book *dep* དེབ་

Directions

north *jang* བྱང་

south *lho* ལྷོ་

east *shar* ཤར་

west *nub* ནུབ་

left *yön* གཡོན་

right *yee* གཡས་

Landscape/weather

lake *tso* མཚོ་

mountain *ri* རི་

hermitage *ri trö* རི་ཁྲོད་

fortress *dzong* རྫོང་

pass *la* ལ་

glacier *kya pa* ཁྱགས་པ་

snowy mountain *gang ri* གངས་རི་

road *lam ka* ལམ་ཁག

river *chu, tsang po* ཆུ། གཙང་པོ་

rain *cha pa* ཆར་པ་

valley *lung pa* ལུང་པ་

village *dong seb* གྲོང་གསེབ་

house *kang pa* ཁང་པ་

cloud *pin mo* སྤྲིན་མོ་

snow *ngey* གངས་

bridge *sam pa* ཟམ་པ་

hot spring *chu tsen* ཆུ་ཚན་

nomad *drok pa* འབྲོག་པ་

prayer flag *lung ta* རླུང་རྟ་

yak (male) *yak* གཡག

yak (female) *dri* འབྲི་

yak (cattle hybrid) *dzo, dzo mo* མཛོ། མཛོ་མོ་

Camping equipment

cup *ka yeu* དཀར་ཡོལ་

bowl *por ba* ཕོར་པ་

bottle *shel dam* ཤེལ་དམ་

film *lok nyen* སློག་བརྙན་
kerosene *do num* རྡོ་སྣུམ་
petrol *num* སྣུམ་
knife *di dri* རི་གྲི་
map *sa tra* ས་བཀྲ་

match *mu si* མུ་སི་
tent *kur* གུར་
tent (nomad) *pa kur* སྦྲ་གུར་
thermos *cha dam* ཇ་དམ་
stove (cooker) *tab* ཐབ་

Gazetteer

Amdo province ཨ་མདོ་
Chamdo ཆབ་མདོ་
Chongye འཕྱོངས་རྒྱས་
Chüsül ཆུ་ཤུར་
Damshung འདམ་གཞུང་
Drepung monastery འབྲས་སྤུངས་
Drigung འབྲི་གུང་
Mt Everest ཇོ་མོ་གང་དཀར་
Ganden monastery དགའ་ལྡན་
Gongkar གོང་དཀར་
Gongkar airport གོང་དཀར་
Gyantse རྒྱལ་རྩེ་
Jidding དགེ་ལྡིང་
Jokhang ཇོ་ཁང་
Mt Kailash གངས་རིན་པོ་ཆེ་
Kham province ཁམས་
Kharta མཁར་ཏ་
Lhasa ལྷ་ས་
Lhatse ལྷ་རྩེ་
Litang ལི་ཐང་
Lake Manasarovar མ་ར་ཕམ་ཡུལ་མཚོ་
Markham སྨར་ཁམས་
Medrogongka མལ་གྲོ་གུང་དཀར་
Mindroling monastery སྨིན་གྲོལ་གླིང་
Nam Tso གནམ་མཚོ་
Nangartse སྣ་དཀར་རྩེ་
Nakchu ནག་ཆུ་

Nedong སྣེ་གདོང་
Norbulingka Palace ནོར་བུ་གླིང་ཁ་
Nyalam གཉའ་ལམ་
Penam པ་སྣམ་
Potala Palace པོ་ཏ་ལ་
Rinpung རིན་སྤུངས་
Rongphu monastery རོང་ཕུ་
Sakya ས་སྐྱ་
Samding monastery བསམ་སྡིང་
Samye monastery བསམ་ཡས་
Sera monastery སེ་ར་
Shalu monastery ཞ་ལུ་
Shekar ཤེལ་དཀར་
Shigatse གཞིས་ཀ་རྩེ་
Taktse སྟག་རྩེ་
Thang province གཙང་
Tingri/Dingri དིང་རི་
Tolung Dechen སྟོད་ལུང་བདེ་ཆེན་
Tsetang རྩེད་ཐང་
Tsurphu monastery མཚུར་ཕུ་
Ü province དབུས་
Western Tibet མངའ་རིས་
Lake Yamdrok ཡར་འབྲོག་མཚོ་
Yangpachen ཡངས་པ་ཅན་
Yarlung ཡར་ལུང་
Yumbulagang ཡུམ་བུ་ན་སྒང་
Zhangmu འགྲམ་

TRAILBLAZER

Australia by Rail	4th edn out now
Azerbaijan	2nd edn out now
The Blues Highway: New Orleans to Chicago	1st edn out now
China by Rail	2nd edn Apr 2003
The Inca Trail, Cusco & Machu Picchu	2nd edn out now
Japan by Rail	1st edn out now
Kilimanjaro – treks and excursions	1st edn Jan 2003
Land's End to John o'Groats	1st edn mid 2003
Mexico's Yucatan & the Ruta Maya	1st edn mid 2003
Nepal Mountaineering Guide	1st edn early 2003
Norway's Arctic Highway	1st edn early 2003
Sahara Overland (English edn)	1st edn out now
Sahara Abenteuerhandbuch (German edn)	1st edn Oct 2002
Siberian BAM Rail Guide	2nd edn out now
Silk Route by Rail	2nd edn out now
The Silk Roads – a route & planning guide	1st edn Jan 2003
Ski Canada – where to ski and snowboard	1st edn out now
South-East Asia – a route & planning guide	1st edn Jan 2003
Trans-Canada Rail Guide	2nd edn out now
Trans-Siberian Handbook	5th edn out now
Trekking in the Annapurna Region	3rd edn out now
Trekking in Corsica	1st edn out now
Trekking in the Dolomites	1st edn out now
Trekking in the Everest Region	4th edn Jan 2003
Trekking in the Greek Pindos	1st edn mid 2003
Trekking in Ladakh	2nd edn out now
Trekking in the Moroccan Atlas	1st edn out now
Trekking in the Pyrenees	2nd edn out now
Trekking in Langtang, Gosainkund & Helambu	1st edn out now
UK Walking Guides – new six title series out in early 2003	
Vietnam by Rail	1st edn out now

For more information about Trailblazer and our expanding range of guides, for where to find your nearest stockist, for guidebook updates or for credit card mail order sales visit our Web site:

www.trailblazer-guides.com

ROUTE GUIDES FOR THE ADVENTUROUS TRAVELLER

TRAILBLAZER

The Silk Roads – a route & planning guide
Paul Wilson & Dominic Streatfeild-James
320pp, 50 maps, 30 colour photos
ISBN 1 873756 53 4, £11.99, Can$29.95, US$18.95 *1st edition*
The Silk Road was never a single thread but an intricate web of
trade routes linking Asia and Europe. This new guide follows all the
routes with sections on Turkey, Syria, Iran, Turkmenistan,
Uzbekistan, Kyrgyzstan, Kazakhstan, Pakistan and China.

Trekking in Ladakh *Charlie Loram*
288pp, 75 maps, 24 colour photos
ISBN 1 873756 30 5, £10.99, Can$22.95, US$18.95 *2nd edition*
Fully revised and extended 2nd edition of Charlie Loram's practical
guide. Includes 70 detailed walking maps plus information on get-
ting to Ladakh.
'Extensive...and well researched'. **Climber Magazine**
'Were it not for this book we might still be blundering about...'
The Independent on Sunday

Trekking in the Everest Region *Jamie McGuinness*
288pp, 50 maps, 20 village plans, 30 colour photos
ISBN 1 873756 60 7, £10.99, Can$27.95, US$17.95 *4th edition*
Popular guide to the world's most famous trekking region. Includes
detailed walking maps, where to stay and where to eat along the way
plus information on trek preparation and getting to Nepal. Written by a
professional trek leader.
'The pick of the guides to the area' **Adventure Travel**

Trans-Siberian Handbook *Bryn Thomas*
432pp, 48 maps, 32 colour photos
ISBN 1 873756 42 9, £12.99, Can$28.95 US$19.95 *5th edition*
First edition short-listed for the **Thomas Cook Guidebook Awards**.
New fifth edition of the most popular guide to the world's longest rail
journey. How to arrange a trip, plus a km-by-km guide to the routes.
Updated and expanded to include extra information on travelling
independently in Russia. New mapping.
'Definitive guide' **Condé Nast Traveler**

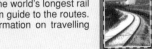

The Inca Trail, Cusco & Machu Picchu *Richard Danbury*
2nd edition, £10.99, Can$24.95, US$18.95
ISBN 1 873756 64 X, 288pp, 45 maps, 24 colour photos
The Inca Trail from Cusco to Machu Picchu is South America's most
popular hike. This practical guide includes 20 detailed trail maps,
plans of eight Inca sites, plus guides to Cusco and Machu Picchu.
'Danbury's research is thorough...you need this one'. **The Sunday
Times**

Trekking in the Moroccan Atlas *Richard Knight*
1st edition, £11.99, Can$26.95, US$17.95
ISBN 1 873756 35 6, 256pp, 50 maps, 30 colour photos
The Atlas mountains in southern Morocco provide one of the most
spectacular hiking destinations in Africa. This new guide includes
route descriptions and detailed maps for the best Atlas treks in the
Toubkal, M'goun, Sirwa and Jbel Sahro regions. Places to stay,
walking times and points of interest are all included, plus town
guides to Marrakesh and Ouarzazate.
'Excellent book'. **The Sunday Times**

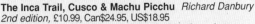

TRAILBLAZER

Adventure Motorcycling Handbook *Chris Scott*
4th edition, 288 pages, 28 colour, 100 B&W photos
ISBN 1 873756 37 2 £12.99, Can$29.95, US$19.95
Every red-blooded motorcyclist dreams of making the Big Trip – this book shows you how. Choosing a destination, bike preparation, documentation and shipping, trans-continental route outlines across Africa, Asia and Latin America, and back-country riding in SW USA, NW Canada and Australia. Plus – first-hand accounts of biking adventures worldwide. *'The closest thing to the Bible for overland adventure motorcyclists...'* **BikeNet**

Sahara Overland – a route & planning guide *Chris Scott*
1st edition, 544 pages, 24 colour & 150 B&W photos
ISBN 1 873756 26 7 £19.99, Can$44.95 US$29.95
Covers all aspects Saharan, from acquiring documentation to vehicle choice and preparation; from descriptions of the prehistoric art sites of the Libyan Fezzan to the ancient caravan cities of southern Mauritania. How to 'read' sand surfaces, using GPS – it's all here along with 35 detailed off-road itineraries covering over 16,000kms in nine countries. *"THE essential desert companion for anyone planning a Saharan trip on either two wheels or four.'* **Trailbike Magazine**

Trekking in the Pyrenees *Douglas Streatfeild-James*
2nd edition, £11.99, Can$27.95 US$18.95
ISBN 1 873756 50 X, 320pp, 95 maps, 55 colour photos
All the main trails along the France-Spain border including the GR10 (France) coast to coast hike and the GR11 (Spain) from Roncesvalles to Andorra, plus many shorter routes. 90 route maps include walking times and places to stay. Expanded to include greater coverage of routes in Spain. *'Readily accessible, well-written and most readable...'* **John Cleare**

Trekking in Corsica *David Abram*
320pp, 67 maps, 48 colour photos
ISBN 1 873756 63 1, £11.99, Can$27.95 US$18.95 *1st edition*
A mountain range rising straight from the sea, Corsica holds the most arrestingly beautiful and diverse landscapes in the Mediterranean. Among the many trails that penetrate its remotest corners, the GR20, which wriggles across the island's watershed, has gained an international reputation. This new guide also covers the best of the other routes. With 67 route maps and 9 village plans. Includes full colour flora guide.
'Excellent guide' **The Sunday Times**

Trekking in the Dolomites *Henry Stedman*
1st edition, £11.99, US$17.95, Can$27.95, 30 colour photos
ISBN 1 873756 34 8, 256pp, 52 trail maps, 13 town plans
The Dolomites region of northern Italy encompasses some of the most beautiful mountain scenery in Europe. This new guide features selected routes including Alta Via II, a West-East traverse and other trails, plus detailed guides to Cortina, Bolzano, Bressanone and 10 other towns. Also includes full colour flora section and bird identification guide.

Trans-Canada Rail Guide *Melissa Graham*
240 pages, 31 maps, 24 colour photos
ISBN 1 873756 39 9, *2nd edition*, £10.99, US$16.95
Expanded 2nd edition now includes Calgary city guide. Comprehensive guide to Canada's trans-continental railroad. Covers the entire route from coast to coast. What to see and where to stay in the cities along the line, with information for all budgets.
'Invaluable' – **The Daily Telegraph**

Index

COLOUR SECTION (following pages)

C1 **Top left** Resting beside the sacred Lake Yamdrok
Top right Accommodation at Tashi Dor monastery, near Lake Nam Tso
Bottom The magnificent north face of Mt Everest, seen from Rongphu monastery

C2 **Top** Prayer ceremony in the Jokhang, Tibet's most sacred temple
Bottom Monks conversing inside Tashilhunpo monastery, Shigatse

C3 **Top left/right** Father and daughter relaxing at Sera monastery, outskirts of Lhasa
Bottom Sharing a campsite with yak herders – a true highlight of any overland trip

C4 **Top left/right** Worshippers on their daily kora (pilgrimage circuit), Barkhor Square, Lhasa
Bottom Children collecting yak dung for the evening fire

C5 **Top** View from Samding monastery over a dry section of Lake Yamdrok to Mt Nojin Kangtsang
Bottom left Nine-storey Gyantse Kumbum inside the Pelkhor Chode complex at Gyantse
Bottom right Gilded copper temple rooftop inside Tashilhunpo monastery, Shigatse

All photographs © Kym McConnell & Wendy Miles

SCALES FOR MAPS (following pages)

Map 1 Lhasa–Ganden (1:450,000)
Map 2 Lhasa–Gongkar (1:500,000)
Map 3 Tsetang–Yarlung (1:450,000)
Map 4 Nam Tso (1:500,000)
Map 5 Yamdrok–Gyantse (1:500,000)
Map 6 Shigatse (1:500,000)
Map 7 Lhatse–Sakya (1:500,000)

Map 8 Dingri–Shekar (1:500,000)
Map 9 Rongphu–Everest (1:300,000)
Map 10 Nyalam–Zhangmu (1:500,000)

1:500,000: 10mm = 5km
1:450,000: 10mm = 4.5km
1:300,000: 10mm = 3km

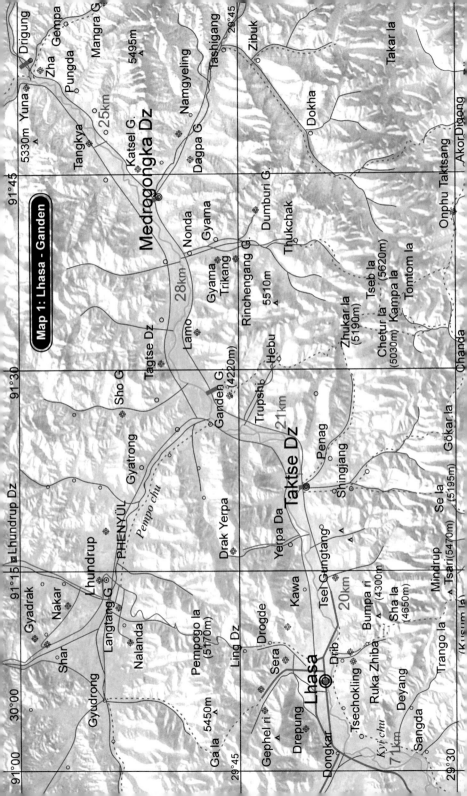

Map 1: Lhasa - Ganden

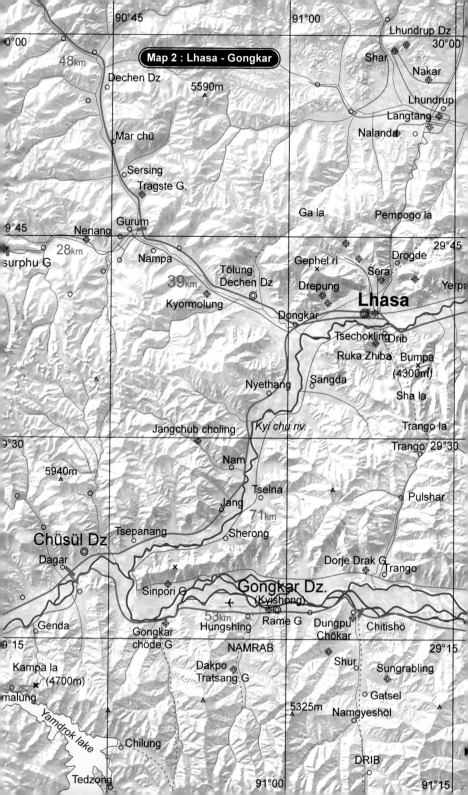

Map 2 : Lhasa - Gongkar

Map 3: Tsetang - Yarlung

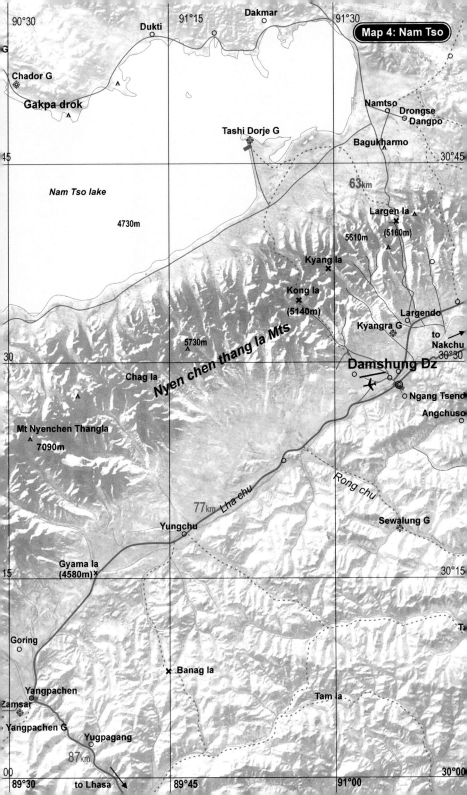

90°30   Dukti   91°15   Dakmar   91°30

G

Chador G

Gakpa drok

Namtso   Drongse
Dangpo

Tashi Dorje G

Bagukharmo

45   30°45

63km

Nam Tso lake

Largen la
4730m   5610m   (5160m)

Kyang la

Kong la
5730m   (5140m)

Largendo

Kyangra G

Nyen chen thang la Mts   to
Nakchu

Chag la   30   **Damshung Dz**   30°30

Ngang Tsend

Angchuso

Mt Nyenchen Thangla
7090m

Rong chu

77km *Lha chu*

Yungchu   Sewalung G

Gyama la
15   (4580m)   30°15

Goring

Banag la

Yangpachen
Zamsar   Tam la

Yangpachen G

Yugpagang
00   87km   30°00

to Lhasa   89°45   91°00

89°30

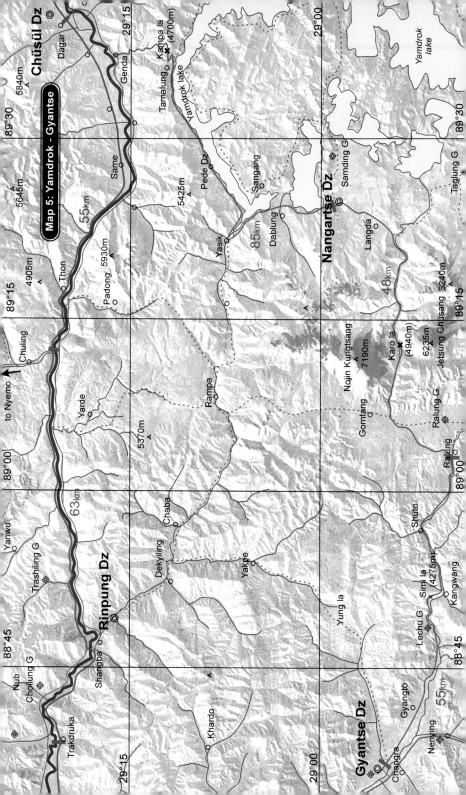

Map 6: Shigatse

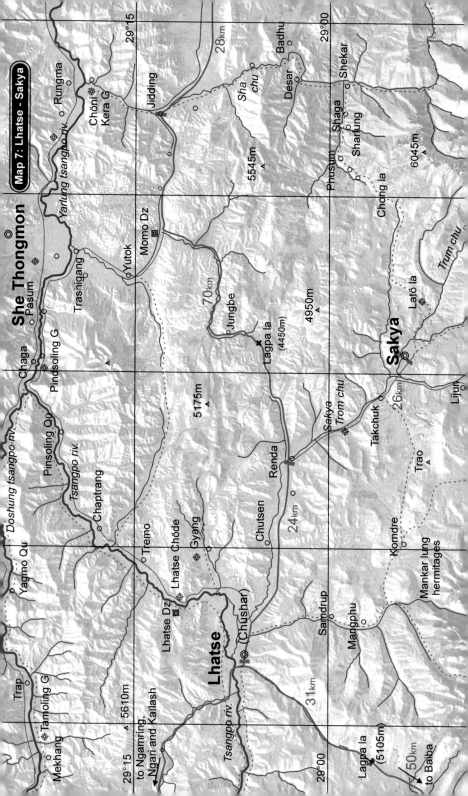

Map 7: Lhatse - Sakya

Map 8: Dingri - Shekar

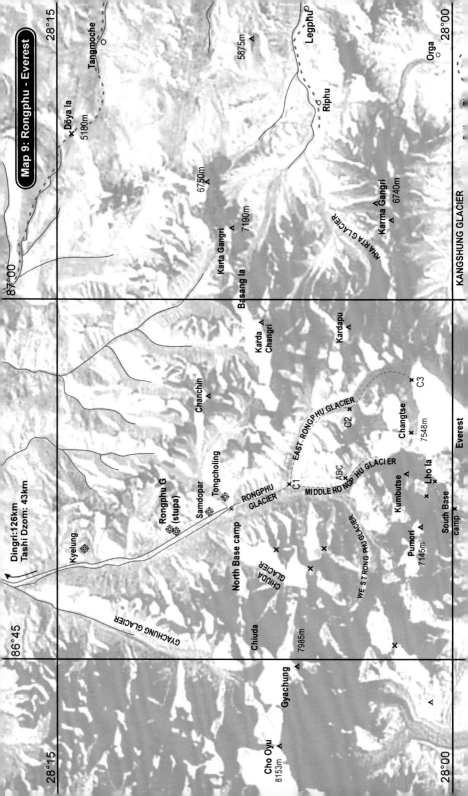

Map 9: Rongphu - Everest